Black Is a Country

Black Is a Country

Race and the Unfinished Struggle for Democracy

NIKHIL PAL SINGH

HARVARD UNIVERSITY PRESS
Cambridge, Massachusetts, and London, England

Copyright © 2004 by the President and Fellows of Harvard College
All rights reserved
Printed in the United States of America

First Harvard University Press paperback edition, 2005

Library of Congress Cataloging-in-Publication Data

Singh, Nikhil Pal.
    Black is a country : race and the unfinished struggle for democracy / Nikhil Pal Singh.
      p. cm.
    Includes bibliographical references and index.
    ISBN 0-674-01300-X (cloth; alk. paper)
    ISBN 0-674-01951-2 (pbk.)
    1. African Americans—Civil rights—History—20th century.
  2. African Americans—Politics and government—20th century.
  3. Democracy—United States—History—20th century.
  4. Racism—Political aspects—United States—History—20th century.
  5. United States—Politics and government—20th century.
  6. United States—Race relations—Political aspects.   I. Title.

E185.61.S6144 2004
323.173—dc22   2003067740

The worlds within and without the Veil of Color are changing, and changing rapidly, but not at the same rate, not in the same way; and this must produce a peculiar wrenching of the soul, a peculiar sense of doubt and bewilderment. Such a double life, with double thoughts, double duties, and double social classes, must give rise to double words and double ideals, and tempt the mind to pretense or to revolt, to hypocrisy or to radicalism.

—W. E. B. DU BOIS, *THE SOULS OF BLACK FOLK*

The history of subaltern social groups is necessarily fragmented and episodic. There undoubtedly does exist a tendency to (at least provisional stages of) unification in the historical activity of these groups, but this tendency is continually interrupted by the activity of the ruling groups; it therefore can only be demonstrated when an historical cycle is completed and this cycle culminates in a success . . . only "permanent" victory breaks their subordination.

—ANTONIO GRAMSCI, *SELECTIONS FROM THE PRISON NOTEBOOKS*

In America, "Black" is a country.

—LEROI JONES, *HOME: SOCIAL ESSAYS*

Contents

Black Is a Country

Introduction: Civil Rights, Civic Myths

> The black revolution is much more than a struggle for the rights of
> Negroes. It is forcing America to face all its interrelated flaws—rac-
> ism, poverty, militarism, and materialism. It is exposing evils that are
> deeply rooted in the whole structure of our society . . . and suggests
> that radical reconstruction of society itself is the real issue to be
> faced.
>
> —MARTIN LUTHER KING JR., "A TESTAMENT OF HOPE" (1969)

Martin Luther King Jr. announced his opposition to the Vietnam War
in the spring of 1967. In the court of public opinion, the response was
swift—he was vilified. King's decision to break his long silence about
the war was overshadowed by his assassination one year later. But as
the campaign against him in the press, in Congress, among civil rights
leaders, and by the FBI showed, King was neither beyond a fall from
grace nor immune to allegations of sedition. *Life* magazine called
his antiwar statements "demagogic slander" fit for "Radio Hanoi."
Lyndon Johnson remarked that King was "destroying his reputation"
and had finally "thrown in with the communists" (which FBI Director
J. Edgar Hoover had claimed all along). Many of King's longtime
supporters accused him of betrayal and wrong-headedness, saying,
"Peace and civil rights don't mix."[1] The man who only a few years
earlier had been charged with saving the soul of America was readily
cast beyond the borders of acceptable discourse.[2]

King spoke "as a citizen of the world . . . aghast at the path we have
taken" and "as an American to the leaders of my own nation."[3] In
adopting this dual stance, King tied the U.S. extension of colonial
war in Vietnam to the failure to achieve racial equality and justice at
home. The fear of communism, he argued specifically, had distorted
the American revolutionary tradition, transforming it into a counter-
revolutionary animus.[4] The costs of this animus were stark: an ex-
haustion of precious economic resources, an elevation of violence and

militarism as pre-eminent responses to human conflict, and a fatal loss of belief in the project of societal reform.[5] "If America's soul becomes poisoned," King summarized, "part of the autopsy must read Vietnam." The patriotic conviction that had once driven him into the civil rights struggle now required him to go "beyond national allegiances."[6]

We can wonder whether, had King lived beyond 1968, his stature would have risen with the burgeoning peace movement, or whether he would have been diminished and eventually broken, like earlier black radicals such as Paul Robeson and W. E. B. Du Bois, by attacks that he was traitorous and un-American. King refused to see his antiwar stance in these terms or as inconsistent with his earlier views. The movement that he had come to personify was never limited to securing the rights of black people, he said. Black struggles for justice, dignity, and self-respect had always been about achieving a broader transformation of the United States into an equitable society. At the same time, where King had once extolled the uplifting power of the American Dream and cast himself in a long line of successful black strivers from Booker T. Washington to Ralph Bunche and Jackie Robinson, he now embraced the traditions of black dissidence.[7] Struggling for justice as a black person in America, he said, was a calling that went beyond "race, nation or creed." In his last public address, King tellingly identified himself with Du Bois, as an activist for peace who had ended his life as an exile from the land of his birth.[8]

Embracing what he called "a world perspective" on violence and inequality, King could no longer avoid a decisive confrontation with the ethical and political shortfalls of U.S. power abroad and the truncation of reformist commitment at home. His subsequent sermons and speeches elaborating on these views were widely aired not in the United States, but in Canada, by the Canadian Broadcasting Corporation (CBC). King opened one of these addresses with: "Over and above any kinship of United States citizens and Canadians as North Americans, there is a singular historical relationship between American Negroes and Canada. Canada is not merely a neighbor to Negroes, in our struggle for freedom, Canada was the North Star." Here, King, the chief symbol of U.S. racial-national integration, consciously deconstructed the unifying term—"United States citizens"—emphasizing that "Negroes" had a separate existence within, and a tortured relationship to, the United States as a nation. This "singular" history, he implied, made other sorts of allegiances and affiliations possible, even necessary. Indeed, King's own experience now seemed to bear this out.[9]

Today, no figure more fully embodies the notion that racial equality is a U.S. national imperative than Martin Luther King Jr. King's most cited rhetoric tied the fortunes of blacks to the status of the U.S. nation-state and to its dominant and defining systems of belief: Christianity, liberal-individualism, and democratic-capitalism. Civil rights reforms, he argued, were urgent matters of national redemption and moral regeneration that would open up a world for individual black achievement ("the content of our character") beyond the barrier of race ("the color of our skin"). At the 1963 March on Washington, King likened the black freedom movement to a person trying to cash a check that had been repeatedly stamped "insufficient funds," defining the fulfillment of black aspirations as litmus test for the United States as an affluent, consumer society.[10] This is the King who is today remembered—even commemorated—with a national holiday, making him the only African American memorialized for the nation at large.

Yet this is also the King who has become part of a mythic nationalist discourse that claims his antiracist imperatives as its own, even as it obscures his significantly more complex, worldly, and radical politics. Indeed, just as King's antiwar stance has been minimized or forgotten, so has the steady incorporation of currents of democratic socialism and black nationalism into his thinking. By the end of his life, King viewed the idea of obtaining civil rights for black individuals as an inadequate framework for combating the economic consequences and cultural legacies of white supremacy. The latter, he believed, had powerfully skewed the economic and political structure of U.S. society, leading to a toleration of massive poverty at home and to an imperial arrogance in world affairs. To combat these, King argued, black people would have to "organize our strength into compelling power." This meant continuing the unfinished struggles for juridical protection and electoral influence. It also meant pursuing the more difficult project of valorizing and institutionalizing the forms of black "collective wisdom and vitality" that had accumulated through long decades of struggle.[11]

In formulating these more challenging views, King drew inspiration from earlier black radicals, like Du Bois, who had been marginalized by Cold War politics even as he sought to open a dialogue with young, black-power radicals who rejected his beliefs in nonviolent protest and racial integration, but who had difficulty formulating coherent theoretical or programmatic approaches to transforming society.[12] Rather than seeing the later King as quixotic or aberrational, we might recognize how for a brief moment he opened a bridge between past and future black radicalisms and their more expansive dreams of freedom. As King understood, black freedom dreams had a habit of exceeding the sanctioned boundaries and brokered compromises of the established political order. Recognizing their persistence and reclaiming their relevance as he did is one of the tasks of this book.[13]

Taking the disjuncture between King as a redemptive national icon and King as an unsettling figure in opposition to the nation-state seriously opens the door to a substantially different interpretation of the civil rights era and its contemporary legacy. The diverging views and conceptions of King typify the successes and failures of the civil rights era itself. On one hand, antiracism and a belief in black equality have attained wide legitimacy in the national public sphere. Overt and direct expressions of antiblack racism are unacceptable, and official public utterances and juridical practice must take account of formal black equality with respect to nationality. At the same time, the assumption that time-honored national norms and ideals have been the effective guarantors of racial justice has an air of unreality that continues to whitewash our history.

Perhaps because he approached, but did not attain (at least in his life), the status of citizen of the world, King has become a symbol of the universalizing force of American norms and institutions. The triumph of the civil rights movement under King's leadership is now said to reveal certain truths about the nation and how its values of tolerance and inclusive boundaries have been reconstituted in our own time.[14] As Taylor Branch puts it, "His oratory gave King authority to reinterpret the core intuition of democratic justice. More than his words, the timbre of his voice projected him across the racial divide and planted him as a new founding father."[15] King's democratic challenge, in other words, was powerful and recognizable insofar as it conformed to the retrospective illusion of shared national identity across time: appearing as "the fulfillment of a project" and as the "completion of a destiny."[16] As a new founding father, the mythic King allowed Americans not only to celebrate their progress into a more inclusive and tolerant people, but also to tell themselves that this is who they always were.

This "King-centric" account of the civil rights era has become central to a civic mythology of racial progress in late twentieth-century America.[17] Beginning with the decision in *Brown vs. Board of Education* in 1954, what might be termed the short civil rights era is imagined to have taken place primarily in the Jim Crow South from the mid-1950s to the mid-1960s, in a series of social movements to desegregate public life and register black voters. With a familiar cast, including a weary Rosa Parks, idealistic, well-dressed black students, and the charismatic minister, the movement is said to have culminated with the 1963 March on Washington, the passage of landmark national legislation and social policy, the Civil Rights Act of 1964 and the Voting Rights Act of 1965, followed by Lyndon Johnson's War on Poverty. This brief period is now viewed as the apex of the historical arc of black struggles for citizenship in the United States: the moment when questions of black political participation and civic equality became central to U.S. civic identity; a long overdue vindication of what King once called "the amazing universalism" of the founding documents and the American Dream.[18]

But this is not the end of the story. Just as there is a rise, there is a fall; just as there is a hagiography, so there is a demonology. Around 1965, we are told, the civil rights movement turned north (and west), where it stalled in the face of intractable problems of black urbanity: residential segregation, chronic black underemployment, and seething ghetto resentment. These explosive conditions, suggested the Kerner Commission Report on the urban disorders of 1968, had in three short years left the progressive optimism of what some had called a Second Reconstruction in a shambles. America, the commission stated, was "two societies, separate and unequal."[19] At this point a series of sudden, coincidental shifts are said to have occurred: from civil rights to black power; south to north; nonviolent to violent; tolerant to divisive; integrationist to black nationalist; patriotic to anti-American, all conspiring to fracture the movement, undermine political support, and create a widespread public backlash against what were now seen as excessive black demands.

If King has come to stand for the idea of an America in which racial equality has already been achieved, the image of black militancy born from a ghetto underclass has both legitimized the withdrawal of public commitment to laws and social policies designed to promote racial equality and helped to renew an age-old racist imagination. The alleged descent from interracial coalition politics and nonviolent protest to militant separatism and urban conflict fostered the public conception that black protest went too far in the 1960s, becoming illiberal in its means and ends. In turn, the civil rights movement—with King frozen in time before the Lincoln Memorial—is represented as part of an achieved national, political consensus, shattered only when blacks themselves abandoned the normative discourses of American politics.[20]

This narrative is built on a number of misleading representations of modern U.S. racial history. It relies on an abbreviated periodization of the civil rights era, as well as fallacies about the South as an exception to national racial norms. It fails to recognize the historical depth and heterogeneity of black struggles against racism, narrowing the political scope of black agency and reinforcing a formal, legalistic view of black equality. It obscures a violent history of black opposition to white supremacy well underway in urban areas, particularly in centers of wartime production, since World War II. Indeed, interracial discord—particularly in northern cities—stimulated by both *de jure* and *de facto* racial hierarchies of state and private agencies in housing and labor markets, as well as by policing and criminal justice practices, was clearly manifest decades before the southern civil rights movement. The eruptions of black ghettos in the 1960s, far from being irrational, inexplicable phenomena, were the result of well-established patterns and recurrent racial conflict.[21]

After World War I black migration and the attendant racialization of city life began to undermine the Jim Crow–era rationalizations of racial division as a regional idiosyncrasy rather than an issue of national concern and import. Bracketed by Roosevelt's New Deal and Johnson's Great Society, what I call the long civil rights era was in this sense the product of a dual phenomenon: the Keynesian transformation of the liberal capitalist state during the 1930s and the emergence of black social movements that were urban, national, and transnational in scope and conception. The first created the conditions in which the classical liberal injunction to insulate market transactions from centralized state intervention was viewed as untenable, and in which nationalist principles of a social-democratic kind began to achieve an expanded purview over weakly integrated, racially stratified, state and local powers. The second constituted the social fact of racial inequality as a symbolic index against which the achievement of U.S. civic ideals could be measured and the legitimacy of U.S. global aspirations could be assessed.

The nationwide reform of society that began under the New Deal was augmented by the American rise to globalism at the end of World War II. During the war, black activists drew strong links between fascism, colonialism, and U.S. racial segregation that could not be wished away. With the onset of the Cold War, U.S. State Department officials routinely argued that white supremacy was the "Achilles heel" of U.S. foreign relations. From the highest levels of government and social policy, it appeared that the stability of the expanded American realm of action in the world was linked to the resolution of the crisis of racial discord and division at home.[22] This fact accelerated the internal decomposition of the *de jure* racial order and the development of new intellectual and legal frameworks that reflected efforts to include black people in the nation by de-racializing institutions of government and civil society. Two decades of racial reform followed that saw the end of legalized Jim Crow; the securing of black political rights, representation, and social freedoms; the widespread entry of blacks into trade unions, the military, and the civil service; and the recognition of black artists, performers, and athletes at the center of a national popular culture.

Even as an officially sanctioned apartheid was being dismantled, however, new structures of racial inequality, rooted in a national racial geography of urban ghettoes and suburban idylls, and intractable disparities of black and white wealth and employment were being established. For three decades, reformist and putatively race-neutral social policies formulated in the New Deal era actually reinforced and expanded numerous racial disparities.[23] Those denied protection under the Social Security Act of 1935 were disproportionately black farm workers and black and female domestic workers living in the South. Despite institutionalizing collective bargaining and a host of new protections to trade unions, the 1935 Wagner Act did nothing to stop existing union practices of racial discrimination and exclusion. After the creation of the Federal Housing Authority in 1937, appraisers used race as an evaluative tool, expressly warning against extending a new generation of federally backed loans to central city areas they described as "honey-combed with diverse and subversive racial elements."[24]

After World War II, government housing and highway policy encouraged the growth of lily-white suburbs, helping to build equity in property for generations of working-class and lower middle-class whites systematically denied to blacks. Urban renewal projects designed to respond to the severe urban housing shortages faced by racial minority communities in the 1950s and 1960s catered instead to commercial, commuter, and business interests. These projects routinely bisected black neighborhoods with freeways and tramlines and invariably destroyed more housing than they created.[25] Finally, throughout this period, trade unions favored agreements that protected the benefits and seniority of organized, predominantly white workers and eschewed organizing efforts to end discriminatory hiring practices that might have resulted in more unorganized workers of color gaining union protection.[26]

In the arena of foreign relations, the United States' struggle for global hegemony increased pressure on the federal government to abolish the formal vestiges of racial inequality, helping to advance the assault on the juridical underpinnings of racial segregation. At the same time, the imperatives of fighting the Cold War severely constrained domestic political dissent in conformity with the new doctrines of national and global security and in conjunction with an unprecedented reliance on U.S. military power in the world at large. A rigid test of anticommunist patriotism undermined the forms and expressions of radical antiracism that had reached their apogee in the 1930s in association with anti-imperialist and class struggles across the globe.[27] As King pointed out, the destructive nexus of racism, capitalism, and imperialism that tied the fates of the U.S. black revolution and the Vietnamese struggle for national liberation was not a new development, but was the return of what had been repressed within Cold War intellectual and political culture. That the state-sponsored civil rights imperative began to fade at this moment was less the result of popular anger at black deviations from a normative nationalist trajectory than of the difficulty surmounting accumulated national and global contradictions of racial-imperial history: what King called "the tragic evasions and defaults of several centuries."[28]

The extant national narrative of racial progress and backlash in the short civil rights era obscures the more complex and contentious racial history of the long civil rights era. In particular, the notion of a backlash against the excesses of black radicalism willfully ignores historically entrenched opposition to even the most moderate civil rights reforms throughout the white South and much of the urban North across the entire post–World War II period. From the inception of New Deal liberalism, white Southerners were weakly committed to the reformism of the federal state, viewing it as a threat to the prerogatives of white supremacy long defended under the auspices of states' rights. When the federal courts mandated school desegregation, whites across the South immediately began massive resistance campaigns and years of successful stalling tactics. Meanwhile, despite their historic support for New Deal liberal social policies, unionized, white ethnic, and working-class voters violently policed the racial boundaries of their neighborhoods and occupational sinecures for more than a generation. As revealed by the well-known scenes of white rioting in Cicero, a Chicago neighborhood, in 1966, the northward turn of the southern civil rights movement only stoked long-burning embers of urban racial conflict.

In the late 1960s, Richard Nixon's political strategist, Kevin Phillips, predicted that these two constituencies—white southerners and urban white ethnics—would propel a dramatic political realignment away from New Deal liberalism and toward a new republican majority.[29] While neither group of working-class whites especially sympathized with the market-fundamentalism and antistatism of conservatives like Barry Goldwater and Ronald Reagan, a new conservatism constructed much of its political identity through displays of hostility to what it called black "special pleading" in the marketplace and black misbehavior in the public square. Even before Nixon deployed Phillips's Southern Strategy to win the 1968 election, Ronald Reagan pioneered these tactics as California's governor, when he opposed fair and open housing legislation as a violation of market freedoms. Reagan not only defended the rights of "homeowners in a 'free society' to 'discriminate against Negroes if they chose,'" he also promised a crackdown on what he would characterize as unlawful and subversive activities in Berkeley, Oakland, and other hotbeds of radical, antiracist activism.[30]

The historical shift represented by the Reagan presidency of 1980–1988 was condensed in the fateful shift from the 1960s War on Poverty to the 1980s War on Drugs. A signal accomplishment of these years was the reinvention and renewal of discredited racial logics of the past. When Reagan, a short fifteen years after the passage of the Voting Rights Act, launched his 1980 presidential campaign in Philadelphia, Mississippi, calling himself a states' righter, and George H. W. Bush eight years later made a furloughed, recidivist black rapist and murderer named Willie Horton into the face of liberal-induced social decay, they engaged the power of unreconstructed, if increasingly well-coded, racist appeals. Such coding of course was not without precedent in an American racist discourse that long favored innuendo, inside jokes, and conspiratorial hysteria over the direct public disclosure of racist intent and feeling. Invidious racial imagery of a black underclass—comprised of wild youths and welfare queens—became an effective right-wing tool to advance broad attacks on tax-supported government services and transfer payments aimed at ameliorating the social conditions of the working poor and unemployed. Insofar as urban black existence remained a concern of government during this period, it was largely in the realm of criminal justice. During these years black incarceration rates quadrupled; today, more than one million black persons are in prisons and jails, making blacks approximately 50 percent of the entire U.S. prison population.[31]

Yet perhaps the greater success of post–civil rights conservatism was its ability to co-opt the discourse of civil rights liberalism and to make its arguments about racial conditions without endorsing racial inequality. Basing resistance to black calls for social justice on a defense of market individualism and national unity, rather than on claims of black inferiority, conservatives changed the debate about race from an argument about how to best redress the economic and political injuries of racism to one that equates ending racism with eliminating racial reference within juridical discourse and public policy. Reagan appointee and conservative U.S. Supreme Court Justice Antonin Scalia put it best in 1995: "In the eyes of the government, we are just one race here. It is American."[32]

Scalia's invocation of the idea of an American race underscores a dogmatic vision of national unity—one whose power has arguably increased after the terrorist attacks of September 11, 2001—that expressly precludes more complicated histories of racialized national identity. For the majority of blacks, the consequences of this have been severe. Since the 1990s, a form of antiracism that is seen as equivalent to American nationalism has been the rationale for overturning policies and programs once deemed essential to fulfilling an antiracist national agenda. The pretext for reform in one period has become the basis for abandoning it in another. Race now means racism, especially when it is used to define or defend the interests of a minority community. Meanwhile, "civil rights" has been appropriated as the slogan of statewide ballot initiatives to end race- and gender-based hiring and college admissions provisions that are said to violate principles of abstract national equality.

In a sweeping rollback of civil rights–era jurisprudence, in the 1990s the U.S. Supreme Court overturned minority-business set-aside programs, minority voter redistricting efforts, and court-ordered desegregation mandates. Meanwhile, the new Democratic administration of President Bill Clinton went his predecessors one better, promising to "end welfare as we know it." Both the legal decisions and the policy shift were filtered through a logic of neoliberal discipline that vehemently opposes government intervention into the "natural" workings of the marketplace, implicitly reopening an expanded field for the play of "private" racist beliefs and practices. Emboldened by the Supreme Court, voter initiatives and legal challenges to affirmative action have been successful in California, Washington, and Texas, and at the time of this writing are being advanced in several states. The now widely held view that any race-based amelioration constitutes a form of reverse discrimination indicates that the public effort to secure social, civil, and political redress for racially aggrieved communities has reached an historic impasse, if not end.[33]

Most recently the U.S. Supreme Court affirmed the legality of affirmative action while narrowing the technical means of its application. In *Grutter v. Bollinger,* the Court upheld the principle of race-based admissions at the University of Michigan Law School on the grounds that the social management of diverse institutions (in particular the U.S. military) requires that pathways to leadership are "open to talented and qualified individuals of every race and ethnicity." At the same time, in *Gratz v. Bollinger* the court struck down the more expansive policy that applied extra points for race in awarding admission to the University of Michigan's College of Arts and Sciences. Together these decisions encapsulate a societal context in which race remains conceptually available as a tool for elite governance under neoliberalism, and at the same time a wedge issue that effectively limits broader, democratic redistributions of social goods.[34]

In sum, the prevailing common sense of the post–civil rights era is that race is the provenance of an unjust, irrational ascription and prejudice, while nation is the necessary horizon of our hopes for color-blind justice, equality, and fair play. While this view has critics, including those who advocate multicultural educational and social policy agendas attentive to the particular needs, concerns, and social locations of minority populations, it is ascendant in American law, politics, and public intellectual discourse. Though nominally anti-racist, the rise of what might be called color-blind universalism conspicuously coincided with the dramatic rollback of federal civil rights enforcement during the Reagan and first Bush presidential administrations, massive cutbacks in federal aid to cities, and the recoding of black existence in urban areas as a major threat to public safety and political virtue (that is, the moral panics over crime and welfare).[35]

In the post–civil rights era, the rising incomes that characterize the partial integration of a black middle-class into the circuits of U.S. prosperity remain weakly related to the accumulated propertied wealth of generations (and thus are more vulnerable to economic downturn). Meanwhile, the lower-middle-class fractions of this class continue to depend on a diminishing realm of public-sector and manufacturing jobs. Blacks without a college education, who comprise the far higher percentage of the working and workless poor, are not only overrepresented in U.S. prisons and in the U.S. Army, but also in the low-wage, nonunionized economic sectors that have seen slow growth and stagnant wages since the early 1970s. Despite a decline in biological arguments for black inferiority, the belief that blacks are culturally deficient—less intelligent, less industrious, and less patriotic than whites—remains widespread.[36] The soft racism of bootstrap survival still marks the stories of black social ascent, even as black achievement becomes condescending proof that race no longer matters. Meanwhile, racism's hard edge remains very much alive in the spatial isolation, hair-trigger profiling, and incarceration of underemployed urban black youth, whose social and economic repression returns (as it always has) in the racial fantasies of our national, popular culture.[37]

The unraveling of the social and political consensus that enabled the limited reforms of the earlier period has exposed the shaky political, institutional, and ideological foundations on which much racial progress has been built. The contemporary reversals of prior movements toward racial equality reveal the gains of the short civil rights era as provisional codifications of a more complex social reality, temporary achievements of longer-fought and still-persisting social conflicts. More than the pronouncements of presidents and the courts, a history of black subaltern struggle, white resistance, and open and surreptitious racial discord shaped the uneven transformations in post–World War II U.S. racial formation.[38] For a brief period, the demands and critiques of black intellectuals, activists, and masses of black people who took to the streets could not be ignored by a nation-state intent on legitimizing its claims to global power and domestic consensus. Yet, in the crucible fired by the clash of black protest and white supremacy and cooled by the workings of political administration and juridical response, national integration, let alone racial justice and equality, has been the exception more often than the rule.

Prominent black neoconservative and U.S. Supreme Court Justice Clarence Thomas gives voice to much of current political wisdom when he asserts that the long and cruel history of racial differentiation and inequality in the United States will be overcome once whites and blacks are "blended into a common nationality."[39] Yet the historical and political process of translating black difference into normative, national subjecthood in the United States remains poorly understood, even as it seems to have been deferred once again. What is generally overlooked in formulations such as Thomas's is the fact that this nation-state has been a powerful mechanism for at once instituting racial division and domination and enabling universalistic visions of inclusion and opportunity. Yet, as King recognized at the end of his life, the redemptive investment in the force of American universalism may not be so easy to sever from histories of U.S. force and violence in which blacks have stood among the casualties and victims.

Indeed, when seen in this light it becomes possible to re-examine King's duality and hence his paradigmatic status. Even before his controversial stand on Vietnam, King declared that "there is no more civil rights movement . . . President Johnson signed it out of existence when he signed the voting rights bill."[40] But this was far from an admission on his part that the struggle against white supremacy had ended. Civil rights, King argued, were just the beginning of a struggle that revolved around housing, employment, and economic justice, the root struggles of the long civil rights era. Lest we forget, King's last visit to Memphis was to support a strike of predominantly black sanitation workers. As he recognized in his radical last years, "justice for black people will not flow into society merely from court decisions nor from the fountains of political oratory."[41] "It is time that we stopped our blithe lip service to the guarantees of life, liberty and the pursuit of happiness . . . equally native to us is the concept that gross exploitation of the Negro is acceptable, if not commendable."[42]

Attacking the presumptions of the "amazing universalism" of the American dream he had championed only a few years before, King argued that the U.S. nation-state was neither a stable mediator of social antagonisms nor the ultimate horizon of black hopes for justice. In doing so, he drew on an intellectual and historical tradition of black protest that dramatically exceeded the terms of normative U.S. social, economic, and political discourses. King may have rejected what he regarded as a misconceived and dangerous emphasis on violence by younger black militants, but he largely accepted their argument, which linked the racism, poverty, and inequality concentrated in black urban areas to "world perspective" on U.S. force and violence used to maintain global inequalities. King, in other words, rejected the view of racial justice now attributed to him: that all that was required was to cross the threshold in which domestic racial differences and divisions were apprehended as the commonalities of some great national abstraction (that is, the state, the founding documents, our nation's ideals). "The implications of true racial integration," he wrote, "are more than national in scope."[43]

If we are to better understand the successes and failures of official efforts and insurgent struggles to transform black people from a subject population into citizen-subjects in our own time, we must respect these insights. One of the tasks of this book is to remember the long history in which black global dreams have foundered on the shoals of America's racial dilemma. In light of the new round of schemes to perfect the world in America's image, the legacies of America's racial dialectic casts a healthy skepticism on the notion that there exists a universalizing tendency within this nation that inevitably wins out, and instead shows how exclusions of the past are reproduced and transferred to the present. Perhaps it will only be by recognizing the limits of U.S. nationalist traditions as a source of justice for all that we will begin to approach once more the possibility of an effective antiracism and a renewal of progressive politics in our own time.

CHAPTER ONE

Rethinking Race and Nation

Let America be America again.
Let it be the dream it used to be . . .
(America never was America to me.)

—LANGSTON HUGHES, "LET AMERICA BE AMERICA AGAIN" (1937)

A recent career retrospective exhibition commemorating the life work of black artist Jacob Lawrence included Lawrence's mid-1950s series, "Struggle . . . From the History of the American People." The series of paintings focuses on the establishment of democratic rights in American history from the revolutionary period to the present. Paintings depict scenes from black history, from slave resistance to civil rights marches: founding national events, like the Boston Massacre, where Crispus Attucks became the first black person killed in the American Revolution, as well as the signing of the Declaration of Independence, where no blacks were present. The museum catalogue singled out this series as one in which Lawrence "went beyond African American history to deal with the American experience as a whole."[1] Such a description is characteristic in the history of black arts and letters. It suggests that universal expression or representation in art or social thought necessarily transcends what is an implicitly narrow racial or minority experience. Lawrence's ability to depict the progress of democracy must, in this view, derive from an expansive, national historical experience, rather than from the confines of a racialized one.[2]

It's unclear, however, whether this is an adequate way to understand the relationship of black struggles for equality to the constitution of national democratic norms and foundations. Is the relationship really one of racial particularity to a national universality? Could we not turn this on its head and recognize how, from Lawrence's point of view, the "history of the American People" might reflect on the denial, rather than the extension, of democratic rights, especially to black people, for the greater part of U.S. history? In such a reading, Lawrence's celebration of rights-making struggles from the American Revolution to the modern civil rights movement could be understood as a particular apprehension of universality by black people, one that consistently exceeded the American application of democratic rights to white men for the better part of the nation's history.

In other words, Lawrence's social vision, rather than manifesting a specific communal experience fully realized in the context of an always more inclusive nation-state, is actually more inclusive at the outset. In contrast to the purported universality of a nation that for most of its history upheld a localized and particularistic distribution of rights, Lawrence's rendering could be said to derive from an admittedly particular collective history that yields a wider, more universal understanding. Rather than marking the movement from the particular subject (black experience) to the universal one (American experience as a whole), Lawrence's work presents a compelling and particular universalism that paradoxically provides more secure, normative foundations for forging a common political life among diverse peoples than those varieties of universalism simply dubbed "American."[3]

Based on his work, Lawrence appears to have been aware of the degree to which social collectivity is constituted on the terrain of linguistic narration and aesthetic representation. He emerged to prominence during the late 1930s through the New Deal's Federal Art Project, as part of what his mentor Charles Alston described as a "new and socially conscious generation of Negro artists." Lawrence established himself as a painter of the black public scene in Harlem—its streets, sidewalks, tenements, and pool halls. His early success was largely the result of the ways he presented stark, visual representations of the modern black experience—especially the definitive movement from country to city—as a narrative portrait of the emergence of a distinct people. His choice of subjects: "The Migration of the Negro," "Harriet Tubman," "Frederick Douglass," "John Brown," "Toussaint L'Ouverture" were not primarily evidence of his identification with the U.S. nation-state, but the visual analogue to the relatively autonomous movement of what was then called Negro History.[4]

Nor did these thematic choices and images lack their own internal coherence as a normative basis, or frame of reference, for modern black life in the United States. It is interesting to note that "Struggle . . ." was the final narrative series Lawrence undertook, and the only one he abandoned without finishing.[5] In fact, it would take some time before Lawrence was simply embraced as an American artist. Although this now appears progressive and inevitable, the reality is of course more complicated. Where Lawrence's blackness once signaled a certain deficit in relation to national belonging, it can now act as a surplus or supplement. Today there is no more powerful way to represent the political universality of the U.S. nation-state than to have black people stand in for the nation at large. Yet, the projection of images of black inclusion (often through the elevation of exemplary individuals) minimizes a contentious, unfinished history of collective struggles against white supremacist monopolies on nationalist ideals and practices. More ironically, enlisting blacks in the story of the nation's transcendence of the racial past perpetuates the idea that the exemplary national subject is still somehow not black and that visible racial difference remains the real deficit and obstacle to be overcome.

This discussion of Lawrence is just a brief illustration of a characteristic approach to representing race in the post–civil rights era. Signaling the successful culmination of the struggle for racial equality, black achievement—aesthetic, political, athletic—can now embody and sanction unremitting U.S. national pride. Civic myths about the triumph over racial injustice have become central to the resuscitation of a vigorous and strident form of American exceptionalism—the idea of the United States as both a unique and universal nation—once thought mortally wounded by the Vietnam War and the divisive racial politics of the late 1960s. This has involved a mostly successful appropriation of Martin Luther King Jr. as a figure affirming the accomplishments of color-blind nationalism, along with sharp and sustained attacks on any form of race-conscious advocacy, from campus-based identity politics to urban black nationalisms to the legacies of black power politics. Writing in a strong vindicationist mood, a host of U.S. public intellectuals have seized on what one calls "the universalist tenor of the civil rights movement" to once again lay claim to a conception of America as the world's exemplary nation-state.[6]

Today it is axiomatic in discussions of American history and politics that the U.S. nation-state has a universalizing propensity at its origin. "American universalism," historian John Higham summarizes, is "our egalitarian ideology . . . molded by the Enlightenment and forged in the revolution . . . simultaneously a civic credo, a social vision and a definition of nationhood."[7] The inclusiveness of U.S. nationality and citizenship is said to derive from an egalitarian tradition of civic nationalism that distinguishes the United States from nation-states with ethno-racial conceptions of the polity, or ones in which national belonging is defined by kinship, primordial attachments, and a metaphorics of blood. Civic nations like the United States are theoretically open to anyone, and the political community that comprises the nation-state is made up of no one in particular. According to Philip Gleason, a proponent of this view, U.S. citizens are fundamentally without "any particular linguistic, religious, racial or ethnic background." American nationality in this view is the antithesis of a system of ethnic and racial marks.[8]

American universalism has been conceptualized as deriving in different measures from Christianity, liberalism, and democratic-republicanism. Historians and political theorists disagree about the proportions of this mixture and the lines of cleavage within it, particularly between liberalism and republicanism, but these elements have tended to fuse in holistic accounts of U.S. national identity.[9] In the story's most conventional version, the absence of feudalism and its aristocratic remnants, the transplant of the most ideologically and economically advanced fragments of British merchant and agrarian capital, the uniqueness of the federalist solution to questions of state power, and the early extension of the franchise (to white men) all combined to produce the world's most vital market society and most open political culture. European history, in this sense, was little more than a rehearsal for an Enlightenment project to be realized in America. Thus, Bruce Ackerman suggests that it is high time we overcome our status as "an intellectual colony, borrowing European categories to decode the meaning of national identity."[10] Or, as another scholar asks: "Was this not the place where the Enlightenment first came down to earth?"[11]

The linked assertions that America is an exceptional and an exemplary nation-state have a long pedigree, from the Puritan Covenant, to Thomas Paine's famous description of America as "an asylum for mankind," to Arthur Schlesinger Jr.'s declaration that America remains "the hope of all continents, creeds and races."[12] These claims, I submit, can never be proven or falsified. Rather, they should be understood as performative, that is, they seek to produce what they purport to describe. They are civic ideologies, normative and pedagogical statements that attempt to create or reinforce a particular narrative of national identity.[13]

The reiteration of American universalism has long been central to the making of Americans at both individual and collective levels. This story of nationhood must be told over and over, because there is nothing natural about the nation or the fashioning of its predominant civic identities. Nations, in this sense, are the quintessential artifacts of modernity—social creations engineered and lived primarily through the techniques of narration and representation. Intellectual descriptions of national history, identity, and community help resolve a special problem for the liberal-democratic or "civic" nation: the production and reproduction of a people who recognize themselves as consenting to a common enterprise in advance of the institutional forms that claim their allegiance.[14]

If the earliest conceptions of America's exceptional universalism were built around claims about religious tolerance and the absence of feudal distinctions of birth and rank, contemporary versions have been fashioned from the story of racial and ethnic inclusion. Today no better proof of American universalism is offered than the idea that dominated or excluded groups have struggled against discrimination and inequality in the name of the superior ideas and values of the nation.[15] David Hollinger states the core premise: American nationalism is based on a nonethnic national ideology that rests on a "universalist commitment—proclaimed in the Constitution and the prevailing political discourse—to provide the benefits of citizenship irrespective of any ascribed or asserted ancestral affiliations."[16] Surely, the argument goes, this principle and the benefits it confers are of the utmost importance to those who have suffered or continue to suffer racial discrimination. Ample testimony can be drawn from a long history in which black activists and intellectuals have grounded their arguments within the prevailing discourses of American politics. For if this is the case, then there can be little doubt that the U.S. nation-state and its liberal-democratic principles provide the necessary horizons and instruments for achieving racial justice.[17]

But what if this story itself is symptomatic of an equally longstanding failure in U.S. political culture, a failure to apprehend and interpret the enduring, invidious power of racial domination? What if there is a recurring oscillation between the universalizing abstractions of liberal-democracy, in which individuals are considered equal with respect to nationality, and a persistent regression, in which the actual individuals and communities who benefit from national belonging are implicitly or explicitly constituted in white supremacist terms? If this is the case, then the idea that American universalism, and the moral and political primacy it attributes to individual freedom and civic egalitarianism, have worked to overcome racial division and racism is faulty—not merely an apology for racist practice, but implicated in creating and sustaining racial division. We will only understand this if we begin to unravel the historical process by which race and nation, racism and nationalism, rather than being antithetical principles, have been articulated together in U.S. history.

American Race/American Racism

No single argument could possibly condense the full scope of American "multiracism" over centuries of continental expansion, racial slavery, imperial conquest, and international labor migration.[18] It is crucial to begin with the recognition, however, of the extent to which a normalizing claim to whiteness preceded the assertion that U.S. nationality and citizenship transcend allegedly prior differences of kinship, ethnicity, race, or nationality. Beginning in the early republic, whiteness was invested both literally and symbolically with the attributes of property. If property rights were the foundation of liberal theories of political order, property-in-oneself was the basis for conceptualizing republican government and political democracy. One owned oneself insofar as one was white and male. Self-ownership, in turn, was a cornerstone of both the market contract and the social contract. It signified at least a potential, if not actual, access to Indian lands and African slaves. And it underwrote the most dramatic feature of the American Revolution, a "universal" right to participation in politics.[19]

In this founding liberal-republican schema, the development of an order of difference with respect to phenotype, affect, intelligence, and what W. E. B. Du Bois called "gross morphology" was codified as racial difference and legally constituted as an obstacle to both market activity and the exercise of citizenship rights for those marked as "other" by their color. Here, the incipient scientific racism of Thomas Jefferson's *Notes on the State of Virginia* (1785) emerges as at least as important as the nonracial, revolutionary lines he authored in 1776. Like the two Martin Luther Kings discussed previously, the two Jeffersons suggest a complicated history of interdependence between race and nation, racism and nationalism, as ways of imagining kinship, community, economic activity, and political society. This is not to say that the American civic-nation had a racial basis at its inception. Rather, racial definitions enabled the very process of thinking about U.S. national belonging as both a normative and a universal condition.[20]

In the U.S. context, the ideal national subject has actually been a highly specific person whose universality has been fashioned from a succession of those who have designated his antithesis, those irreducibly *non-national* subjects who appeared in the different guises of slave, Indian, and, at times, immigrant.[21] The capaciousness of American nationalism was due not to its inclusiveness, but to its ability to accommodate significant national, class, and religious diversity among its settler populations. Here, the forging of national subjectivity, famously described by Hector St. John Crevecoeur as the "melting" of men of all nations and ranks into a "new race of men . . . an American race," was derived from a carefully delimited heterogeneity, or what Crevecour qualified as that "mixture of English, Scotch, Irish, French, Dutch, Germans and Swedes."[22]

Of course, it's not enough to stop here. The power of American nationalism, for its defenders, is that it has enabled the "widening of the circle of we."[23] The contours of the national "we" have been constantly recomposed as those previously excluded have asserted their own claims to be a nothing-in-particular American, or true national subject. This is where things get interesting, because the process of reshaping the boundaries of nation has also involved rearticulations of race. This process allowed for the incorporation of not-quite-white, but not-quite-not-white Irish, Jewish, and Southern and eastern European immigrants into the canons of whiteness through the nineteenth and early twentieth centuries, making them Americans first in a legal and then in a cultural sense.[24] The question remains, how does this process work—or does it—for groups that have been more durably caught within the world-system of racial marks, particularly peoples of African descent?

If whiteness became the privileged grounding and metaphor for the empty abstraction of U.S. citizenship, blackness presented an apparent contradiction and a fixed limit against which it was enacted and staged, beginning with the consolidation of a slave regime based on African origins and the codification of racial rules of descent. While other racialized groups have since been similarly subordinated, and in the case of American Indians violently expelled from the nation's borders, blacks presented the anomaly of an exclusion that was at once foundational to and located within the polity.[25] Despite the wish of iconic U.S. presidents like Jefferson and Lincoln that black slaves be emancipated and then removed ("beyond the reach of mixture," as Jefferson put it), an enduring black presence within the nation-state has led to an extraordinary cultural and political dynamic.[26] In this dynamic, African—and later Negro, black, and African American— struggles against civil death, economic marginalization, and political disenfranchisement accrued the paradoxical power to code all normative (and putatively universal) *redefinitions* of U.S. national subjectivity and citizenship. Lurking within the original conceptions of American freedom, providing the underlying logic of the brutal civil war of national unification, unsettling the fragile legitimacy of the U.S. defense of the free world after World War II, and inhabiting contemporary justifications for dismantling the welfare-state is the question of the status of black existence: the problem of race in the United States.

From this standpoint, then, comes another reading of America's universalism: it is built around an exception, leading to torturous but creative efforts to accommodate the racism internal to the nation-state's constitution. For most of U.S. history this problem was simply resolved by defining black people apart from any representation of the national interest. At the delicate intersection of public opinion formation and public policy formulation—national sovereignty and state institution building—was a broad racial consensus based on black exclusion. This may be the most succinct definition of racism as a social and institutional fact: the construction of black people as subjects proscribed from participating in the social state in which they live, and that part of the public whose relation to the public is always in radical doubt.

Prior to slave emancipation and political enfranchisement that culminated in the constitutional revisions of the Reconstruction era, the vast majority of blacks in the United States were excluded from the nation-state as a guarantor of natural rights and political participation. The slave was not merely the other of the republican citizen, but was the symbol of what was incommensurable with political society, a representative of a boundary to national belonging, a zone where the radical Enlightenment ideal of "the rights of man and citizen" was irrelevant. This was evident in the evasions of the Constitution, which refused to refer directly to slavery even while including the "three-fifths" clause that rendered slaves as part persons, part property.[27] Senator Henry Clay was more straightforward in 1850, pronouncing, in response to rising sectional tensions, that slavery was "an exception (resulting from stern but inexorable necessity) to the general liberty in the U.S."[28] The paradox of a parenthetical black presence—never absent but never fully present—was best captured by the antebellum blackface minstrel show, a popular form that underlined the creation of a national popular culture whose basic grammar and content was predicated on what was excluded from that culture.[29]

By making ex-slaves into citizens and enfranchising black men, the Civil War and Reconstruction era established a new cultural and political trajectory. Of paramount import was the augmentation of a universalizing nationalist imperative in which the masses of black people—no longer located outside the U.S. nation-state, its imagined community, public sphere, and political society—entered America's shared, if fiercely contested symbolic, social, and political space. At the same time, freeing the slaves also freed racism as a constituent element of national popular politics.[30] In the South the attack on Reconstruction was swift and immediate after the northern armies withdrew in 1877. It led to the organization of new segregated institutions, white supremacist ideologies, legal rationalizations, extralegal violence, and everyday racial terror, which elaborated black racial difference as the basis of a new order of unequal social relations. While the severe policing of racial boundaries was already a fact of life in many northern states where free blacks lived, the end of Reconstruction led to the nationalization of a new racial regime in which blacks were reconstructed as "anti-citizens . . . enemies rather than members of the social compact."[31]

There's a difference between being socially unintelligible and being society's enemy.[32] As enemies of a newly emerging liberal-nationalist order, blacks virtually had no room to maneuver politically, but their collective situation could at least be grasped as one subject to politics and to their collective influence as political subjects. Nothing can better explain the intensification of white supremacist activity during this period—lynching, segregation, "scientific" racism, the white riot, and pogrom—than the real possibility of black participation in the common social and institutional life of the nation-state. As Senator William Windon of Minnesota put it in a telling admission in 1879: "the black man does not excite antagonism because he is black but because he is a *citizen*."[33]

Periods of democratic upheaval, in which an activated citizenry threatened to overturn or radically reorder governmental powers in the name of civic-egalitarian principles, such as Jacksonian democracy, the Populist movement of the 1890s, or the labor movement of the early twentieth century, not only failed to challenge racial hierarchies, but often heightened them, succumbing to explicit "master race" appeals that helped to shape the future course of democratic expansion. At the same time, it was often the guardians of established property relations who paternalistically presented themselves as the true champions of defenseless blacks and Indians, in the context of an overall defense of social order and as a counterweight to socially disruptive political challenges from below.[34] The political divide between northern and southern elites that led to the Civil War complicates this argument, but the compromises that led to a segregationist South after the Civil War reverted to the pattern. Once the radically democratic hopes of interracial populism were undermined, segregation was advanced by both northern industrialists and rising New South boosters as a more moderate form of white supremacy, a check on the "democratic" excesses of the white rabble and a political solution that would guarantee the orderly succession of property relations in the South that liberals believed would be the true source of social progress.[35]

It might seem puzzling or contradictory that proposals to ameliorate racial subordination have been tied to the reinforcement of hierarchies of property, and democratic social movements tied to the reproduction of hierarchies of race. The destruction of the fleeting experiments with interracial politics during Reconstruction and the end of interracial populism and trade union organization during the 1880s and 1890s led to the wholesale exclusion of blacks from participation in the egalitarian struggles that were beginning to reshape the republic at the end of the nineteenth century. The attitude of American Federation of Labor (AFL) founder Samuel Gompers was typical when he said that blacks did not need to be afforded trade union protection because they had "no understanding of the philosophy of human rights." At the 1901 convention of the National American Women's Suffrage Association (NAWSA), President Carrie Chapman Catt divorced the suffrage movement of white women from the "hasty and ill-advised" enfranchisement of black men, which, she said, had led to "inertia in the growth of democracy" and "the introduction into the body politic vast numbers of irresponsible citizens." One time populist-egalitarians like Tom Watson were irresistibly drawn to herrenvolk ideas. Even the incipient socialist movement had little interest in racial inequality. As Eugene Debs, otherwise one of the most radical political thinkers of his generation, put it, "we have nothing special to offer the Negro."[36]

What historians and theorists have represented as a deep-seated conflict between liberalism and civic-republicanism in American political life has actually been mediated through a series of negotiated compromises around racial boundaries. That these have been forged at the expense of black equality is ignored by partisans on both sides of the debate.[37] To understand this more fully we need to unpack a series of oppositions inscribed in the wider debate surrounding liberalism and republicanism in U.S. political thought: the market versus the state, the private and the public, the defense of liberty and the goal of equality. If the ideal inhabitants of the nation-state are citizen-subjects, abstract, homogeneous, and formally equivalent participants in a common civic enterprise, then the ideal inhabitants of the market are private individuals endowed with an unknowable range of different attributes and engaged in competition and personal advancement. The principles that apply to the market and those that apply to the nation-state, in other words, are in direct conflict much of the time. While the market presumes the atomistic freedom of individual competition and advantage, the state presumes equality with respect to nationality and the forging of a common communal life through politics. The market derives its theories from eighteenth-century liberalism, while the modern political state is an achievement of democratic revolutions and republican theories of good government. Both the state and the market posit an abstract individual subject, but within the market that abstraction opens the way for the play of differences, while the political state is organized around the principle of sameness.

While these two realms are imagined as separable, they are deeply intertwined. The political state not only literally underwrites social faith in the market (in the form of money), it creates the basis of accumulation, stabilizing market exchange in a sphere of civic order and preventing the war of all against all. What needs to be grasped is how in the United States the market and state combinatory (i.e., the capitalist state) constitutes and maintains racial inequality. This is most easily perceived in relation to the operations of the state, in which racial exclusion has taken the force of juridical sanction. In this case, alleged sensuous particularities of black embodiment (odor, unsightliness, sexual excess) have provided a variety of rationales for denying abstract equality and political participation within the national community. But antiblack racism has also operated at the level of market activity and so-called private life, where blacks have been prevented both formally and informally from acting as proprietors of their own capacities, sellers of their labor-power, and sensuous participants within exchange relations. In these cases, racial stigma has been applied to blacks as a group, preventing them from being perceived as qualitatively differentiated individuals.

Indeed, what makes racial ascription and antiblack racism so powerful and so difficult to undo is that it has possessed this double optic, working its pernicious effects, both as an inscription of embodied particularity and as an abstract universality. In the process, it has helped to suture the otherwise problematic split between the public and the private that characterizes the development of modern bourgeois society. Thus, on the one hand, racial differentiation has underwritten the abstract egalitarianism that animates the idea of the democratic public, providing the latter with a particular, putatively "real" sensuous precedent, the idea of different skin and physical embodiment. On the other hand, racial differentiation is itself a form of abstraction, providing what is imagined to be an infinitely differentiated realm of private individuality and sensuous embodiment with a normative framework (that is, whiteness).

Liberalism as a theory of market society and democratic-republicanism as a theory of political society collude in the perpetuation of racial inequalities by denying their own theoretical limitations and by locating the cause of racial division in the other theory. Thus, liberalism would understand racial inequality to be the result of state interference with otherwise neutral market principles, suggesting that such discrimination would disappear if the market were only allowed to operate according to those principles. The liberal's answer to racism, in other words, is to remove the barriers to market freedoms and private individuality. On the other hand, democratic-republican, civic-nationalist, and communitarian arguments understand racial inequality as a subset of the inequalities generated by the market itself, which has engendered competition and distinction among a range of excluded groups and prevented their unified political pursuit of the common good. The answer for the republican theorist is removing the barriers to democratic politics and public power.

In each instance, to combat racial ascription, it is merely necessary to affirm the universality and rightness of the original theory and to bring it into line with practice, just as in both cases, the specific fate of racially aggrieved populations causes no special alarm within the terms of the theory. Since these frameworks of theory, social action, and institutional development are in practice interdependent rather than oppositional, each provides the other with a kind of plausible deniability around the historical persistence of racism and the problems it poses for producing the good society. The irony is that even when liberals and civic republicans take racism into account, it does not contradict their own fundamental premises, but instead reconfirms their universal validity. In each case, racism winds up being little more than an aberration of, or deviation from, what is otherwise a fundamentally sound liberal or civic-nationalist project, rather than something that has shaped and animated U.S. society at every turn.[38]

Racism and the reproduction of racial hierarchy are blind spots for the forms of liberal and democratic political theory and practice that are said to constitute American nationhood. What needs to be recognized is that white supremacy is neither the essence of U.S. nationality nor its antithesis, but an ever-active ideological formation that has structured market behavior and social movements within the constitution and governance of the U.S. nation-state. More precisely, racial classification has provided what Evelyn Brooks Higginbotham terms a "metalanguage" of American culture and politics. As such, it has operated as a durable medium of symbolic constitution, cutting across conventional boundaries between the economic and the political, the private and the public, with the power to shape both the dispensation of value and the formation of groups.[39]

To put this a different way, racism (here, more specifically antiblack racism) and conceptions of racial hierarchy have provided decisive symbolic and cultural elements for creating hegemonic political and economic arrangements throughout U.S. history.[40] The liberal-republican antithesis in American politics, in this sense, converges around a two-pronged acceptance of racial exclusion—the uses of blackness as a market differential (for example, housing markets, labor markets, capital investment), and as an index of political community (for example, residential segregation, civic participation, public investment). Just as the question of black employment (including the deployment of black strikebreakers, practices of "lily-white" trade unionism, the protection of occupational sinecures) has been integral to more than a century of conflicts between labor and capital, the question of black social and political participation has been a flashpoint in struggles over the proper scope of government authority (including debates about federalism, state's rights, and private entitlements to discrimination).

This approach can help explain the steady reproduction of racial ascription in U.S. political culture across time. Often this has been understood too simply as a function of an invariant need to constitute a compelling collective identity for the nation. In other words, racism is often conceived as a distortion arising from the symbolic identity requirements of civic-egalitarian dynamics and democratic sovereignty. Racism, in this view, provides specific cultural content to an otherwise empty democratic universalism, enabling the forms of boundary-drawing and fusions of past and present crucial to fashioning the story of a particular national "we."[41] But this is not the whole picture. Racism has also been central to the constitution and defense of material investments and market inequalities (in the United States and globally). This begins with the world trade in black skin and includes imperialist land grabs, quests for markets and raw materials, use of racist ideologies and practices to drive down the price of labor at home and abroad, and phenomena of property devaluation and residential segregation tied to concentrations and population movements of peoples of color. Just as racism fills the empty universalism of democratic theory, it provides an otherwise abstract capitalist market with one of its most reliable mechanisms of value-differentiation.

Insofar as liberalism insists on divorcing universal questions of individual rights from a historical context of unequal property relations and what Karl Marx termed primitive capital accumulation, it is not only ill-equipped to combat white supremacist constructions of peoplehood, but invested in their reproduction. Recent scholars have taken this further, suggesting that it is not possible to separate the core ideas of liberalism from the milieu of imperial expansion in which they were fashioned. Uday Singh Mehta thus argues that a politically exclusionary impulse can be found *within* the "theoretical framework of liberalism" itself. This is not, he suggests, because liberal ideals (i.e., universal suffrage, individual freedom, self-determination, etc.) are themselves fictitious or hypocritical, or even because they are practically difficult to implement. Rather, liberal universalism has been based upon a distinction between "anthropological capacities and the conditions for their political actualization." Behind the liberal notion of universal human capacity has been a thicket of delimiting "social credentials"—cultural, historical, material, biological, and psychological "preconditions"—for which race (and gender) have proved to be highly durable shorthand and broadly disseminating rubrics.[42]

To develop this argument further it is necessary to frame our questions not only in terms of the domestic politics and ideologies of the nation-state. To be sure, racist and white supremacist appeals have been most visible as an intra-national cultural projection about the boundaries of communal belonging. However, they have also been central to the definition of legitimate supranational political aims and economic ambitions, or the internationalist and imperialist constructions of modern nationhood. It is useful, for example, to recognize that the "separate-but-equal" segregationist compromise codified by the U.S. Supreme Court in *Plessy vs. Ferguson* (1896) virtually coincided with the formal entry of the United States into the world imperialist competition in the Spanish-American war of 1898. Just as "Indian removal" at the frontier and the Anglo-American slave trade outlasted the temporary fissures of U.S. national independence at the end of the eighteenth century, "the white man's burden" in foreign relations—taken up in Cuba and the Philippines—was paired with an acceptance of internal exclusion at the end of the nineteenth.[43] At least until the mid-twentieth century, American national subjectivity was organized by the competing universalisms of liberalism-democracy supplemented by a range of racial dividing practices that constituted "the people" and imagined the world in specific racial-cultural terms.[44]

Americans have largely lived in denial about the centrality of their racial-imperial project to national self-conceptions. One of the main bulwarks against admission has been the typical argument of U.S. exceptionalism: the United States it is said, has never pursued the kind of territorial colonialism of European nation-states. The turn-of-the-century acquisitions of Hawaii, Cuba (for practical purposes), the Philippines, and Puerto Rico forces some qualification of this claim. Yet, even this might be considered a minor episode in U.S. history. What can hardly be disputed, however, is that relative absence of territorial conquest abroad was enabled by an unprecedented expansion of the contiguous national territory, from the revolution and westward expansion to Indian wars and removal policies to the seizure of northern Mexico from the Southwest to the Pacific Coast.[45]

A major psychic motivation for denying the role and scope of American empire is that so much of this activity proceeded under the terms of a now-discredited, overt, and extreme racism. Here, in fact it is less easy to differentiate the United States from Europe. Both viewed themselves as carrying a superior civilization to subject peoples, through conquest, forced labor, and extermination of indigenous populations. Even when engaged in so-called great power rivalry, each advanced a transnational racial vision of the historical progress of European-derived, or in the case of the great U.S. imperialist Teddy Roosevelt, "Anglo-Teuton" peoples. The boundaries of the civilizing process were secured by a remarkably simple axiom: the uncivilized (that is, racialized) subject was a person who could be killed with impunity. They were, in the words of the great British imperialist poet Rudyard Kipling "lesser breeds without the law."[46]

The racism of imperialism presents a significant problem for its latter-day defenders. This is one reason that no matter how much historians may now claim that statist liberalism triumphed over republicanism in the twentieth century, when it comes to imperialism, America is still cast as a republic, not an empire. Here we see similar tactics of bait-and-switch, in which a domestically racist republicanism can, from another vantage point, become the source of aggressive claims for U.S. anti-imperialism (just as a globally expansionist liberalism is often heralded as the intellectual harbinger of a more benign racial order at home). Once we recognize that racist commitments have routinely transcended such oppositions, however, a different picture can emerge. Rather than canceling out the other's racism, racist practice has been more likely to demonstrate a cumulative logic. In this sense, rather than seeing domestic racism simply fueling empire, we can recognize how imperial expansion at the turn of the century and Jim Crow had reciprocal effects. Both gave new life to racist schemas of thought already deposited in the American past.

The flowering of U.S. liberal internationalism in the twentieth century, encapsulated by Woodrow Wilson's "Fourteen Points," was nominally anti-imperialist, offering general support to the principle of national self-determination in international affairs. This should not mislead us, however. Wilson's views were partially born of strategic considerations, particularly of the threat posed by the radical, left-wing anticolonialism of the Bolshevik revolution under V. I. Lenin, which quickly gained adherents among intellectuals and insurgents of the colonial peripheries. Defeated by the more robust vision of imperialist rivalry favored by Senator Henry Cabot Lodge, Wilson failed to transform U.S. foreign policy and public opinion, which returned to isolationism within a hemispheric dominion after World War I. Indeed, even in its most enlightened form, Wilsonian internationalism failed to address colonial and minority questions, as both the United States and European powers remained notoriously hostile to the grievances of colonial subjects and rising nonwhite powers such as Japan. A Southerner, Wilson's own racial antipathies were well known. He enforced rigid segregation on the capitol during his years in the White House and he regarded U.S. black soldiers as an especially dangerous group, a fertile conduit, he said, for the spread of Bolshevism in the United States. This viewpoint gained a wider purchase through popular period works depicting western civilization imperiled by the twinned threats of international revolutionary politics and white racial degeneration. Following World War I, the combination of Red scares and race riots fueled a counter-subversive imagination that would inextricably link antiblack racism and anti-radicalism for years to come.[47]

From the turn of the century until the New Deal era, black political actors faced a world defined by competing versions of capitalist imperialism (in which the entitlements of national belonging had little or no relevance or value for non-national subjects) and a nation-state organized around herrenvolk republicanism (in which civil, legal, and political institutions were effectively established as a white monopoly and institutional preserve).[48] In fact, whiteness was arguably solidified as a structure of privilege during this period, as immigration restriction and virulent Americanization campaigns hastened the assimilation of previously stigmatized European immigrants and the intensification of the legal and cultural codes of U.S. biracialism at the national level. Even though whiteness and Americanness were never perfect synonyms, during the imperial scramble for territories they increasingly operated in concert as signs of universality, humanity, and civilization as the nation entered the globalizing epoch. The power of whiteness was enhanced by its mutability in a context of national and global expansion, even as the idea of blackness was more powerfully fixed as its antithesis.[49]

Thus, just as the state and the market have converged around practices of racial ascription and hierarchy, so have the realms of the domestic and the transnational. Indeed, the great power of modern racism as a mode of symbolic action—a way of organizing ideas in relation to practice—is that its purview has been at once so great and so varied. No amount of qualifying American nationalism with the terms "liberal" or "democratic" can mitigate how the accumulated history of racial inequality has weighed on the movements of U.S. history into the present day. The long centrality and normativity of whiteness in U.S. political culture has not been inconsistent with the history of American liberal-democracy, but integral to it.[50]

With the explosive racial conflicts of the past half-century supposedly behind us, contemporary affirmations of the United States as an exceptional and exemplary nation have returned to the old habits of downplaying the enduring power of racial domination in shaping U.S. social and political history. Evidence of antiblack racism in political life or the marketplace is defined as latent rather than manifest, contingent rather than normative, practical rather than theoretical, temporary rather than permanent, a result of minoritarian commitments to race rather than to endemic, racist constructions of the polity. As philosopher Michael Waltzer writes, "With severe, but episodic exceptions" tolerance has been the national norm. Gleason acknowledges a "latent predisposition" to racism within U.S. nationality but concludes that a commitment to universal "defining principles . . . has worked historically to overcome exclusions and to make the practical boundaries of American identity more congruent with its theoretical universalism." And, Hollinger concludes, "The 'we' that corresponds to American citizenship—mediates more directly than most other national communities do between the species and those varieties of human kind defined in terms of ethno-racial affiliations."[51]

By failing to acknowledge or to assess the articulations of race and nation, racism and nationalism, reiterations of American universalism evade the issue. This has coincided with a shifting of the burden of racial ascription onto black people themselves. No longer do the racial practices of the dominant society deform the lives of peoples of color, it is said, but their own single-parent households, lack of work ethic, criminal tendencies, and welfare dependency are to blame. Blacks need to stop crying racism and pull themselves up by their bootstraps just as wave upon wave of new Americans have done. One of the staunchest defenders of American universalism over the past half-century, Arthur Schlesinger Jr. expresses a widely held view when he argues that race-conscious blacks, "nourishing prejudice, magnifying difference and stirring up antagonism," have come to represent a significant threat to the defining ethos of American nationhood.[52]

Arguments such as these have resentfully displaced the singular history of U.S. racism in a manner similar to the post-Reconstruction era attacks upon blacks. Then, war-weary whites angrily sacrificed black equality to the project of national reconciliation. Blacks, it was said, were free, now they needed to get back to work. Something like this has occurred in the postcivil rights era, when the lack of statutory (or *de jure*) racial inequality, or an absence of explicit white supremacist discourses, is said to sufficiently demonstrate harmony between the universalistic theory of U.S. nationhood and its social functioning and political practice. Substituting "American" for "white" as the term signifying an inclusiveness "beyond race," this claim overlooks the historical reproduction of a "possessive investment in whiteness," which continues to limit equal access to housing and labor markets (in the absence of *de jure* racial discrimination) and which produces a form of majority tyranny in politics that blocks even moderate efforts toward racial redress and equality, such as minority redistricting and affirmative action.

Less obvious, but equally important (especially in the context of the current world crisis), is that assertions that true Americans embody a universalism beyond race have contributed to the belief of U.S. policymakers and public intellectuals that they speak and act on behalf of the entire world, even as they recognize the humanity and uphold the interests of the few—those who are believed to share common political traditions, or who have obtained legitimacy through market success. As Schlesinger puts it once again in a characteristic passage defending the historic imperatives and presumptions of U.S. nationhood:

> Our task is to combine due appreciation of the splendid diversity of the nation with due emphasis upon the great unifying Western ideas of individual freedom, political democracy and human rights. These are the ideas of American nationality—and today empower people of all continents, races and creeds. "What then is the American, this new man? Here individuals of all nations are melted into a new race of men." Still a good answer—still the best hope.[53]

Further contextualization and a closer reading of this passage are in order. In resurrecting the idea of an American race, Schlesinger draws on Crevecour's *Notes of an American Farmer* (1788), one of the first of many works to define the process of perfecting the republic as a special alchemy of melting or mixture. "What then is an American, this new man?" Crevecour asked. "He is an American, who leaving behind him all his ancient prejudices and manners, receives new ones from the new mode of life he has embraced, the new government he obeys, and the new rank he holds . . . Here individuals of all nations are melted into a new race of men."

This is the now-familiar template of American universalism. The "new race" is precisely national and universal to the extent to which it incorporates anterior differences of nationality, class, status, and custom. Yet, Crevecour also made it very clear in the lines that precede these oft-quoted ones that his universal American was "either a European, or a descendant of a European." The ability to leave oneself behind and enter into the national abstraction was to be the property of particular subjects and unavailable to others. Crevecour's transcendent Americanism was no empty container, but rather dependent on a prior order of ascription, transnational in scope.[54]

What is interesting about the idea of an American race is that the language of race is used to mark not particularity and exclusion but universality and inclusion. The significance of this is missed by those who understand racial differentiation solely in relation to domestic political order, or as the failure of American universalism that results from the need to construct a sufficiently concrete or particular basis for national identity. The idea of an American race also works from the outside in: a supranational lineage originating in northern or western Europe is imagined to be its germ. Rather than excluding, the language of race here encompasses a wider world of transnational affiliation that enables the United States as an admittedly particular nation-state to claim a transhistorical trajectory in the service of humanity itself. But, we must ask, what other function does the term "Western" serve when placed in front of the terms "freedom" and "democracy," than to signify the boundaries of humanity as a transnational racial community?

Ironically, even the most careful defenders of American universalism end up circumscribing the ethnos to which America corresponds. David Hollinger, for example, acknowledges that the distinction between civic nationalism and ethnic nationalism that he sees underpinning American universalism is less than securely fixed. Recognizing that all solidarities are constructs rather than primordial, Hollinger nonetheless suggests that it is important not to underestimate the "cultural continuities that have developed in relation to the American nation-state." "The distinction between civic and ethnic eventually breaks down," he writes, "because over the course of time civic affiliations can help to create those that are eventually recognized as ethnic."[55] Time, however, is the refuge of the racial imagination. At what point in time do those marked with the gross morphologies of dark skin, almond-shaped eyes, wide or flat noses, many of whom have participated in the civic life of the United States for generations, become part of its ethnos? A more difficult question: If the radically open-ended vision of civic-nationalism has been repeatedly undermined from within and without by cultural continuities of whiteness as a supremacist discourse, what does this tell us about the vaunted universalism of the United States?

The idea of cultural continuities can be specified more precisely in relation to the constitution of what Etienne Balibar calls the "fictive ethnicity" of a nation-state. Fictive ethnicity is a concept that helps to explain why liberal, civic-nationalism is paradoxical in its universalism, or why racism has so often emerged as its supplement.[56] Civic nationalism, like all forms of nationalism, is not simply based upon an empty abstraction; it also creates institutions and draws upon and reinforces particular cultural narratives, practices, and histories. This is the point at which a process of subjective normalization occurs and political struggles over the meaning and content of nationalist lineage generally ensue. In other words, it will not do to separate nationalism into civic and ethnic strands. When talking about nationalism, we must talk about the emancipation of the individual as an abstract citizen-subject as we simultaneously acknowledge the process by which a collective identity is created by state institutions and their rubrics of cultural legitimation.[57]

The liberal-democratic nation-state and its structures of citizenship are examples of what Balibar calls "fictitious universalism," or the universalism appropriate to those domains that encompass "effective processes of institutions and representations . . . [that] liberate individual subjectivity from narrow communitarian bonds, and at the same time impose normal, i.e. normative and normalized patterns of individual behavior."[58] The political community of the modern civic nation has been imagined first as something that can contain inequalities generated by the protections of private accumulation and market activity.[59] At the same time, the civic nations of Europe and America have also formed against one another as a dominant "core" in a world system in which territorial conquest, forced labor, and colonization have been central to a history of nationalizing otherwise heterogeneous social territories and articulating them into a common entity, often called "the West." In other words, these nations have formed the kind of collective identity for which the historical frameworks of race and legacies of racism have been employed to produce both a concept of the people and the legitimacy of the state.

To put it more simply, ideologies and practices of racism have been central to the formation of nation-states in the epoch of capitalism's global expansion. The mediation performed by the U.S. nation-state, especially in the era of its own global ascendancy, has not been between ethnos and species, then, but between honored individuals and communities within the nation-state and a privileged series of "family resemblances" and "special relationships" beyond national borders. Forms of intranational and transnational identification have in turn worked to restrain a movement of U.S. nationalism, from an over-inclusiveness that potentially extends to the entire world to a resolute affirmation of particular national interests and identities.[60] This is why racialization has been a persistent feature in the nationalization of U.S. (and European) social formations; it has helped to define a normal state of national belonging both as a product of a unique history and local circumstance and as a defining aspect of one's humanity, or membership in a global civilization. It remains a paradox that the racism that produced these definitions as exclusive conditions constantly threatens to bring them into crisis because the national, the civilized, and the human are also understood to be universal and universalizing conditions.

We will not understand the historical functioning and durability of race (and its cognate terms) until we recognize that it is at once larger and smaller than the nation-state. We might think of race, racism, and fictive ethnicity as mysteries lodged within the "hyphen" joining the nation and the state, society and the market, liberalism and democracy. For what is the hyphen but the place of what is occluded from view, or ancillary to politics, and yet also what allows us to assemble these unstable conjunctions? On the one hand, the hyphen allows us to imagine that the universalizing value of national sovereignty can be separated from the racial depredations of modern imperialism. On the other hand, it suggests that the global expansion of Enlightenment universals and capitalist markets progressively overcomes parochialism and ethnocentrism, rather than unendingly renewing them.

Despite living in a democratic age, we remain haunted by a legacy of white men of property who adjudicated the "fitness" for self-government of their social inferiors. The racism that has shaped the world's "core" nation-states has in this sense not only helped to limit the most profound social injuries of the market to those cast outside the sphere of democratic sovereignty, it has also helped to ensure that rising democratic demands for social protection have never been commensurate with market expansion. Racialized peoples in turn are those who have been defined by a status that is never individuated enough to grant rights, nor collective enough to justify sovereignty. In the U.S. context, this has entailed the production of a host of "exceptional" figures and legal fictions exorbitant to liberal-democracy: the three-fifths person (African slave), the "domestic dependent nation" (American Indians), "separate but equal," (black citizen), "foreign in a domestic sense" (Puerto Ricans), the "immigrant ineligible for naturalization" (Asians), and of course the "free white person."

It may not be possible to fully disaggregate racist commitments and histories from the liberal-democratic components of U.S. national identity. Rather than being definitively separated from Europe, the United States emerged as a major tributary of the modern European stream of racist projections of an idealized humanity against an abject prehumanity or subhumanity. American universalism then, in both its liberal and democratic articulations, has degenerated into racism not because it has failed to be "true" to itself, but because racial demarcation has historically been a central measure of the inner constitution of modern, civic identity. As a consequence, when considering the historical and political status of racial exclusion and inequality perpetuated under the auspices of U.S. liberal-nationalism, the reassertion of American universalism provides few answers; it only begs more questions.

Black Critique: The Dialectic of Race and Nation

The traces and remains of the racist past are deeply engrained in U.S. society and culture. Against the historical backdrop of U.S. racism and the racialized social conflicts since mid-century, it is easy to see why a "new founding" would be necessary and desirable. Yet, the record of the post–World War II efforts to overcome historical racism is mixed at best. Often it has appeared that there has merely been an effort to sanitize the past and to restore tired truths rather than to establish new foundations. Today, struggles against racial discrimination are believed to reside so securely within the boundaries and history of U.S. political culture that they are no longer even believed to be necessary. The color-blind equation of antiracism with an argument against any form of racial differentiation further suggests that black people do not possess any distinct historical, cultural, or political claims on the U.S. body politic.

This perspective was emergent in its basic contemporary form in the first major work of modern racial liberalism, Gunnar Myrdal's two-volume, seven-year collaborative effort, *An American Dilemma: The Negro Problem and Modern Democracy* (1944). More than any other single work, this study sought to provide the intellectual foundations for the effort to overcome racial segregation and abolish *de jure* racial hierarchy at the start of the long civil rights era. Beginning work in the late 1930s, Myrdal and his associates established a formulation in which racial justice in the United States was assured by the power of "the American Creed," or the U.S. commitment to Enlightenment universals of liberty and equality. As Myrdal summarized: "When in this crucial time the international leadership passes to

America, the great reason for hope is that this country has a national experience of uniting racial and cultural diversities, and a national theory, if not a consistent practice, of freedom and equality for all. What America is constantly reaching for is democracy at home and abroad. The main trend in its history is the gradual realization of the American Creed."[61]

Myrdal's distinction between theory and practice was a canny one. It has been a powerful intellectual device for shoring up the universal basis of American national norms in the face of contrary evidence. With it, Myrdal and his collaborators established the framework in which the liberal emphasis on racial reform in the United States has been understood ever since, namely, as something that is paradoxically already accomplished and never quite complete. By identifying the "American Creed" as the main trend in U.S. history, Myrdal further posited the overcoming of racism in America (and in the global realm under U.S. leadership) as a teleological certainty. Thus, despite a commitment to reform, in Myrdal's hands the messy actualities of the struggle against racial injustice and for racial democracy were demoted within the classic form of Whig history. As he put it, "since Revolutionary times; steadily, although with long periods when gains were made and there were actually losses, the ideals of the American Creed have been winning out."[62]

Recent incarnations of American universalism are the products of the political and ideological course of racial liberalism that coalesced in the years before World War II, based on the idea that modern life inevitably yielded a steady transition from the evils of racial differentiation into holistic national sameness. One of the cruelest ironies of new liberal approaches to race was that its powerful new impetus toward social reform could not differentiate itself from the longer-standing wish that "Negroes" themselves would simply disappear. Kenneth Stampp's plaintive statement that "black men were after all simply white men with black skin" was a manifestation of this wish. Or, as St. Louis Cardinals manager Eddie Stankey offered in response to the persistent race-baiting of the growing number of black Major League baseball players in the wake of Jackie Robinson's success, "Negro players shouldn't be touchy about those things. They've just got to forget they're black." What the nation now demanded, Nathan Glazer warned the advocates of black power in the 1960s, was "the final liquidation of Negro separation."[63]

Modern racial liberalism's best intentions have been betrayed by its own metaphors, whether they are metaphors of forgetting, liquidation, or today's preferred term, blindness. Why a visual impairment that interferes with the perception of normal variations in the color spectrum has become the preferred image of racial neutrality, if not racial justice, defies common-sense. The imperative to be color-blind only makes sense if we assume that to perceive color automatically leads to hierarchies of value. In the United States, only one socially significant tradition is built on this assumption: white supremacy. Under the universal, color-blind regime, in other words, we are forced back on an unstated belief in the order of white over black. In this looking-glass world, the struggle for racial equality is turned on its head. Today, to see antiblack racism as something that still generates social inequalities marks one at best as oversensitive, with suspect judgment, and at worst as racist, still invested in an invidious logic of race.

The liberal-nationalism underpinning the past half-century of U.S. racial reform has been ill-equipped to address the historical question of racial injustice. Viewing race and nation as incompatible rubrics of communal life, liberal-nationalists have argued that transforming racial subjects into national subjects is the most urgent antiracist task. Yet, at the same time, they have imagined the nation and, as important, the normative national subject as entities that exist beyond any kind of ethnoracial history. While post-World War II liberals and conservatives have imagined solving the "Negro problem" with integration and color-blindness, rather than expulsion and whiteness, they have been unable to come to terms with the legacy of racially coded difference itself.

The urgent admission of blacks into an order of abstract equality or citizenship has taken the form of a claim that "the Negro" is simply an "American." It offers to overlook the negative particularities of racial ascription on the condition of an absolute rejection of any positive particularities that may have accrued to black cultural and communal practices over time. This stance thus ironically perpetuates a situation in which blacks remain the group in the United States denied ethnic honor (the honor of having "ethnicity") and in which whiteness remains the (unstated) cultural norm.[64]

During the Cold War, Myrdal's principal black collaborator, Ralph Bunche, exemplified this strategy of inclusion in his 1949 address to the graduating class of Fisk University: "The Negro graduates of Fisk University are better Americans than they are Negroes. They are Negro primarily in a negative sense. They reject that sort of treatment that deprives them of their birthright as Americans. Remove that treatment and their identification as Negroes in American society would become meaningless—at least as meaningless as it is to be of English, or French, or German, or Italian ancestry."[65]

Bunche's statement again illuminates the conventional means of producing the fictive ethnicity "American," in relationship to a prior order of identities it has left behind and supposedly rendered meaningless. More specifically, it aligns the black future with the bountiful freedoms of the settlers, those whose ethno-national origins either never were, or long ceased to be, incompatible with American identity. (Indeed, it is interesting that Bunche did not compare blacks with American Indians, or to Japanese or Chinese migrants, whose ancestries still prevented them from becoming "naturalized" citizens.) Even more significant in this regard was his conflation of being a Negro with an ongoing sense of abjectness, or the negation of normative nationality. One could hardly imagine saying, for example, that one was "English" primarily in a negative sense; rather, being—or once having been English—could be a source of pride, a tributary of American expansiveness, rather than something to be downgraded or concealed, a source of American shame.

Under the regime of modern racial liberalism, it has been difficult to uncouple the idea of successful black assimilation from violent imageries of black erasure long central to American exceptionalism. Specifically, normative attempts to write blacks into a national narrative of immigrant incorporation and ethnic succession have invariably left behind the traces of prior histories of racialization. This has been manifested in an intellectual division of labor in which discussions of intranational differences often proceed under the separate headings of "race" and "ethnicity." Race and ethnicity have become ways to handle different kinds of difference. As a normative category, ethnicity has become a generic marker or symbolic residue of a kind of difference that no longer makes a difference, thus contributing to the transcendent idea of America as a container of only positive and uncomplicated diversities. Race by contrast remains a code for histories of color: legacies of conquest, enslavement, and non-national status that disturb the national peace, whose narratives must thus be silenced within public culture, or hived off from the national story into a separate world of their own.

The splitting off of racial history has, in our own time, yielded a kind of national schizophrenia in which racial difference is either shouted down in a chorus of national unanimity (color-blindness), or shunted into zones of institutionalized marginality—the ghetto, the prison, even the ethnic studies program. In the mid-1950s, E. Franklin Frazier discerned the rise of the first tendency in his telling suggestion that the unremitted pursuit of equality after World War II had led many middle-class blacks and black intellectuals to become "exaggerated Americans."[66] Bunche typified this, not only in his forcible negation of racial difference, but also in upholding an idea that has subsequently become central to modern defenses of American universalism, namely, that black struggles against inequality and racial discrimination have no meaning beyond affirming the normative values and identities of the national community.

As an exclusive emphasis, this approach has an air of wish fulfillment about it and tends to operate at the expense of a more complicated and disturbing story. Few of this political faith consider what has happened to black intellectuals and activists who have presented the challenge of a consistent and exacting universalism, but the list would include exile, repression, ostracism, and assassination. And few ponder the compelling question posed by Langston Hughes: "What happens to a dream deferred?" Unilateral decrees of American universalism not only force us to dispose of questions of racial inequality prematurely, but they also require us to misread the innovative, politically productive dynamic in which black publics have asserted their own racial particularity in the name of wider struggles for social justice. The effort to articulate a black standpoint on public life—what Jean-Paul Sartre (perhaps unfortunately) labeled "racist anti-racism"—has been a characteristic response to its opposite: a universalizing antiracism complicit with the nonrecognition of black social existence.

If we take the articulations of racism and nationalism in U.S. history seriously, then under what intellectual terms and social conditions has the U.S. nation-state been a liberating ideal and institutional form? Specifically, what would an account of American national identity look like if it engaged with the recurrent force of white supremacy, particularly from the perspective of the social struggles that have most vigorously opposed it? For while black intellectuals and social movements for equality have undoubtedly drawn from vocabularies that signify an adherence to universal values in the U.S. political imagination, including Christianity, liberalism, democratic-republicanism, and varieties of Euro-American cosmopolitanism, they have also drawn on universalizing discourses that surpass the sanctioned national and transnational boundaries of U.S. political and intellectual culture, including Islam, international socialism, black nationalism, and varieties of third worldism.

From the compulsive (one wants to say compulsory) standpoint of American univeralism, one can only regard the latter incarnations of black politics as aberrant or incoherent—irrational excesses born of racial subjection. As a result, the dominant flavor of the contemporary discussion of race and nation reproduces one of the foundational exclusions of U.S. political culture, in which liberal nationalist conventions monopolize the discussion of civic identity and political expression at the expense of a full rendering of black political subjectivity. The casualties of this account, as King's career showed, are political expressions of black discontent that deviate from a normative trajectory. These are regarded as signs of frustration and futility, or worse, ingratitude and insubordination. To salvage King for the purposes of nationalist memory it has thus been necessary (and easy) to forget how he scandalized the nation with his searing prophecy that the promises of the Great Society had been shot down on the battlefields of Vietnam, as well as his recognition that the black struggle for "civil rights" in the United States was only a small part of a much longer, more global, and mostly unfulfilled struggle against the psychic, material, and juridical legacies of white supremacy.

Efforts to write racially excluded populations into national histories reinforce the false idea that the nation-state is the sole arbiter of universal values and legitimate political aims. At the same time, it would be a mistake to overlook the political inventiveness, collective irony, and socially significant identity that have resulted from black people's struggles to make the U.S. nation-state their own. Keeping both in mind modifies either an American universalist or a strictly ethnocultural account of black modernity. It also foregrounds the fact that the forms of collective identity and practice instituted by racial difference are not organic, essential, or self-evident, but are historically specific and variable creations. Like nation, race has been subject to ongoing material reconstitution and symbolic representation shaped by internal political conflicts and divisions and by the disorganizing and aggregating pressures of more powerful social forces.

Black activist intellectuals and social movements have confronted the assertions of the universal moral, political, and ethical values of the nation-state in the breech created by the reproduction of historical racism. In doing so they have produced what can be characterized as a distinctively dialectical discourse of race and nation. To paraphrase an early formulation of Du Bois, black political discourse has represented the hopes of black populations and shaped understandings of racial exclusion in relation to the "ethical currents" moving the U.S. nation-state as a whole. The imagery of parts and wholes should not mislead us, though. This has been a relentlessly "negative dialectic," in which black intellectuals and activists recognized that racial belonging operates at scales that are both smaller and larger than the nation-state, and voiced visions of communal possibility that consistently surpassed the conceptions available in the prevailing idioms of U.S. political culture.[67]

In other words, struggles to claim universality for black people have challenged not only particularlism masquerading as a universalism, but a universalism distorted by its long monopolization against blacks. The repetition of this confrontation has yielded distinct patterns and expressions of black, antiracist discourse and communal identity that cannot be reduced to the nationalist teleology of American universalism and its dominant discursive frames of market-individualism and civic-nationalism. This is the more crucial point: black freedom struggles have not only been about obtaining market access, equal citizenship, or integrating black people into common national subjectivity. Rather, they represent the counter-statements of political subjects who have struggled to widen the circle of common humanity. To put this another way, if American universalism has been marked by its persistent degeneration into racial exclusion, black political life has been marked by the opposite movement: the generation of new universals from the forcible enclosures of racial stigma.[68]

The critical task thus becomes to trace the movements of black social thought and action in their self-consciously dialectical relationship to the official civic ideology, rhetoric, and norms of U.S. nationalism and government practice. "What to the Slave is the Fourth of July?" (1852), Frederick Douglass asked in one of the earliest, most outstanding examples of this mode of discourse. Beginning with praise for the nation-state, the founding documents, and civic and religious traditions as the emblems of a superior universalization already achieved, Douglass located himself *outside* what he called "*your* National Independence," "*your* political freedom," and "*your* great deliverance." The "existence of slavery," Douglass argued, in a searing litany, placed American universalism in doubt and disrepute: "[it] brands your republicanism as a sham, your humanity as a base pretence, and your Christianity as a lie; . . . it makes your name a hissing, and a by-word to a mocking earth."[69]

Douglass relented as he wound down his address, expressing "hope" that the insurrectionary universalism and progressive historicism of U.S. liberal-republicanism and Enlightenment discourse assured "the doom of slavery."[70] Yet, he never stopped arrogating for himself the right to view the nation from "the standpoint" of "the victims of American oppression."[71] This meant that he did not articulate his demand for inclusion from an identifiable location within the nation-state as a cultural emblem and institutional guarantor of human rights, but instead asserted a prior—even utopian—claim on humanity and human rights that the nation-state denied. Insofar as the humanity of black people (both slave and free) had been put into question, Douglass implied, the U.S. nation-state and its particular amalgam of political and religious discourses always had a relative, rather than an absolute, value as a frame of reference, source of authority, and site of public conflict and struggle.

For Douglass, as for King more than a century later, the final court of appeal lay beyond the nation-state—in a global realm in which "no nation can shut itself up from the surrounding world," where "oceans no longer divide, but link nations together."[72] In the absence of stable reform, even Douglass, the ex-slave and outstanding black exponent of radical liberalism and national-racial integration, would, like his twentieth-century counterpart, invoke a vision of black self-determination that exceeded the boundaries and truncated universalism of the U.S. nationalist project: "With the Gulf of Mexico on the South and Canada on the North, we may still keep within hearing of the wails of our enslaved people in the United States. From the isles of the sea, and from the mountain tops of South America we can watch the meandering destiny already on this Continent, and in the adjacent islands, all of 12,370,000 Negroes, who only wait for the life-giving and organizing power of intelligence to mould them into one body and into a powerful nation."[73]

Black nationalism, defined here as the imagination of black communal autonomy arrayed against the primacy of U.S. nationalist discourse and political culture, has been dismissed as a minor tendency in the thought of both Douglass and King, as well as of a host of other black thinkers and activists who personify the black face of American virtue. American liberal intellectuals (and some black nationalists) have divided a black protest tradition into liberal/integrationist/ Americanist and radical/separatist/ blackist variants. Yet, this division does an injustice to the array of black activist intellectuals (including King and Douglass) who embodied this split within a single career.

Specifically, the integrationist/separatist opposition obscures the constitutive tension that has shaped black encounters with the U.S. nation-form and its dominant political discourses. These encounters have been experienced by black intellectual activists as a double-bind, in which a too-honest assessment of U.S. racial exclusion risks looking like a fatalistic disavowal of national progress, while concessions to optimism appear foolish and exaggerated. As hard as achieving affective equanimity has been, it has also been problematic for black freedom struggles to separate liberal demands for tolerance and individual rights from group demands for recognition and social equalization. To the extent that black activist intellectuals have negotiated these emotional and conceptual dualisms, they have generated their own significant languages of politics with distinct lines of influence, division, and debate.

The opposition between the leadership paradigms of Booker T. Washington and Du Bois at the beginning of the twentieth century has generally been a starting point for these considerations. Indeed, the Washington and Du Bois conflict might be viewed as an inceptive black variation on the conflict between liberal and civic-republican tendencies in American political thought. Behind the mask of a folksy racial provincialism ("casting our buckets down where we are"), Washington supported the orthodox liberal conception that the cultivation of proprietary individualism and good market behavior ("property, economy, and Christian character") was the key to racial uplift. As founder of the Negro Business League in 1900, he foresaw black entry into industrial labor and the development of nascent forms of black capitalism premised on intraracial class stratification and a model of segregated capital accumulation. In a social context in which 90 percent of all blacks were poor, landless, racially terrorized agricultural laborers, however, Washington's true appeal was less as the harbinger of a vital black capitalism than as the deliverer of docile black labor. (which he tellingly advertised as "the best free labor in the world, not given to striking"). Perhaps not surprisingly, he gained significant backing from politically and economically powerful whites throughout the nation, particularly northern industrialists, while obtaining for himself considerable powers of appointment and intellectual authority over a small, but politically stunted, black intelligentsia until his death in 1915.[74]

Although the influence of Washington's economic thinking lingered within versions of black nationalism from Garveyism to the Nation of Islam to contemporary black neoliberalism, it was Du Bois who created the more enduring philosophy and tradition of black civic struggle. Penning the first significant intellectual defense of federal interventions during Reconstruction, Du Bois presented a frontal challenge to the antistatist liberalism of his era that made such an easy peace with segregation. Challenging the idea that racial exclusion could be addressed through a simple market calculus, Du Bois emphasized the importance of rights and duties associated with membership within the national, political community. As one of the chief conveners of the Niagra Movement (the precursor to the NAACP) in 1906 with Monroe Trotter, Du Bois was one of the principle black authors of the democratic-republican demand for "every single right that belongs to a freeborn American, political, civil and social."[75]

While Du Bois emphasized the collective struggle for political rights and social equality across the broad front of civil society—including black entry into trade unions—his early thought maintained a strong antidemocratic cast that many would claim it never lost. Just as the parallel civic-egalitarian struggles among middle-class women and white male workers retained strong racialist commitments, early black public activism under Du Bois's leadership was built on the idea of substituting hierarchies of gender and education for those of race and accumulated wealth ("a dictatorship of character and intelligence across the color-line"). Du Bois's famous emphasis on the black "talented-tenth" as a fount of racial genius and a leadership vanguard thus narrowed the scope of intraracial democracy within an incipient black public sphere for at least at least a generation, privileging what was essentially an elitist and patriarchal mode of discourse.[76]

In several important respects, however, Du Bois's ideas were in continuous revolution. Although he held strongly to the possibilities of U.S. national reform in the era before World War I, by 1919 he bitterly recognized that his patriotic call on blacks to close ranks with the nation during the war had yielded few social and political gains. "What we cannot accomplish before the choked conscience of America," he wrote then, "we have an infinitely better chance to accomplish before the Organized Public Opinion of the World."[77] Over the following decades, he too would emphasize what he termed "the world view" of "the unsolved problem of race relations." "Our good will," he wrote, "is too often confined to that labor which we see and feel and exercise around us, rather than directed to the periphery of the vast circle, where unseen and inarticulate, the determining factors are at work." He spent the rest of his life in a conscious search for forms of discourse and political struggle adequate to what he called "the ever-widening circles" of common humanity, including an embrace of an ever-more strident socialism.[78]

World War I and its aftermath were profoundly disillusioning for U.S. black intellectual activists, because many had hoped and expected national military service would result in an augmentation of citizenship rights. The war marked the beginning of a sustained period of radicalization and adversarial internationalization for black politics as socialists and black nationalists entered the field of racial struggle in significant numbers for the first time. As Du Bois observed in *Darkwater* (1920), his most bitter and caustic book, "as far as black and brown and yellow people are concerned," World War I was little more than a "jealous and avaricious struggle for the largest share in exploiting the darker races."[79] This period witnessed the remarkable emergence of Marcus Garvey's United Negro Improvement Association (UNIA), which, despite its meteoric rise and fall, left an unmistakable imprint on black politics and intellectual life during the interwar period. Although he feuded bitterly with Garvey, Du Bois agreed with much of the latter's race-based internationalism. Garvey's prophetic statement, "I know no national boundaries where the Negro is concerned" resonated with Du Bois's contemporaneous claim that "a belief in humanity is a belief in colored men."[80]

By the 1930s, a highly internationalist and leftist cohort of black intellectuals had begun to produce a sophisticated body of work analyzing racism and colonialism as a global history of Euro-American dominance. Works like George Padmore's *Lives and Struggles of Ne-*

gro Toilers (1935), Du Bois's *Black Reconstruction* (1935), Ralph Bunche's *A World View of Race* (1936), C. L. R. James's *Black Jacobins* (1938), Eric Williams's *Capitalism and Slavery* (1944), Du Bois's *Color and Democracy: the Colonies and Peace* (1945), and Oliver Cox's *Caste, Class and Race* (1948) outlined the spatial and temporal coordinates of a modern world-system, racially ordered by the international slave trade in African bodies, and the conquest of the aboriginal peoples in the Americas. Where Du Bois and James emphasized the ways that racial and colonial projects truncated the radical universality of the national forms of political modernity bequeathed by the American and French Revolutions, Cox and Williams argued that the global, long durée of economic modernity twinned the processes of capital accumulation and racial domination at its inception.[81]

The conventional opposition between a nation-oriented racial integration and an autonomy-driven black nationalism is an impoverished framework for understanding the modern forms of black politics that crystallized at the intersection of nation-based class conflicts and anticolonial ferment in the inter-war period. What may have been most innovative about the black political imagination that developed between the Great Depression and the end of World War II was its increasingly sophisticated meditation on what the communists called "the national question." Black movements and intellectuals at once weighed the positive aspects of the emergence of black people into the national consciousness of American publics and policy-makers during the New Deal era against the increasingly powerful and distinctive expressions of the political self-consciousness of black people as a *people* within a world-system who were effectively denied national status, or as Du Bois put it more sharply, "a nation without a polity, nationals without citizenship."[82]

While the modern black freedom struggle is as old as the Atlantic slave trade and encompasses a history of resistance, refusal, revolts, and runaways, black modernity—in the narrow sense of gaining collective access to the means and instruments of modern, democratic politics—is inextricable from the vicissitudes of U.S. national history since the mid-1930s. This was hastened by the increasing heterogeneity and political radicalism of black freedom struggles, both in terms of class composition and ideological adherence and by the emergence of a transformational dynamic between increasingly self-conscious black publics and wider U.S. and global publics.

As Ralph Ellison wrote in 1942 in his journal, *Negro Quarterly,* black people were creating "themselves as a free people and as a nation." The use of the term "nation" by black writers during this period signaled a kind of self-invention and communal imagination that differed from older uses of "race" and pressed a claim to political sovereignty for blacks in the United States similar to that of colonial subjects throughout the world. That Ellison refused to specify the source of national identification evoked the ambiguity of the ultimate political horizons of black nationhood, even as he affirmed his belief that the Negro's "historical role" was "integrating the larger American nation and compelling it untiringly toward freedom."[83] Caribbean intellectual activist and U.S. sojourner C. L. R. James framed the matter in his own inimitable Marxian analysis of black protest activity he witnessed and encouraged in these years: "The history of the Negro in the U.S. is a history of his increasing race consciousness, a constantly increasing desire to vindicate his past, and the achievements and qualifications of the Negro race as a race. This is an inevitable result of his position in American society, of the development of this society itself, and is not only a powerful but a familiar concomitant everywhere of the struggles of nationally oppressed groups."[84]

The last point is easy to misconstrue in the current context, where attacks on the notion of a racial essence, the so-called "illusion of race," and uncomplicated notions of black racial unity are routine. But modern "race-making," to use Thomas Holt's phrase, has in different ways, at different times, involved large-scale processes of symbolic mediation frequently ascribed to nation-building, including the formation of publics and translocal imagining of community. To speak of an emergent black public sphere or black nationality at the inception of the long civil rights era is not to endorse a separatist politics of black nationalism, nor does it infer a singular or corporate black racial identity; in fact, it may do the opposite. The modernity of the black public/nation may actually result from the very heterogeneity (in terms of region, occupation, class, and gender) increasingly arrayed and negotiated under the sign "Negro," or "black," as well as from a growing awareness of the lack of biological foundations for racial differentiation, and a widening of the means and scope of intraracial and interracial communication.

To illustrate this, we might compare and contrast Du Bois's depiction in *Souls of Black Folk* (1903) of the southern black belt as "vast stretches of land beyond the telegraph and the newspaper," where "the spirit of the Thirteenth Amendment is sadly broken," with Richard Wright's epic montage, *Twelve Million Black Voices* (1940), in which the urban black belt is characterized as a place of occupational diversity, intraracial class and gender divisions, and a flurry of new mass-mediated messages, images, and symbols.[85] Wright believed that the black movement from country to city inaugurated a "new worldliness" in black life: "The seasons of the plantation no longer dictate the lives of many of us; hundreds of thousands of us are moving into the sphere of conscious history. We are with the new tide. We stand at the crossroads. We watch each new procession. The hot wires carry urgent appeals. Print compels us. Voices are speaking. Men are moving! And we shall be with them." Wright's own emergence as a "native son" of American letters, and as the first U.S. black writer of unquestioned importance to national and international reading publics, exemplified the process he described, in which black people, he said, were attaining a new and paradoxical power to "*represent* . . . what America is."[86]

It is important to distinguish the black capacity to represent America from the idea that Negroes were simply Americans, as if that relationship was and always is self-evident. Like America itself, the formation of black communal identity in this period was open to multiple determinations. A flawed view of "nation"—whether it is the typical Stalinist view of the black "nation" as a territorial, cultural, and psychological unity defined by population concentration alone, the liberal assumption that race and nation are antithetical principles, or the Garveyite vision equating racial separatism and nation-building—should not obscure the modern dynamic of black nationality. As Du Bois recognized when he began describing blacks as "a nation within a nation" in the 1930s, the term "nation" was above all a mechanism of communication and communal regulation that indicated the uniquely modern densities of black existence resulting from racial segregation (what Ralph Ellison would call "the life" black folks had made on "the horns of the white man's dilemma").[87]

What remained to be determined was the precise relationship between black nationality as a marker of what Du Bois termed "free and favorable development" in civic, cultural, and political life, and U.S. nationhood as an institution of governmental power. One thing is certain: the long civil rights era did not lead to black assimilation into the U.S. nation-state, but to a more complex dynamic of *differential inclusion* in which new forms of black existence were shaped in the crucible of black migration, urban apartheid, and new global imaginings and longings. While the New Deal and World War II, like the Civil War and Reconstruction, enhanced the universalizing force and appeal of American nationalism, this was only one side of a social process that gave rise to black political and intellectual dispositions focused not strictly on securing entry and assimilation into the nation-state, but on strengthening relatively autonomous black communal identities, social imperatives, and political interests.

To insist on the autonomy and worldliness of black communal formation and social movement is to refuse the assumption of a long march toward racial equality and social justice in the United States since mid-century. It is also to insist that antiblack racism remains a structuring feature of this national formation. Of course, the historical forms of racism, racial ideologies, and identities have undergone profound changes. Rather than presume that historical change in matters of race and racial formation has led in a linear or progressive direction in conformity with some set of super-ordinate national principles, however, it is valuable to consider the history of racial reform from the standpoint of those who have been subjected to and have struggled against the social practice of racial discrimination and stigma.

To argue that there is in fact a singular standpoint, one that reflects a corporate black racial interest or identity, would be problematic. Nonetheless, the long civil rights era was marked by the shifting, contested formation of black publics that articulated distinct political interests and broadly shared languages of politics. During this period, black social movements developed as an integral part of the expansion of the economic and political promise of U.S. liberal-democracy at home and abroad. At the same time, they began to contest the monopolization of the universal by particular U.S. interests and agendas. As in the past, this period was marked by tension between unfulfilled black aspirations for justice and black investment in the universal sanction and global reach that U.S. political officials and publics claimed for themselves. This led to bitter splits in black movements and attentive publics—in the late 1930s, during World War II, with the onset of the Cold War in the late 1940s, and again with the emergence of black power in the mid-1960s. Nevertheless, a more or less consistent tradition of radical dissent can be traced, in which black activists and movements produced political discourses that strained the nation-form, stretching the boundaries of U.S. liberal and democratic thought and issuing a political challenge—still unmet—to achieve lasting equalitarian transformations of social life in general, both within and beyond U.S. borders.

As Du Bois argued most eloquently, the world beyond the United States was especially important for blacks at home because it presented the possibility of wider publics—indeed a global majority—who had been denied the historic protections and benefits of nationality. This vision was of course central to the formation of the United Nations after World War II. Despite the United Nations's subjection to the machinations of great power politics, the existence of this world body held profound importance as a court of appeal outside the ambit of the nation-state for racially subjected peoples. Inaugurated by Du Bois's famous declaration in 1946: *An Appeal to the World: A Statement on the Denial of Human Rights to Minorities in the Case of Citizens of Negro Descent in the United States of America and an Appeal to the United Nations for Redress,* successive generations of U.S. black activists and organizations in the 1950s, 1960s, and 1970s sought to transform what they viewed as a too-limited struggle for civil rights into a more expansive claim for human rights. This political trajectory remains alive in the demand for reparations for slavery codified in the recent declaration of the 2001 United Nations Conference Against Racism that defined the transatlantic slave trade as a "crime against humanity."[88]

From this perspective, it is not far-fetched to conceptualize black struggles of the long civil rights era in the U.S. as a central part of the wider, more ambiguous legacy of post–World War II decolonization. Indeed, one of the greatest limitations of the civic mythology of America's exceptional universality is that it obscures this link by denying that U.S. history is part of the genealogy of domination and resistance produced by the expansion of colonial (and neocolonial) capitalism. This further prevents us from recognizing that perhaps the most consistent and enduring strand of modern black activism has been the opposition to imperialism and colonialism. It was manifest across the spectrum of black politics, from the secular communism of Du Bois and Paul Robeson, to the Christian pacifism of King and the revolutionary, black nationalism of Malcolm X and the Black Panther Party.

It led diverse groups of the black activists and intellectuals in the United States to consciously link their own aspirations to national liberation struggles across the world, including India, Ghana, Cuba, Congo, Vietnam, South Africa, and Palestine.

One significant concession might be made to the defenders of American universalism: it may be that black intellectuals and social movements developed the most politically generous versions of it available during this period. At the very least, blacks were the one political constituency that consistently supported the expansion of social as well as civil rights, or the development of a full-employment welfare-state in the United States. By refusing to accept the limitations of liberal reform at home, and by challenging the depredations of U.S. imperial politics abroad, black movements consistently advanced more worldly and expansive political conceptions—toward democratic anticapitalism and anti-imperialism—that were regularly disparaged and rejected as un-American. Thus, it is worth pondering the fact that so many of the most celebrated black artists, writers, and activists of the long civil rights era, including Du Bois, Wright, and King, ended their lives in exile from the promise of American universalism.

Race, Autonomy, and Dissent

Black struggles of the long civil rights era produced a different discourse that was neither derivative of, nor separable from, the political dominance of U.S. nationalism. This has been largely effaced in contemporary discussions of race and nation. An example is former U.S. Senator Bill Bradley's seemingly daring uptake of Langston Hughes's famous poem of the 1930s, "Let America, be America Again," in his nominating speech at the 1992 Democratic Convention, delivered in the shadow of the Los Angeles riots after the acquittal of four white police officers who viciously beat black motorist Rodney King. Bradley offered the poem as an example of black affirmation and redemption of national values and foundations in spite of the frustration and bitterness of racial injustice. Yet, much like the civic mythology that now surrounds King, even as this reading used a black forebear to bear the burden of national unity and reformist hope, it missed the consistency of the poem's mirroring refrain—Hughes's parenthetical lament: "(America never was America to me)."

What black novelist Ralph Ellison described as the "boomerang" of history suggests that for black people in the United States, the word "again" has had a different meaning. Rather than signaling the return and renewal of the supposedly timeless universals of American political culture, it evokes "the changing same" of racism, as both a contemporary practice and as one of the country's most insistent forms of historical memory.[89] The boomerang of history is one of the metaphors Ellison uses in *Invisible Man* (1952) to signify the central paradox that has confronted racially subordinated peoples within the United States, in which declarations of American universalism are the sign of both a long-promised liberation and the "obsessive presence of an insidious discourse."[90]

Ellison suggests that racism creates an impossible bind, in which if you're black, "you're damned if you do, damned if you don't." On one hand, adherence to America's allegedly universal "founding principles" can seem like little more than swallowing exclusion; on the other hand, protesting—even in the name of these self-same principles—risks regurgitating racial enmity. Ellison brilliantly dramatizes this bind in his novel's central allegory. In it the protagonist finds himself working at the factory of Liberty Paints, whose slogan, "Keep America Pure with Liberty Paints," is backed by a promise that its "Optic White" is the "purest of whites." Batches of the paint are soon to be shipped out to beautify (that is, whitewash) a national monument. The protagonist's job is to mix ten drops of a substance called "black dope" into the paint, which binds its white color and ensures its properties of adhesion and coverage. The company uses a different—but to the protagonist, indistinguishable—substance as a solvent for the paint, which thins it into a streaky gray ooze. As he furiously mixes the paint, he grows increasingly unsure whether he's applied the correct black additive: the glue or the solvent.[91]

In this parable, Ellison suggests that the country—as signified by its whiter-than-white national monuments—rather than resolving contradictions of racialized citizenship, oscillates between perpetually retouching the facade of its national idealism and worrying that its ugly divisions of race will be exposed. Facing the contradiction between the image of America as the champion of freedom and equality and the violent realities of everyday racial inequality, racialized subjects have experienced cognitive dissonance. Duke Ellington (in an essay known to Ellison) actually counseled blacks to embrace a "strategy of dissonance." In an ironic twist on the emerging post-World War II tendency to trumpet "an American way of life" as a model for all the world's peoples, Ellington wrote, "dissonance is *our way of life in America*; we are something apart; yet an integral part."[92] Lurking within every assertion of national unity and black centrality to that unity lay the oppressive interrogative long at the center of America's relation to black people: "How does it feel to be a problem?" Like the "black dope" in the Liberty Paint paints, blackness unseen allows an imaginary national fusion; blackness visible threatens to dissolve the body politic.

Though Ellison is frequently presented as the archetypal black defender of American universalism, his narrative, written in the aftermath of the Harlem riot of 1943, projects considerable ambiguity about the future of the black relationship to U.S. liberal-nationalism.[93] The career trajectories of many of America's most significant post–World War II black intellectuals offer grounds for more definitive skepticism. Perhaps the signal black public intellectual of the post–World War II era, James Baldwin, traveled a characteristic path in the course of the short civil rights era from the mid-1950s to the late 1960s, one that began with Baldwin's famous "discovery of what it means to be an American."[94] The philosopher Richard Rorty takes Baldwin's call to "achieve our country," written in the early years of the southern civil rights movement, as yet another black emblem of the redemptive potential of U.S. nationalism and liberal-democratic ideals.[95] But this reading again requires us to forget the *other* Baldwin who, after King's assassination and the urban riots that followed in 1968, declared: "One could scarcely be deluded by Americans anymore, one scarcely dared expect anything from the great, vast blank generality; and yet one was compelled to demand of Americans—and for their sakes, after all—a generosity, a clarity and a nobility which they did not dream of demanding of themselves. Part of the error was irreducible, in that the marchers and petitioners were forced to suppose the existence of an entity which, when the chips were down, could not be located."[96] By the late 1960s Baldwin had gravitated toward black militancy, whose chief avatar, the Black Panther Party, irrevocably scarred the reformist liberal-national imagination. Arguably, Baldwin never again made the error of investing the generalities of American universalism with his political hope. Perhaps he had seen the arc of the boomerang.

These cases exemplify what has become an endemic pattern within the dominant U.S. imagination of racial hierarchy and difference, one at least fifty years in the making. More teleological than historical, more nationalist than universalist, post–World War II American liberalism, from Myrdal's *An American Dilemma* to President Bill Clinton's "National Conversation on Race" has consistently underestimated or devalued the autonomous dimensions of black political discourse, extolling instead American political culture as the ablest, if not the only, ideological source of black struggles for justice and equality. Behind the formal similarity of appropriation, annexation, and misreading in the examples just illustrated—in which black activist projects and discourses become nothing more than a vindication of American universalism—lies a temporal coincidence—the years 1943, 1968, and 1992—that tell a different story, the story of repeated massive civil disturbances associated with racial division and inequality. These years might be made to stand for an alternative (and less assuring) historicism, encapsulating a long civil rights era that begins well before the Montgomery Bus Boycott of 1955, and whose ending has not yet been determined.

The vindicationist history of America's self-transcendence of the racial past that dominates the present is predicated upon a national forgetting of what Frederick Douglass called the standpoint of the victims of American history. The specific danger is that many of the valuable insights derived from the ethics and politics of living and overcoming Jim Crow are now being squandered. More worrisome, the steady denial of the deep legacies of historical racism now contributes to the idea of an America restored to an identity with itself and with the destiny of all of humanity. In the face of this, the stubborn contribution of black activism may be to remind us of the words of Langston Hughes: that such an America never was. Indeed, the dialectic of race and nation rehearsed by generations of black intellectuals and activists forces critical recognition of the nonidentity of America—the failure of American universalism—both in space and in time. It thus reopens the necessary, radical question of authentic freedom: what kind of social world might be that fulfills the diverse and particular needs generated by an unequal history?

CHAPTER TWO

Reconstructing Democracy

We need hardly remind ourselves of the degree to which we form today a nation within a nation. Most of us are in separate churches and
separate schools; we live largely in separate parts of the city and
country districts; we marry almost entirely within our own group
and have our own social activities; we get at least a part of our news
from our own newspapers and attend our own theaters and enter-
tainments, even if white men run them.

—W. E. B. DU BOIS, "THE NEGRO AND SOCIAL RECONSTRUCTION" (1936)

In 1934, at the height of the Great Depression and the start of the
New Deal, W. E. B. Du Bois resigned from the National Association
for the Advancement of Colored People (NAACP), one of the first
civil rights organizations in the world and one that, as editor of its
journal *The Crisis,* he founded. Accepting his resignation with a mix
of sadness and regret, the NAACP board of directors recognized that
Du Bois's departure was the start of a new era. Du Bois, they said,
had "created what never existed before, a Negro Intelligentsia." Even
those who did not read his work or agree with his positions were in
his debt.[1]

Du Bois, however, did not go quietly. The NAACP, he charged, was
at an impasse—"without an organization or a program" to address
the economic and social crisis of the times. Black unemployment was
twice the national average, black migrants streamed from country to
city in search of relief, and Roosevelt's National Recovery Administration showed few signs of addressing the needs of the black population. "The face of reform has been set to lift the white producer and
consumer," Du Bois warned, "leaving the black man and his peculiar
problems severely alone."[2] The situation, he argued, required a new
strategy for black advance—based on the "voluntary, determined, cooperative efforts" of Negroes themselves.[3]

For the remainder of the decade, Du Bois focused on developing a
"special plan" to ensure black progress in the face of deteriorating

economic conditions and the benign neglect of New Deal social policy. Negroes, he argued, needed to pursue independent "organization for normative action" because "our advance in the last quarter century has been in segregated, racially integrated institutions and efforts and not in effective entrance into American national life."[4] Du Bois knew that this argument would alarm civil rights leaders, who would take it as a renunciation of the faith in the gradual acquisition of individual, civil, and political rights and national belonging—the liberal-democratic faith that had guided and sustained black struggles in the United States since Reconstruction. But he doubted that racial inequality would yield substantial ground in years to come. He was also pessimistic that alliances between blacks and other social groups or classes could effectively address the wide-ranging legacies of racial exclusion that had so thoroughly eroded "decent civilized ideals in Church, State, industry, and art."[5]

The task ahead, Du Bois declared, was to develop the political and intellectual capacities of a separate world of black public discourse and political action, which he described in telling language as a "new racial production and reasoned distribution."[6] First, this meant overcoming a deficient political imagination in which black people were only viewed "in relation to the people of the U.S." Second, it meant rejecting the idea that blacks could only progress by standing with another recognized national group, whether it was liberal whites, communist radicals, "exploiting capitalists," or striking workers.[7] Du Bois's new emphasis was separatist and (as his many critics charged) "racialist," but in a way that lacked an exact precedent. This was not Garvey's romantic nationalism, nor the Communist Party's "scientific" defense of separate Negro nationhood in the black belt (the contiguous southern counties where blacks were a demographic majority). Instead, what Du Bois proposed was the political harnessing of what he believed was an already existing, relatively autonomous sphere of black public discussion, interaction, and exchange.

Du Bois never explicitly referred to a black public sphere, but this concept helps illuminate the meaning behind his use of contemporary left-wing slogans describing black people in the United States as a nation within a nation. The rhetoric of "nation" conveyed the magnitude of what was at stake for Du Bois: the formation of black public opinion and capacity for collective action on an unprecedented scale. Du Bois did not define black nationhood in conventional terms—it did not depend on capturing state power or achieving territorial sovereignty. Rather, he used "nation" to signify the moral and intellectual coherence shared by black people as result of their common exclusion within the United States: the fact that Negroes, as he put it, "were confined by an unyielding public opinion to a Negro world."[8] Du Bois recognized that, when arrayed against a U.S. public, blacks were weak and increasingly dispersed throughout the country. He argued, however, that they could attain a wider national and even global reach by cultivating "careful autonomy." At least, he reasoned, if blacks could recognize and assert their own cohesiveness, "no hostile group could continue to refuse them fellowship and equality."[9]

Despite his enormous prestige and intellectual standing, Du Bois's final decades have been neglected.[10] Writing in the early years of the civil rights movement in the late 1950s, Francis Broderick, Du Bois's first biographer, echoed Du Bois's contemporaries, who criticized him for succumbing to racial nationalism. This view anticipated color-blind perspectives from our own time that have seen this period as the culmination of Du Bois's life-long failure to rid himself of the "illusion of race."[11] "Few were listening" to Du Bois, Broderick wrote, because he had "broken with the fighters for integration and with his own great past just as the struggle for integration was about to make real gains." Yet, Broderick added, "When Du Bois broke with the Association and recommended Negro separatism, he was carrying to their logical conclusion racist tendencies apparent in his thought since his days in Great Barrington."[12]

Du Bois was neither out of step with his times nor simply repeating what he had said before. Rather, what he offered was a fascinating contribution to the wider revisions of liberal, democratic (and Marxist) thought underway throughout the North Atlantic intellectual milieu in the 1930s. Du Bois's ideas and the critical discussions they engendered among black intellectuals and activists of the period shed light on the decisive turn in the dialectic of race and nation provoked by the impact of the Great Depression and the New Deal on black life in the United States. Instead of terminating his significance as a black public intellectual, his departure from the NAACP was a new phase in his own long labors of racial reconstruction and a response to qualitative changes in the role of racial differentiation in the formation of modern nations, peoples and publics.

The 1930s was a watershed decade for the development of egalitarian alternatives to classical liberalism. A variety of challengers sought to reform or overturn laissez-faire individualism in favor of what John Dewey called the demands of "organized publics," including "the assertion of the rights of groups" and the creation of civic associations that were not directly political in nature.[13] Through its uses of federal state authority, Franklin Delano Roosevelt's New Deal incorporated many of these challenges, stabilizing liberal ideology by binding it more durably to the centralizing and homogenizing power of U.S. nationalist discourse over the forms of civic life. Du Bois cautioned that antiblack racism was an animating constituent of U.S. public opinion across the broad front of civil society: a "public and psychological wage," as he famously defined it in his most important work of this period, *Black Reconstruction in America* (1935). As long as this was true, people categorized as black would not achieve equality by being incorporated as nationalized individuals (or even by joining trade unions and militant working-class organizations), but only by organizing a black public.[14]

The New Deal era was the culmination of a long age of reform in the United States, and an unparalleled effort to resolve the contradictory imperatives in modern political life between securing the freedoms of market exchange and forming a large-scale community of social equals. Despite the antistate heritage of the liberal tradition, most New Deal liberals began to argue that tensions between market freedoms and social organization could only be addressed by expanding political administration. Dewey, an articulate defender of what he called "renascent liberalism," best summarized the tenor of the new dispensation: "The majority who call themselves liberals today are committed to the principle that organized society must use its powers to establish the conditions under which the mass of individuals can possess actual as distinct from merely legal liberty."[15]

The Great Depression discredited an idea that had already been assailed for a generation, namely, that civil society and market-exchange were capable of generating social stability and economic prosperity without political intervention.[16] The economic crisis was the result of widespread market failure caused by a gap between productive capacity and a lack of effective demand among the population. The resulting imbalance between production and consumption forced down wages and employment, exacerbating the crisis and auguring a long period of civil unrest with potential for social chaos and mass violence. Of particular concern to the new liberals was the specter of a revolutionary rupture in the social and political fabric of the industrialized world, as in Russia in 1917. The task, as British economist John Maynard Keynes put it to Roosevelt in 1933, was "to mend the evils of our condition by reasoned experiment within the framework of the existing social system." Anything short of this, he warned, and "rational change will be gravely prejudiced throughout the world, leaving orthodoxy and revolution to fight it out."[17]

Despite its fidelity to many of the laissez-faire orthodoxies of classical liberalism, Roosevelt's New Deal gradually embraced much of the theory Keynes pioneered, that national government had to create productive and distributive mechanisms to shore up the purchasing power of ordinary citizens within civil society. The most important corollary was that the state needed to facilitate the organization of wage-earners in trade unions to balance economic distribution and strengthen social and communication networks beneficial to governance. As Keynes wrote in *The End of Laissez-Faire* (1926): "The ideal size for the unit of control and organization lies somewhere between the individual and the modern state, therefore . . . progress lies in the growth and the recognition of semi-autonomous bodies within the State—bodies whose criterion of action within their own field is solely the public good as they understand it." Keynes argued that such public or civic entities—within definite and prescribed limitations—could lead to "improvement in the technique of modern Capitalism by the agency of collective action."[18]

Keynes's language of social control and capitalist reform and his concern about the dangers of radical or revolutionary alternatives to the status quo reflect the technocratic, managerial ethos that underpinned much of the "new liberalism," linking it to both the earlier program of the British Fabians and the U.S. Progressives' thirty-year "search for order." As Antonio Negri has suggested, what distinguishes the evolution of the modern welfare state is its acceptance of *class* as a legitimate principle of social conflict that it "sets out to resolve . . . on a day to day basis, in ways that are favorable to capitalist development."[19] At the same time, the immensity of the social and economic crisis of the period promoted more aggressive revisions of older liberal doctrines, leading to a greater emphasis on the role of independent democratic action in the public sphere. As an early critic of the New Deal, even an emphatically liberal thinker like Dewey ultimately questioned the compatibility of capitalism and democracy and sought to reconstruct an understanding of liberty as more than an abstract right of individuals, but as an achievement of collective, democratic "revolts against prior governmental forms."[20]

The intellectual contrast between Dewey and Keynes illustrates the elusiveness at the heart of the New Deal order: it fostered both democratic expansion as well as new aggregations of governmental and corporate powers.[21] The New Deal was not a wholly autonomous political development, but the culmination of a long history of interpenetration of political administration and market society that resulted in the emergence of increasingly large-scale organizations, professional expertise, political propaganda, and bureaucratic authority capable of mediating, if not controlling, the formations of public opinion. These developments were strongly predisposed to a corporatist form of political power that compromised the local autonomy, invention, and critical independence that might be considered hallmarks of more authentically democratic conceptions of public power.

Like most public intellectuals of the period, both Keynes and Dewey were gravely concerned about new dispositions of public power, although neither gave any consideration to its racial implications and logic. Their respective briefs for a reformed or radicalized liberalism provide context for understanding the significance of Du Bois's intellectual contribution and innovation. Du Bois called his "new racial philosophy" an effort "to rationalize the race concept and place it in the modern world." By this he meant the recognition of independent, black political activity as intrinsically valuable, an irreducible part of any change in the form of the state on a par with other world-historical social movements, particularly class struggles.[22] Indeed, Du Bois went further. In the face of official efforts to incorporate class as a nonantagonistic principle of national life, Du Bois argued that movements of the racially excluded represented the cutting edge of democratic transformation—and could be "a method of reorganizing the state." Alongside the period's celebrated advocacy of industrial and political democracy, Du Bois suggested, the task of black struggles would be to teach "cultural democracy to a world that bitterly needs it."[23]

Even as he insisted that being black was a central category of modern social history and politics, Du Bois rejected the idea that he was a racialist. Nonetheless, he recognized the conundrum he posed. Any focus on galvanizing black public opinion as a counter to racial exclusion risked reinforcing, rather than unraveling, the power of racial reference. "This is, or at least we thought it was, the day of International, Humanity and the disappearance of "race" from our vocabulary," he acknowledged thoughtfully.[24] "Yet, so long as we are fighting a color-line," Du Bois wrote, "we must strive by color organization."[25] "Science alone could not settle this matter," nor would the "color bar . . . be broken by a series of brilliant, immediate assaults." Rather, a "long siege was indicated," with "organization in boycott, propaganda and mob frenzy," alongside "careful planning and subtle campaign with the education of coming generations."[26]

These ideas did not directly counter the ethical currents of this era but rather anticipated what was to come, what had already begun. The 1930s witnessed a flurry of new black political activity. Black nationalists and socialists formed unprecedented coalitions in the Provisional Committee to Defend Ethiopia (PCDE) from Italian invasion. Negroes' Cooperative Leagues and Don't Buy Where You Can't Work campaigns in Chicago, Philadelphia, Harlem, and Washington, D.C. (led by figures like future black federal judge William Hastie and a young black activist named Ella Baker) demonstrated the new local power of black urbanites. The explosive Harlem riot of 1935—the first major urban property riot—alarmed the city and country prompting an official civil inquiry led by black sociologist E. Franklin Frazier. The successful culmination of the decade-long organizing campaign of the Brotherhood of Sleeping Car Porters in 1935, under the leadership of A. Philip Randolph, a leading black socialist of the World War I era, established the first, powerful, independent black trade union. The same year, Ralph Bunche, John P. Davis, Randolph, and others sought to organize civic organizations dedicated to black advance on a national scale for the very first time, resulting in the formation of a National Negro Congress (NNC).[27]

Weakened by political divisions, the NNC was overtaken by the nationwide March on Washington Movement (MOWM) by 1941. Under Randolph's leadership, the MOWM gained the first-ever state concessions to a black movement with the formation of a federal Fair Employment Practices Committee (FEPC) to monitor job discrimination in the expanding arenas of defense-related employment. An MOWM youth organizer, future civil rights leader Bayard Rustin, would describe the MOWM as the "symbolic inauguration" of the modern civil rights era.[28] The MOWM, however, would have been unthinkable without novel ideas and projects knitting together heterogeneous agencies of the struggle for racial equality at new scales of association and influence. National Negro Congress organizers, for example, modeled their efforts after the Congress Movement in India and hoped to influence "a nation-wide public opinion." As black voters in the urban north defected en masse to the Democratic Party and the New Deal, Du Bois and other political strategists resurrected the old dream of an independent black politics as a "balance of power" between rival forces in the political realm. Just as in the Ethiopia protest, the older dream of U.S. blacks as a redemptive force in world affairs was transferred from the fatalism and eschatology of Garveyism to the international organizing and publicity campaigns of anti-imperialist solidarity politics.[29]

The MOWM, in other words, was the culmination of a decade of political activity when U.S. blacks became fluent with the instruments and strategies of modern politics, including the press, the picket, the protest march, and the property riot—all of which fully entered the repertoire of black struggles during this period. In this sense, Du Bois's departure from the NAACP is an appropriate symbol for the long civil rights era itself, an era that began with unprecedented democratic challenges by black intellectuals and activists across the broad front of civil society. The cumulative result of these challenges was the rise of a black "counter-public sphere," Nancy Fraser's term for the political space of withdrawal and group formation where "subordinated social groups invent and circulate counter-discourses" and "formulate oppositional interpretations of their needs, identities and interests." Du Bois's effort was precisely to envision such a space in his writings of the period, something that both reflected and contributed to its development.[30]

Du Bois's thought and activism during this period and the debate he engendered among a new generation of black activists and intellectuals remain relevant to ongoing discussions of the tension between a liberal-democratic model of civil society, rooted in the universalization of the nation-form as the only legitimate form of political community, and the recognition of non-national groups, particularly racial or ethnic minorities.[31] Du Bois believed—as he always had—that black democratic participation in politics was the precondition for achieving social justice in the United States. Yet he also believed that what he called the "cultural fact" of black difference (both in the United States and in the transnational arena dominated by the United States and European nation-states) would continue to block full, democratic participation.[32] Rather than try to evade or escape this bind through the negation of "race," he attempted to use race to expand the realm of politics. His was an early effort to move democratic theory and practice beyond its own implicit "commitment to a unified public that tends to exclude or silence some groups" and toward what might be called (mixing his language with ours) a reconstruction of democratic publics.[33]

Transforming the Black Public Sphere

It is generally acknowledged that black civil rights emerged as a national issue in the United States during the New Deal era. The New Deal initiated a revision of classical liberal doctrines along social-democratic lines, overturning definitions of American freedom based on limiting the power of national government and maximizing the freedoms of market-exchange and private property.[34] In the process, it paradoxically undermined racially stratified state and local powers while also linking federal government expansion to the vitalization of citizen-initiated democracy, from trade unions to civic organizations. As a result, New Deal policies became intertwined with struggles for racial equality, even when its policy-makers expressly sought to avoid such associations. As the *The Crisis* would editorialize in 1940: "The most important contribution of the Roosevelt Administration to the age-old color-line problem in America has been its doctrine that Negroes are part of the country as a whole."[35]

The New Deal marked a fundamental departure from the minimal U.S. "state of courts and parties" and the federalist devolution of political administration.[36] With the expansion of institutional capacities came new, unprecedented claims for the federal government as a universalizing agent. This meant that problems of racial division and hierarchy could no longer be seen as peculiar facets of regional development. As the white southern sociologist Howard Odum put it, "what the South called the North had become the larger nation." Progressive voices within the Roosevelt administration (such as former NAACP board member Harold Ickes, Works Progress Administration Director

Harry Hopkins, and Eleanor Roosevelt) recognized that racial division and inequality were not only the particular concerns of black people but also part of the general interest in the exercise of federal state power and the making and un-making of subnational social agencies, especially in labor organization. Roosevelt's promise at Howard University in 1936 that under the New Deal there would be "no more forgotten men and no more forgotten races," was an emblem of how the New Deal included racial inequality as a stake in its project of national, civil, and economic reform.[37]

In these years, the institutions of the federal government grew more hospitable to blacks, particularly in the areas of civil service employment. More than one hundred blacks were appointed to posts in cabinet departments and New Deal agencies, and more than 150,000 blacks were on the federal payroll by the end of the 1930s—triple the number when Herbert Hoover left office in 1932. The creation of the Federal Council on Negro Affairs—Roosevelt's famous "black cabinet," made up of such notables as NAACP President Walter White and National Council for Negro Women Chair Mary McCleod Bethune, partly transcended older practices of honorific appointment, establishing a medium of quasi-official consultation and negotiation between the government and representatives of the black population.

A less direct manifestation of the official openings for blacks was the historic transformation of trade union organizing. Government sponsorship of the associational processes among industrial workers under the Wagner Act, and the founding of the Congress of Industrial Organizations (CIO) in 1935, challenged the traditions of white craft labor organization and racially segregated dual-unionism promoted under the American Federation of Labor (AFL). Dubbing the Wagner Act "the emancipation proclamation" of the U.S. worker, CIO founder and United Mineworkers leader John L. Lewis placed the New Deal expansion of class-based organization and trade union protection in a progressive, nationalist trajectory established by the Lincoln Republic, the moment when black slaves first became citizens and wage laborers. The CIO's organizing drives (a significant number of which were led by communists) spurred the entry of more than 500,000 black workers into the new industrial unions by the end of the decade.[38]

State-initiated reforms, however, were only one part of the story of the 1930s. The New Deal era was preceded by the emergence of new forms of black social existence, racial protest, and disruptive conflict that challenged the limitations of official racial progress. C. Vann Woodward was perhaps the first to describe this period as the beginning of a "Second Reconstruction," but he was predated by two decades by E. Franklin Frazier, who hailed as the "Second Emancipation" the uninterrupted black movement from country to city that began before World War I—the largest internal migration in U.S. history. Between 1910 and 1940, more than two million rural blacks left the southern countryside for cities throughout the nation. By 1935, eleven northern and western cities had black populations of more than 100,000. The great migrations of black people to cities, in particular to northern cities, created the possibility for nationalizing black struggles for equality in the United States by giving black populations the associational freedom required to develop democratic political mobilization.[39]

The new national and urban political context enabled more emphatic articulations of black political aspirations, and as a result, the constitution of black people—for the possibly first time in U.S. history—as an influential public. The regional container of the "Negro problem" was finally bursting as racial injustice and violence could be more readily interpreted by critical audiences throughout the country—particularly black audiences—linked by a national black press, an increasingly confident black intelligentsia, and new forms of labor struggle and mass organization. For perhaps the first time since the fleeting, failed experiments in interracial democratic action under agrarian Populism and the Knights of Labor in the 1890s, black intellectuals and social movements were also becoming meaningful participants in a wider field of democratic contention within the national public sphere.

This situation was partly the result of the stronger institutional links between black populations, civil society, and the federal state, to be sure. At the same time, black people continued to experience a vexed relationship with American nationalism, the dominant discourse of collective-identity formation. (It was not at all clear in fact that blacks were part of the country as a whole.) The emergent black public was thus defined by how it shared racial exclusion as a source of community, and by increasingly effective practices of symbolic representation in which black legislators and interpreters claimed to give voice to the identities and interests of restive black masses. Despite the often self-serving nature of such claims, I suggest that the origins of the long civil rights era reside here: in the development of institutional and information networks that linked black intellectuals and activists with geographically dispersed but densely concentrated black populations who could be mobilized—with unpredictable consequences for the nation as a whole.[40]

Such a development would have been impossible without the work of the first significant intergenerational cohort of black artists, writers, and intellectuals, including Ralph Bunche, E. Franklin Frazier, Richard Wright, Langston Hughes, W. E. B. Du Bois, Mary McLeod Bethune, A. Philip Randolph, Paul Robeson, Walter White, and others who started to command the attention of both a black public as well as national and international publics. The specific importance of black intellectuals to the constitution of a black counter-public sphere cannot be underestimated. The public is less a concrete aggregation of persons than an ethical ideal and symbolic construct that signifies the democratic institution of modern politics itself, to which the watchwords of "publicity," "public opinion," and above all, "publication," attest. Intellectuals in turn can be understood to be among the primary producers of public discourse—theoretical and practical knowledge of the social world—knowledge that becomes a key stake in social and political struggles to conserve or transform that world.[41]

Despite the adverse economic impact of the Great Depression overall, the 1930s saw the expansion of the black intelligentsia. Two hundred blacks received doctorates in the 1930s (and another 128 between 1940 and 1943), compared with a mere 45 between 1900 and 1930. By the 1930s, black illiteracy had decreased to 16.4 percent of the adult population, from a rate of 45 percent at the turn of the century. The 1930s saw doubled circulation figures for black newspapers, and news outlets such as the *Pittsburgh Courier, The Chicago Defender,* and the *Amsterdam News* established a nationwide readership for the first time. By the mid-1930s more than one third of black families subscribed to the commercial black press, which was now entering what some have called its "golden age."[42]

The economic crisis and urban recomposition of black populations precipitated a sharp leftward turn among black intellectuals and across black political thinking and activist practice. Intellectuals as politically diverse as the cautious Tuskeegee sociologist Charles Johnson and the increasingly radical Du Bois recognized that a "revolution in thought from earlier generations" was underway, as black leadership sought to establish new lines of correspondence with those they understood to be black working masses.[43] By choosing the designation "Negro," Bethune challenged traditional gender and class limits of "colored" women's activism, asserting the rights of black women as "citizens and wage-earners."[44] In black arts and letters, established "New Negro" poets such as Langston Hughes and up-and-coming black protest writers such as Richard Wright connected revolutionary expression and social realist conventions to the worsening plight of black farmers and industrial workers. As the elder scion of the Harlem Renaissance, Alain Locke, put it, black artistic expression was "going proletarian." Contrasting the new political mood with the cultural production of the 1920s, Locke wrote, "Our art is again turning prosaic, partisan and propagandistic but this time not in behalf of striving, strident racialism, but rather in a protestant and belligerent universalism of social analysis and protest."[45]

Locke put his finger on something important. A rising cohort of black artists and intellectuals responded to the crisis of the times with their own expressions of militancy frequently at odds with a prior generation of black leaders. The black social scientists at Howard University, including Ralph Bunche, Abram Harris, and E. Franklin Frazier, constituted an especially formidable intellectual force by mid-decade, attacking what they saw as the bourgeois orientation and elite pretensions of the older race leadership, including Du Bois, past NAACP President James Weldon Johnson, Negro history advocate Carter G. Woodson, and Howard sociologist Kelly Miller. The young radicals recognized a need for intraracial unity in their private conversation and correspondence. Yet, they stridently rejected Du Bois's racial philosophy, which, they argued, perpetuated the old "race uplift" tradition: a form of special pleading rooted in racial chauvinism and serving the interests of a black elite.[46]

To the younger generation of intellectuals and activists, Du Bois's political turn not only was eccentric, it rested on an unacceptable racialist premise. The 1930s saw fewer and fewer defenders of the notion of biological racial difference and more scientific criticism of concepts of racial superiority and inferiority. Much of the attack on racial thinking, including the work of many of Du Bois's outspoken critics, was framed by the concept of modernization that would dominate U.S. social science discourse by mid-century. Modernization was a theory of historical transition based on the idea that the economic pressures of capitalist industrialization had shattered traditional social formations rooted in kinship, locality, and religion and ushered in more dynamic forms of secular political identity and large-scale forms of governance, particularly nationalism and representative democracy. Beneath much modern antiracism, then, was the presupposition that race (and racism) were anachronisms of "traditional" society that would automatically give way to societal modernization (urbanization, wage-labor, and national identity), and thus wither away as features of U.S. public life.[47]

Du Bois's own claim on radical modernity—through his inventive mix of communist rhetoric and racial sentiment—did not convince the young radicals who had studied his long and storied career. Du Bois may have helped found a black intelligentsia, but its emerging stars, including Bunche, Frazier, Harris, black socialist George Streator, New Dealer Robert Weaver, and National Negro Congress cofounder John P. Davis, showed him less and less deference in the 1930s. These figures saw themselves as part of a new intellectual vanguard charged with redirecting black political aspirations toward an alliance with the resurgent labor movement under the leadership of the CIO. They agreed with each other that the traditions of black politics before them neglected poor and working-class blacks, who shared more common ground with white workers than with the black elite Du Bois once called the "talented tenth." "If there is any ideology which offers any hope to the Negro," Bunche wrote, "it would seem to be that which identifies his interests with the white workers of the nation." Frazier in turn expressly downplayed race as a distinct sphere of social life and political action: "There are signs that the question of the status of the Negro is losing its purely racial character and becoming tied up with the struggle of white and black workers against the white landlords and capitalists."[48]

A generational revolt akin to Du Bois's own departure from the NAACP, the perspectives of the younger group signaled the increasing heterogeneity and radicalism of black activism and social thought that marks the inception of the long civil rights era. Indeed, the debate that has shaped the course of black politics ever since began at this moment. Were black struggles for equality in the United States to play a leading role in a vast, transnational project of social reconstruction that began with the recognition of black cohesiveness independent of other communities, as Du Bois believed? Or, as the young social scientists argued, were black migration, urban resettlement, and federal government reform initiating a process that would equalize black status within the nation-state as a result of the entry (or integration) of blacks into civic institutions: the family, the school, the political party, and the trade union? On this debate hinged a number of subsidiary, but no less decisive, questions. Would black equality be a by-product of New Deal liberalism, or would it require more radical movements toward socialism? Was either reformed liberalism or socialist radicalism up to the challenge Du Bois provocatively called "the black reconstruction of democracy in America"?

The outlines of this debate began to emerge in the gatherings of radical black intellectuals in Amenia, New York in 1933. Here, younger intellectuals met with the old race leadership (including Du Bois) at the estate of NAACP Chairman Joel Springarn to re-think national civil rights strategies and agendas. The meeting was viewed hopefully as the start of a "second Niagra movement," an allusion to the founding of the NAACP in 1909 and to the historic gathering to consolidate civil rights leadership at Amenia in 1916 after the death of Booker T. Washington. Amenia had also been the site one year earlier of the twenty-third annual NAACP convention. Foreshadowing his break with the organization, Du Bois closed this meeting with a stirring speech arguing that the black activists needed to develop a positive program for social change and to work not at a distance from the masses in legalistic and lobbying efforts but with them in organizing efforts directed at wider publics on both a national and international scale.[49]

Du Bois had hoped that Amenia II (as it came to be called) would bring the young radicals into a new national civil rights initiative under his leadership. Like him, most who attended the 1933 meeting— including Howard's so-called "young turks": Frazier, Bunche, and Harris, as well as John P. Davis, future organizer of the Joint Committee on National Recovery (JCNR), the precursor to the NNC—disparaged weaker civil rights approaches to the crisis of the Great Depression and were looking for new political options and approaches. There are no records of the discussions at Amenia II, but in his reflections on the period, entitled *Dusk of Dawn: An Essay Toward an Autobiography of a Race Concept* (1940), Du Bois described the meeting as an effort to combine the older liberal emphasis on civil rights with a recognition of the importance of political economy to "the welfare of the great mass of Negro laboring people." Du Bois noted that despite agreement on the universal importance of economic issues, the meeting resulted in little consensus and left the participants "whirling in a sea of inconclusive world discussion." "We could not really reach agreement as a group because of the fact that so many of us as individuals had not made up our own minds on the essentials of coming social change."[50]

In a series of articles that appeared in *The Crisis,* Du Bois had already begun to outline his view of the "essentials of social change." Any new program, he argued, had to begin by acknowledging that "there is no universal suffrage in modern industry." The great achievement of democratic politics, in other words, scarcely touched the world of the private corporation. "The disfranchisement of the great mass of workers," Du Bois wrote, "is the most vital disfranchisement in the modern world." Publicly regulated corporations, such as utilities and railroads, were partial exceptions, but even these were organized on an "autocratic basis." "Industrial democracy," Du Bois wrote, meant an expansion of public ownership over the "great public service industries" and increasing worker power through collective bargaining and worker cooperatives. To overcome the split between the universal promise of political democracy and the unencumbered rule of the private market, he suggested, social movements must push further toward socialism, social democracy, and trade unions. In the final analysis, Du Bois concluded, "government ownership is the only solution for this present industrial disfranchisement of the Negro."[51]

Had Du Bois stuck to this line of argument, he might have been in the main current of thought among the younger black intellectuals and part of an array of political forces coalescing on the left of Roosevelt's New Deal coalition. But Du Bois was unwilling to let economic approaches to racial matters rest with variations on the class-conscious imperative to "black-white unite and fight." He agreed that the central contradiction of modern capitalism between the state and the market—the public good and private gain—could only be resolved by a movement toward socialism. He did not believe that the answer to the age-old question, "Where did this leave the Negro?" was self-evident. Du Bois further doubted the younger group's certainty that economic problems "could not be approached from the point of view of race" and questioned the assumption that "white labor" would accept "the new scientific argument that there is no such thing as race." "Socialists and Communists," he wrote skeptically, "assume that state control of industry by a majority of citizens or by a dictatorship of laborers, is going in some magic way to abolish race prejudice of its own accord without special effort or special study or special plan; and they want us Negroes to assume on faith that this will be the result."[52]

Du Bois's answer was to resurrect an idea that most of his young critics would ridicule as quixotic: a vision of a separate black economy—"a cooperative Negro industrial system" based on the organization of black purchasing power.[53] Impressed by the spontaneous militancy of the Don't Buy Where You Can't Work protests, Du Bois argued that by using "economic organization" through consumer cooperatives, black people might achieve long-term economic stability and "provide for their own social uplift." By organizing the spending power of "the two million eight hundred thousand Negro families [that] spend at least two billion dollars a year," he wrote, more favorable terms of social investment and employment could be secured in the face of neglect "by the state and the nation."[54] Conceiving consumption practices as the empirical basis of a relatively autonomous black civil society, Du Bois again used the analogy of nationhood to drive home his point: "No group can approach economic independence or a position of self-sustaining inter-dependence unless it is organized as a nation with law-making powers, armies and police. On the other hand, we should remember that the American Negro numbers about 12,000,000 and thus we are much larger than either Denmark, Greece, the Netherlands, Norway, Portugal or Sweden and very nearly the size of Egypt, half the size of Spain, and one third the size of Brazil. This surely indicates that we must have great economic power."[55]

Du Bois may have been attempting to defend black autonomy in the only language he thought his young compatriots understood: economic determinism.[56] Clearly for Du Bois, the economy was less the foundation of social organization than one of its instruments. His plan, in other words, was offered with normative, not programmatic, intent. As he put it, "I was willing to try to set forth my new point of view while giving anyone else who had an idea full opportunity to express it. I wanted, not dogmatically, but inquiringly, to find out the function of a minority group like ours, in the impending social change."[57]

What worried Du Bois was the status and future of black people within the racialized regime. As he wrote, "We are fleeing, not simply from poverty, but from insult and murder and social death. We have an instinct of race and a bond of color, in place of a protective tariff for our infant industry."[58] Such breezy conversion of economic language into metaphors of racial belonging may be a reason why his critics, many of them social scientists, became so frustrated with him. Du Bois was less interested in the "black consumer" than in what he tellingly termed the black "consuming public."[59] Consumption, in other words, was less an end in itself than a way of considering what it would take for black people to become a public in the political and ethical sense.

Du Bois's turn to consumption was another way to register his belief that a narrow focus on issues of industrial democracy obscured political challenges he grouped under the heading "cultural democracy." "The problem of race," Du Bois wrote, "always cuts across and hinders the settlement of other problems."[60] Bunche's suggestion, for example, that black interests now resided with the "white workers of the nation" was inadequate to this complexity. For one thing, this formulation not only advocated an alliance on the basis of material interests, but it did so on the basis of a prior assumption of shared nationality. It was precisely in the constitution of the cultural subjects of nationalism, however, that racism exerted many of its most powerful and negative effects. This did not mean that race was a more important axis of social differentiation than class. It did, however, mean that racial oppression had a material and symbolic specificity that had to be addressed on its own terms.

The cultural democratic paradox was that in order to address the cross-cutting effects of racism along the broad front of civil society, it was necessary to begin with the "social and civic recognition" of blacks as blacks.[61] This entailed a risky defense of black particularity. But we must interpret this defense in the context of Du Bois's effort to link the social and political experience of blacks in the United States to the central categories of modern civic life: nation, citizen, people, and public. Like Karl Marx, whom he began to study more systematically, Du Bois wanted to stand G. W. F. Hegel on his feet by showing that the excluded category (that is, race) was the basis of a universal political aspiration.

Here, it is worth recounting that Hegel was the principle author of both modern political philosophy and the modern philosophy of history. These two specializations were joined in his infamous argument that Africa had "no history in the true sense of the world . . . no movement or development of its own." As a consequence, Hegel wrote, when contemplating African Negroes "we must forget all the categories which are fundamental to our own spiritual life," especially the idea of a state "based upon rational universality." While Hegel believed slavery had made American Negroes somewhat more "susceptible to European culture" and civilizing influences, he concluded that they would be unable to form political subjectivity or rational or universal ideas because "they lack a focus of communal existence without which no state can exist."[62]

Here is the racist double bind so integral to modern thought. Blacks could not be considered part of modernity because they were incapable of ethical judgment. "Life in general," Hegel wrote, "has no value for them." At the same time, ethical or rational incapacity was proven by the lack of a proper "communal existence" or the prior nonrecognition of blacks as part of social (or human) history. Hegel's philosophy exemplifies how the modernizing narrative of nationality, citizenship, and the public sphere was constituted at its inception by racial exclusion. Black people's social and political aspirations were in turn nullified by a prior description of black pasts as instances of what another founding European philosopher, Immanuel Kant, called "human immaturity, pasts that do not prepare us for either democracy or citizenly practices, because they are not based upon the deployment of reason in public life."[63] Political rationality among blacks within this historical and cultural context was precisely unthinkable. People defined as black could only become modern political subjects if they were first remade—both in the terms of an already sanctioned, political subjectivity and also as somehow no longer black.

Du Bois sought to overturn this notion—of "the Negro" as a cultural and historical void—that was so central to modern historical discourse and cultural conceptions of political practice. He believed, furthermore, that the tendency to denigrate black capacity for independent thought and action undergirded the prevalent assumption among the younger black intellectuals that the problem of race would only be solved by asserting its obsolescence and irrelevance. Frazier, for example, famously described U.S. blacks as "stripped" and "bereft of culture" and repudiated the compensations of "a barren racial tradition" that interfered with "fuller participation in American society."[64] In similar, vitriolic tones, Bunche derided "the extreme provincialism" and "stagnation in social thought" of black leaders and organizations that continued to think in terms of "race." As Bunche put it revealingly some years later, one was a "Negro primarily in a negative sense."[65]

It is undoubtedly the case that such a perspective informed the most influential work of black social thought produced during this period, Frazier's *The Negro Family in the United States* (1939). Frazier's work shared (and contributed to) a view of the "civilizing process" in which black people were something akin to the raw materials in a manufacturing process—things to be acted upon—that needed to be transformed ("assimilated") to something else to become functioning agents within what was understood to be a larger (in this case, primarily economic) system. Frazier regarded the nuclear family, based on the model of the male bread-winner, and the organizing capacity of the trade union as the principle instruments of this transformation. He thus helped to inscribe a view in which the primary obstacles to governmental elimination of racial disparities were understood to be the lack of black male work-discipline and economic opportunity and, more invidiously, the lack of black female sexual discipline, or reproductive excess.[66]

Frazier sincerely believed that objectivist social science could provide a way out of the bind of racialized identity, especially when it was placed in the service of rational state initiative. Indeed, his was a categorically "non-racial," even "de-racializing" theory, one that was supposed to apply to all migrants who transformed from rural peasants to industrial workers in one or two generations. As a component of a broader modernizing view, however, this theory had invidious racial effects against its own conscious intentions. Frazier contended that "gains in civilization" for Negroes would primarily come from social "participation in the white world." Yet, he continued to ascribe to "whiteness" the universal properties of a civilizing agent and to align blackness with typical Victorian markers of social disorder and pathology, particularly sexual excess, deviance, and idleness. Indeed, his very use of the concept of civilization is to be highlighted. As the *Oxford English Dictionary* defined it in the mid-1930s, "To civilize is to polish what is rude or uncouth . . . to domesticate, tame (wild animals) to make 'civil' in the sense of having proper public or social order." The fact that Frazier and many of his young contemporaries understood black social participation in terms of inclusion in the labor movement and the achievement (for black men) of stable, working-class identities did not alter the hierarchical racial (and gendered) antithesis that continued to structure their thinking. In order to enter into "civil society," blacks first had to be "civilized."[67]

Perhaps Du Bois's greatest foresight was in modeling resistance to these historic depredations of racism as they operated within the dominant spheres of knowledge production. As he put it with characteristic flourish in *Black Reconstruction*, "The American black man . . . will enter modern civilization here in America *as a black man* on terms of perfect and unlimited equality with any white man, or he will enter not at all . . . This is the last great battle of the West."[68] One of the intellectual monuments of this period, *Black Reconstruction* was Du Bois's precise attempt to give black history a "movement of its own." Neither a celebration of racial difference nor an evasion of it, it was an effort to invert and transform its symbolic meaning. "So, today, if we move back to increased segregation it is for the sake of added strength to abolish race discrimination; if we move back to racial pride and loyalty, it is that eventually we may move forward to a great ideal of humanity and a patriotism that spans the world," Du Bois wrote, giving an apposite turn to the Hegelian dialectic. "We must unite our own forces no matter how much we segregate our spiritual and social life," he concluded, "so long as we never lose sight of the one great aim: the making of American Negroes into a real force for economic justice to all men."[69]

Du Bois's proposals for developing black consumer cooperation as the basis of black economic and political independence, and as what he called a "training ground" for socialism among black people, may have convinced few of his contemporaries. But that he neither provided a realistic blueprint for "normative action" nor predicted the paths of entry for blacks developing within the state apparatus and labor movement should not obscure the alternative he represented. Like the black public he searched for, the ideas Du Bois put forth were not empirically verifiable, but were an effort to make the unthinkable thinkable, to reconstruct a modern political imagination that had been so thoroughly distorted by racist presumption.

Many of the young public intellectuals arrayed against Du Bois were more practically oriented toward securing black entry into the new institutional arrangements, including political administration, labor organization, and expanded arenas of federal employment. One of the ironies of the coming years would be that many of these younger intellectuals and activists—Du Bois's erstwhile radical critics—would become strong supporters of the New Deal state, even as the old race man continued to resist its blandishments, growing ever more restive in his radicalism.

Race and Class in the New Liberalism

Du Bois's forays into economic theory and socialist politics after Amenia were harshly dismissed. Bunche, who only a few years earlier had written to Du Bois asking how he could best serve the race, penned one of the most influential critiques, identifying Du Bois's position with those of his olď nemesis, Booker T. Washington. "Though Washington and Du Bois differed sharply on the issue of political and social equality for the Negro, and industrial versus cultural education," Bunche wrote, "they were never very far apart in their basic philosophies. Both confined their thinking within the *periphery of race*."[70] Frazier, who was emerging as the country's premier black social scientist, confirmed this assessment, concluding that "there was no difference between the economic program of Du Bois and Washington," adding that Du Bois's conversion to socialism was superficial and theoretically incoherent.[71] In a review of *Black Reconstruction* (1935), Harris, who had once worked with Du Bois to democratize the political structure of the NAACP, completed a circuit of repudiation. Du Bois, Harris wrote, was "a racialist whose discovery of Marxism as a critical instrument has been too recent and sudden for it to discipline his mental processes or basically to change his social outlook."[72]

Frazier's searing critique, "The Du Bois Program in the Present Crisis," published in 1935 under the auspices of The Conference on Social and Economic Aspects of the Race Problem, reflected the summary judgment of the younger black intellectuals. Du Bois, Frazier wrote, embodied an antiquated model of race leadership that did not fit "the new social and economic scene." Du Bois was an intellectual who "loves to play with ideas, but shuns reality," Frazier wrote; his socialism was romantic, not scientific, and his Marxism a "literary device." He warned that Du Bois's program of a "separate non-profit economy within American capitalism" threatened to distract the Negro from a "realistic conception of the capitalist economy and the hopelessness of his position in such a system." "In the end," Frazier noted, with damning understatement, Du Bois "remains a liberal." He did not understand how "the status of race" was "determined by those economic forces which have shaped the country as a whole," and thus could not "furnish the kind of social criticism which is needed today in order that the Negro may orient himself in the present state of American capitalism."[73]

In a companion essay to Frazier's, the black socialist George Streator underlined the main theme of many critiques of Du Bois: the defense of "Negro racialism" was "reactionary" because it obscured the fact that "the Negro is nine-tenths a laborer." "The Negro masses will get a new leadership," Streator concluded, but "it will come from the rank and file, and from those educated young colored people who discover where their real class interests lie."[74] The black activists and intellectuals who gathered under the auspices of the Joint Committee on National Recovery (JCNR) to "survey the problems of the Negro under the New Deal" shared this view and self-conception. Introducing the conference, John P. Davis argued that racial discrimination permeated every aspect of the New Deal, affecting blacks across every region and occupation, whether they were organized or unorganized workers, living in rural or urban areas. At the same time, with an eye to creating a program of action, Davis argued that class, not race, was most fundamentally at stake. "Today we find ourselves subject as other groups of workers and farmers, to economic exploitation within a capitalist nation, but as well doubly exploited because of the accident of race." Yet, "there can be little doubt," Davis concluded, "that the inequalities experienced by the Negro masses under the New Deal stem from economic and not racial causes."[75]

Two years after Amenia, the 1935 JCNR was the most comprehensive and ambitious black intellectual gathering of the decade. Most of the key exponents of a new black activism attended, including Frazier, Bunche, Randolph, and Du Bois, as well as Socialist Party Chairman Norman Thomas, Communist vice presidential candidate James Ford, and the Trotskyist Worker's Party representative, Ernest Rice McKinney. The discussions were again exploratory, but the conference established the impetus for organizing a National Negro Congress the following year to press what Davis termed "the aspirations and the demands of the masses of Negroes in America whose condition is shown to be indescribably miserable." Despite Davis's disclaimer that the proceedings were "bound by no intellectual limitations," as a member of the Communist Party he forcefully argued that black "aspirations and demands" could be achieved only if capitalism was first discarded. The sole group who could achieve this, in his view, was class-conscious workers. Thus, Davis argued, "The problem of achieving a solidarity of Negro and white workers becomes one which principally concerns us."[76]

Despite sectarian rivalries and differences of tone and emphasis, this argument was repeated by every speaker (with the exception of Du Bois, who sounded the race-first theme). As McKinney put it, "The Negro worker must realize his class position as a worker and not attempt to maintain a race position as a Negro, first, last and always."[77] More cautiously, Randolph warned that racial discrimination in the trade union movement was "the greatest challenge to its profession of democracy and its claim of representing a progressive force in American society."[78] Randolph argued that Negroes lacked "the experience, class perception, courage and vision that are only born in a struggle for power." That struggle was one they needed to wage with all workers—white and black—most of whom still lacked union protection. Thomas emphasized the necessary "comradeship of workers irrespective of race, creed and color" and attacked the communists for their occasional fealty to principles of black cultural autonomy and self-determination.[79] Avoiding further allusions to self-determination, Ford attacked Du Bois for his defense of "Black Patriotism and race solidarity" and defined the communist position on the "Negro Question" as the achievement of an integrated popular front of all progressive forces under the leadership of the working class.[80]

In the most substantive presentation at the JCNR, Ralph Bunche offered a penetrating, Marxist-influenced critique of the New Deal's liberal reform project, which he called a form of "middle-class planning . . . fatal to the interests of labor."[81] Bunche was well aware of the racial evasiveness and inequalities at the heart of the New Deal order. He documented these in detail, arguing that the labor provisions of the National Recovery Administration (NRA) had perpetuated "occupational and wage differentials," attacking the disproportionate representation of blacks on relief roles, and denouncing the outright theft of the Negro farmer's share of the Agricultural Adjustment Administration (AAA) "crop-reduction contracts." Still, like Davis,

Bunche insisted that the failings of the New Deal were economic, not racial, and a result of its state capitalist approach to social reform. "In fact," he wrote, "New Deal planning only serves to crystallize those abuses and oppressions which the exploited Negro citizenry of America have long suffered under laissez-faire capitalism and for the same reasons as in the past."[82]

Bunche's remains one of the most brilliant critiques of the limits of the liberal reform project and of the New Deal's corporatist tendencies. The New Deal, he argued, was but a "domestic phase of the almost universal attempt in capitalistic countries to establish a new equilibrium in the social structure." The goal of this equilibrium was to reduce growing class antagonism and to create a situation in which "conflicting group interests and inequalities will be merged in a higher national purpose." A Marxist at this stage in his career, Bunche saw this solution as not only unstable, but also as designed to confine working-class economic and political aspirations within the "limits of middle-class democracy." In other words, Bunche implied that the New Deal's transformation of liberalism was really more of the same. Facing "an economy of chaos," he concluded, the New Deal was little more than "a mass of self-contradictory experimentation."[83]

According to Bunche, because the New Deal was conceived to preserve "the existing social structure," it was irrelevant to talk of Negroes's specific aspirations under it. The problem remained the colossal failure of the "old individualistic-capitalistic system" to safeguard the "economic destinies and welfare of the American people." Despite amassing considerable evidence to the contrary, Bunche, in other words, dismissed the idea that the New Deal posed any particular danger to Negroes. "Insofar as the program has applied to Negroes," he wrote, "it has followed the traditional patterns of racial discrimination and segregation." The real danger he sensed was that the "working-masses" would "become ever more dependent upon the intervention of the state in their struggle to obtain social justice from the owners and directors of industry."[84] Not only would this fail to settle "any of the fundamental conflicts within the modern capitalistic state," it was the recipe for an American-style totalitarianism.

In sum, while Bunche completely documented the New Deal's invidious racial differentiation, he too presented it as incidental to the more fundamental question of economic inequality. What was ironic was Bunche's unwavering conviction (at the very moment he was helping to plan a National Negro Congress) that there should be no new politics of race in response to the New Deal, but should instead be a translation of the political aspirations of black people into the terms of the wider political-economic struggle between a national labor movement and national capital. With regard to the independent articulations of black "needs and aspirations" manifest in the economic boycotts, or the Du Boisian idea of consumer sovereignty, Bunche's repudiation was animated by a racial abnegation that once again linked blackness to an image of abjection. It is "absurd," he wrote, "to assume that the Negro, deprived of the advantages of full participation in American life today, will be able to gain advantages by setting himself up in a black political and economic outhouse."[85]

Like the other young radicals of the JCNR, Bunche underestimated the novelty and significance of the New Deal's liberal experimentalism and the new agencies of black struggle, just as he overestimated the power of dominant economic groups—particularly the owners of capital—to harness the new governmental powers to their needs and interests. The latter error typified the cruder kind of Marxist analysis, which failed to recognize that economic power was by itself insufficient to produce a sphere of public order. In the struggle to produce a community of people or a public, moreover, far more than economic identity was at stake. Bunche was not wrong in many aspects of his analysis of the New Deal, especially his fears about the blunting or co-opting of working-class militancy. However, like many of his fellows in the JCNR, he displayed a profound disregard for the messy heterogeneity and racial specificity of popular-democratic movements.

Despite Bunche's fears about the co-optation of the sphere of working-class politics by the liberal state, the vision of progressive alliance politics and radical trade unionism embraced by members of the JCNR in 1935 and later by the National Negro Congress was broadly consistent with the politics of the Popular Front. The Popular Front became the official position of the Soviet Comintern and the U.S. Communist Party between 1935 and 1939. It held that the struggle against fascism in Europe necessitated abandoning the hard-line, separatist politics of working-class struggle that had characterized the "Third period," from 1928–1935, in favor of interclass, democratic coalition politics. Although no detailed or especially coherent theoretical doctrine accompanied the Popular Front, in practice it augured a period of temporary co-existence and alliance between defenders of capitalist reform and proponents of socialist transformation.[86]

The most sophisticated and prescient theorist of the Popular Front (writing from a fascist prison cell through this period) was the Italian Marxist, Antonio Gramsci. A contemporary of Dewey's and Keynes's, Gramsci suggested something convergent with their ideas: modern politics was characterized by the blurring of the boundaries between civil society and the state. As a result, Gramsci argued, workers' movements needed to abandon abstract proletarian internationalism and the vision of immediate, revolutionary seizure of state power (which he termed "a war of maneuver") in favor of protracted struggle (or a "war of position") across the institutions of civil society in their respective countries. This insight is relevant to understanding the New Deal period in the United States, because Gramsci was one of the rare Marxist theorists to recognize that the art of politics was not solely about economics, but about organizing society in general, or what he famously termed the struggle for "hegemony." In this struggle, economic power alone did not determine the success or failure of a social movement, but so did symbolic power, or the ability of movement intellectuals to provide a compelling moral and intellectual vision for society—or the nation—as a whole.[87]

Refining an old Marxist insight, Gramsci believed that the key limitation of U.S. workers' movements had been the inability to resolve "exigencies of a national character . . . to fuse together in a single, national crucible with a unitary culture, the different forms of culture imported by immigrants of different national origins."[88] This too was a prescient observation, one supported by numerous accounts ascribing historic defeats of the U.S. labor movement, particularly after World War I, to failures to overcome divisions of skill, ethnicity, and race in the workplace. Several recent, important histories have argued further that the CIO's signal achievement in the 1930s was precisely this: the "fusing together" of previously insurmountable working-class heterogeneities into a new structure of feeling that one dubs "working-class Americanism."[89]

The question remains: Who was the true beneficiary of this transformation, and what did it really mean for blacks? The Popular Front hastened the development of alliances and interactions between Marxists and liberals in the New Deal state and blurred the boundaries between the discourses of Marxism and liberalism in American left and progressive movements. Roosevelt used this blurring to his advantage. As he put it slyly, "I am a juggler, and I never let my right hand know what my left hand does."[90] The New Deal itself was predicated on a model of collective economic citizenship and the subordination of class division to what Bunche called the higher national purpose. Particularly in its public works and public arts initiatives, the New Deal expressly harnessed the cultural and regional signs of "working-class Americanism" to the ends of nationalizing governance. In turn, neither the upsurge in working-class immigrants voting for the New Deal nor the unprecedented defection of black voters to the Roosevelt coalition during the 1930s led to the development of new expressions of working-class cultural and political autonomy, but rather to the growing dependence of workers on the liberal state (as Bunche foresaw). A proletarian or working-class public sphere that might have become the basis for an independent working-class politics (that is, a Labor Party), let alone the public recognition of class division as an enduringly recalcitrant problem of social order and political rule, was never achieved. The working-class—especially in its institutionally recognized forms—was effectively incorporated into the life of the state.[91]

This blurring of the ideologies of left-wing transformation and liberal reform, in other words, occurred in a context in which liberalism (and not Marxism) assumed a far more expansive and hegemonic scope, especially with respect to the question of class division. This is not surprising: once the nation-state was imagined as the absolute horizon of class struggle (as it was by both liberals and Marxists during this period), nationalist discourses necessarily took precedence over class struggle, just as class struggles on a global scale were increasingly "nationalized" after World War II. In the United States, the old communist slogan, "nationalist in form, proletarian in content," proved as fallacious as the Stalinist dictum, "socialism in one country" was in the Union of Soviet Socialist Republics. This was sealed even before the onset of the Cold War, with the solidification of an Anglo-U.S. bloc against both Nazism and Stalinism, both of which were condemned as insurrectionary and antidemocratic models of political power. In this context, most democratic socialists, trade unionists, Keynesian liberals, and liberal intellectuals, including former Marxists, like Bunche, viewed the New Deal much more favorably by the end of the 1930s.

The New Deal established a new political center of gravity and model in the United States and in the world-system at large. Roosevelt's promise "to give to 1936 what the founders gave to 1776—an *American way of life*" was strictly neither a left-democratic (that is, Deweyan) nor corporatist (that is, Keynesian) revision of liberal doctrines, but a uniquely successful nationalist revision of liberalism that has been central to the defense of the "virtues of liberalism" ever since. Keynes's prophecy that this political experiment could provide the model for "rational change throughout the world" was also largely borne out, as the symbolic and institutional infrastructure of the New Deal welfare state became the basis for the transnational power of the American warfare state during and after World War II. To paraphrase Antonio Negri, insofar as the modern welfare state became the framework of an institutional compromise in the so-called free world after World War II, it must be considered "American by birth."[92]

Most important, the New Deal advanced a powerful intellectual and political synthesis of liberalism and nationalism, and in doing so, augmented the old American exceptionalist belief that the United States was the world's exemplary nation-state and the bearer of universality in the world-system. The parallel slogans of the Popular Front—that the United States was a "nation of nations" and that communism was "twentieth-century Americanism"—make sense in this context as failed efforts to envision a Marxism that could compete in a public sphere understood in U.S. nationalist and world-ordering terms. The architects of the New Deal had learned better than their Marxist adversaries the Gramscian lesson that class struggles were less a simple reflection of the ontology of labor relations than the result of contests over symbolic power—struggles over the classification of relevant subnational groups. The social identity of classes, in other words, was revealed to be an effect of political struggles and institutional practices—not a sociological given waiting for the right programmatic consciousness. Roosevelt's skill at "juggling" reflected the New Deal's effectiveness in establishing control, organization, and predictability in the social patterning and flows of communication between business and labor and in its ability to define and regulate the visions and divisions of class such that workers saw themselves as wage-earners, consumers, and, most important, as Americans all.[93]

The architects of the New Deal, however, were more effective in claiming that the nation took precedence over class divisions than in reclassifying racial difference so it could be similarly incorporated as a nonantagonistic principle of national social life. An unstable mix of urban liberalism and herrenvolk republicanism, the New Deal was marred by a set of ad-hoc, race-specific omissions and adjustments that proved increasingly consequential over time. Roosevelt refused to champion antilynching legislation, and none was passed before World War II. Despite campaigning on the issue, New Dealers accepted compromises with the South in their struggle for a tough Fair Labor Standards Act (FSLA), which would have abolished regional differentials in wages and working conditions that were the legacies of slavery and segregation. The New Deal's most enduring achievement—universal social security—exempted domestic and agricultural laborers, who were disproportionately black. Housing loans and subsidies under the Federal Housing Administration (FHA) were allocated on racial lines, expanding rather than diminishing residential segregation throughout the country, particularly in urban areas. Crop reduction payouts under the Agricultural Adjustment Administration (AAA) were notoriously discriminatory and barely trickled down from plantation owners to poor tenant farmers and predominantly black sharecroppers. Much maligned from its inception, the Fair Employment Practices Committee (FEPC), created by executive decree in 1941 in response to pressure from the MOWM, was abolished a short five years later by an anti-New Deal alliance of northern conservatives and southern, soon-to-be Dixiecrats.[94]

Because the New Deal failed to actively pursue racial equality, racial hierarchy continued to serve as an explicit limit within the expanded field of government practice. Roosevelt was uncharacteristically blunt about this in response to NAACP President Walter White's petition for federal antilynching legislation. According to White, Roosevelt admitted, "I did not choose the tools with which I must work. I've got to get legislation passed by Congress to save America. The Southerners by reason of the seniority rule in Congress are chairmen or occupy strategic places on most of the Senate and House Committees. If I come out for the anti-lynching bill now, they will block every bill I ask Congress to pass to keep America from collapsing. I just can't take that risk."[95] The state patriotism that so resonated with an imperative of economic equalization, in other words, was captive to white supremacist demands for differential recognition and distributions. At stake in FDR's disclaimer was not merely the practical or contingent failing of an otherwise consistent, universalism; it exemplified how the higher purpose of U.S. nationalism was simultaneously subject to civic-democratic and racist-democratic articulations.

In the end, the New Deal not only evaded issues of racial reform, in some respects it expanded and legitimized racist practice on a wider scale. The degeneration of New Deal professions of universalism into defenses of racially ascribed collectivity would be hastened by its own strident appeals to national security in the war years, which would lead to clampdowns on the black press and to the internment of the Japanese. The charge that the New Deal was itself un-American, a form of creeping state socialism, further weakened even moderate commitments to racial equality, such as that represented by the FEPC. The old association of antistatist federalism and the defense of local "racial mores" remained one of the most powerful equations in U.S. political culture, only slightly more powerful than the increasingly popular one that linked challenges to racial hierarchy with communist subversion at the end of the 1930s. Vulnerable on both counts, the New Deal consequently adopted a defensive posture around reforming the racial order. It suggested that insofar as benefits came to blacks, they would come quietly and gradually as gains to all workers, even as blacks continued to suffer differential treatment.

Contemporary intellectuals committed to the reformist, social-democratic legacy of the New Deal era have lamented the passing of this era and what they argue has been one of its legacies: "The substitution of race for class as the great unsolved issue of American life."[96] In this view, the founding of the CIO in 1935 was the high-water mark in the imagination of a different post–World War II trajectory, a nation united around the quest for color-blind justice and economic equality. But the lessons of this period and its incipient socialist trajectory are more ambiguous. Even at its most insurgent, labor was a (decidedly junior) partner in a New Deal state rife with racial conflicts, attacked by conservatives and business interests, and locked in fatal compromises with the Jim Crow South. At the same time, with its own pursuit of progressive unity riven by hate strikes, the labor movement often discovered that the particular demands and needs of black workers and activists were the most expendable.

Ironically, the parallel political trajectories of both the New Deal and Popular Front actually made it more difficult to assess the interrelation, compatibility, and commensurability of race and class struggles that preoccupied someone like Du Bois. If the "substitution of race for class" defined the subsequent period of social conflict and struggle, it was facilitated by an earlier substitution of class for race in the logic of liberal reform and its official, left opposition. At the same time, it is important to emphasize that race entered national politics during this period not at the expense of class, but in tandem with the increasing importance of a racially and ethnically diverse, working-class people to the governance of the polity.

Indeed, Du Bois's work implied that rather than being substituted for class, racial struggles were the locus of the most insurgent democratic aspirations in the public sphere. Rather than simply embracing the faith in a unified class struggle, he believed it was necessary to engage in classification struggles within the public sphere around the meanings of race and class. Specifically, Du Bois rejected both the liberal and Marxist faith that racism and race relations would disappear as the category of race lost the force of official sanction and political reference, and he anticipated (correctly) that race and race relations would be the terrain on which a wider array of social and political conflicts were mediated, interpreted, resolved, and displaced.

By the end of the 1930s, race, not class, was the recalcitrant element in the New Deal's liberal-nationalist synthesis of political rule and the site of the most vexing public conflicts of the period, including black consumer boycotts, property riots, protest marches, and white hate strikes and housing protests. But to place race and class in simple opposition is misleading. Rather, to paraphrase Stuart Hall, race was revealed as a modality in which class was lived and a medium through which class relations were experienced. This neither displaced nor simply intensified labor's struggles over wages and working conditions of the 1930s, nor did it fall neatly on either side of the Stalinist/liberal divide that would define the coming period. It did mean, however, that class relations had been "systematically transformed by race." This left the issue of which forms of social struggle would be most relevant—and for whom—entirely unsettled. In other words, Du Bois's old question, "Where did this leave the Negro?" lingered.[97]

Toward a Black Reconstruction

As black historian St. Clair Drake reminisced, "By 1932 I didn't know any black social scientist who privately or publicly didn't claim to be some kind of Marxist."[98] The differences in kinds of Marxists, as the debate between Du Bois and his contemporaries demonstrates, proved more consequential as the decade proceeded. No stranger to intellectual combat, Du Bois willingly engaged his adversaries. Cleverly, he reversed their arguments against him, beginning with an indictment of their economism. It was they who were "thinking in terms of work, thrift and investment and profit," he wrote. "They hope with the late Booker T. Washington to secure better economic conditions for Negroes by wider chances of employment and higher wages." Only this time, an "alliance with labor rather than capital spells their salvation." "The difficulty with this latter solution," Du Bois concluded, "is that the same color line, the same racial repulsion persists in the labor movement as in the case of other cultural contacts."[99]

If, as Du Bois accused, the NAACP leadership was too "deeply American with the old theory of individualism, with a desire to be rich, or at least well-to-do, with suspicion of organized labor and labor programs; with a horror of racial segregation," the young radicals were too hasty to reject the legacy of the black civil rights initiative, "one of the finest efforts of liberalism to achieve human emancipation."[100] Although Du Bois agreed that class struggle and economic organization were now essential to any philosophy of social change, he rejected the left's presumption that civic organization and citizenship rights were bourgeois conceits that invariably forestalled more radical forms of social change. He was also troubled by occasional lapses into provocative language, in which blacks were depicted as "shock troops" of a coming social revolution. The idea of "immediate, violent and bloody revolution is a silly program even for white men," Du Bois wrote, "for American colored men, it is suicidal."[101]

Yet Du Bois rebuked his adversaries more subtly: they actually did not go far enough in their critique of liberalism. Du Bois agreed that the denial of citizenship rights did not exhaust the inventory of modern racialism, whose causes and effects were often most acutely registered in the economic realm, particularly at the point of production. But he was skeptical of the class-based argument because it failed to see that modern racialism retained a cultural and symbolic logic of its own, with powerful social and political effects on the formation of political subjects, particularly citizens, the subjects of nationalism. Thus, as long as American working-class publics were influenced by racialism (and Du Bois claimed that this was a manifestation of their own bourgeois aspirations and their national identification), they would not only fail to achieve class-consciousness, but remain one of the most visible barriers to black advancement.

Du Bois perceived that economic determinist and class-based arguments overlooked a fundamental issue. To paraphrase a contemporary political theorist, in making war on the political in the name of the social and economic, the left in general and Marxists in particular failed to address how nationalism and democracy mediated the formation of socially significant identity.[102] Citizenship rights alone would not solve racial exclusion, Du Bois concluded, but not simply because the law concealed a more fundamental economic reality— but because "back of law must lie public opinion." Rights, in other words, were only as good as the publics that upheld them.[103] The ethical ideal of liberalism that Du Bois wanted to preserve was the possibility of democratically constituted publics, something which had been abrogated by racism. To live up to such an ideal meant confronting how the circle of the national "we" was persistently closed off through the mechanisms of racial exclusion.

Du Bois concluded that black social death in the United States exposed the deep tension in modern political thought between democracy and nationhood—the public use of reason and the exercise of popular sovereignty. This meant that it would always be easier for blacks to identify with the struggles of U.S. workers in general than it would be for U.S. workers in general to identify with the struggles of blacks. "No revolt of a white proletariat could be started, if its object was to make black workers their economic, political, and social equals," Du Bois wrote. "It is for this reason that American socialism for fifty years has been dumb on the Negro problem." The race problem and the labor question were linked, Du Bois insisted, but this did not mean race could be collapsed into class. Instead, the racialized dimensions of class formation had to be recognized.[104]

Marxism, Du Bois summarized, "did not envisage a situation where instead of a horizontal division of classes, there was a vertical fissure, a complete separation of class by race, cutting square across the economic layers."[105] Moreover, as he had long argued, class-based reforms and struggles tended to be "confined to that labor which we see and feel around us, rather than directed to the vast circle where unseen and inarticulate, the determining forces are at work."[106] This obscured what he called in *Black Reconstruction* (1935) the "real modern labor problem": "That dark and vast sea of human labor in China and India, the South Seas and all Africa; in the West Indies and Central America and in the United States—that great majority of mankind, on whose bent and broken backs rest today the founding stones of modern industry—shares a common destiny; it is despised and rejected by race and color; paid a wage below the level of decent living; driven, beaten, prisoned and enslaved in all but name; spawning the world's raw material and luxury."[107]

The true proletariat was not only transnational in scope but, in some sense, also black. Du Bois thus envisioned democratic struggles against racial exclusion subsuming class struggles. "The democracy which we have been asking for in political life," Du Bois wrote, "must sooner or later replace the tyranny which now dominates industrial life."[108] Although there was no "indication that a Marxian revolution based on a united class-conscious proletariat was anywhere on the American far horizon," in "the hearts of black workers" were "ideals of democracy in politics and industry" that might "in time make the workers of the world the effective dictators of civilization."[109] In this way, Du Bois again reversed the emphasis of his critics—that race consciousness among blacks should yield to a unified class struggle— arguing that the "first proof" of socialism would be "the abolition of color and race prejudice among the laboring class."[110]

Du Bois's reviewers attacked what they saw as the hyperbolic claim in *Black Reconstruction* that "the record of the Negro worker during Reconstruction" was "one of the most extraordinary experiments in Marxism that the world, before the Russian Revolution, had ever seen."[111] Specifically they criticized the two most provocative arguments of the book: 1) that the slaves emancipated themselves in a social movement that was akin to a "general strike" when they abandoned the plantations during the Civil War; and 2) that post–war, black-led Reconstruction governments were analogous to "dictatorships of the proletariat." In *The Nation*, Harris's long-time collaborator, white historian Sterling Spero, hailed publication of the book as a "literary event," only to clinically dismantle its quasi-Marxian conceptualizations as yet another series of romantic illusions. If "Marx's hero was the proletariat," Spero concluded, "Du Bois's hero is the Negro. Du Bois, fresh from his reading of Marx, makes the Negro the proletariat. Everywhere throughout the book, in many ways an extraordinary work, Du Bois's race consciousness distorts his Marxism; so that the net result of *Black Reconstruction* is to add more confusion than light to the understanding of one of the most crucial epochs of American history."[112] Spero's fixation on Du Bois's "race consciousness" reveals that the crux of this disagreement was not only about Marxism, but also about what Spero regarded as Du Bois's wild inflation of black democratic agency. Spero was definitive: "The Negro masses did not play a conscious and decisive role in their own emancipation" but were the objects of large-scale social transformation that led to the triumph of capitalism throughout the nation-state. Harris drove home the point: "the Civil War completed our bourgeois revolution"—nothing more, nothing less. Insofar as black men had benefited, Harris concluded, it was as heirs to its legacy of "middle-class ambition" that "has until this day confined his radicalism mainly to militant civil libertarianism."[113] Once again, Du Bois had shown himself up as a liberal.

What Jacques Ranciere has said about the works of the lyric social historians of the "masses" like Michelet or E. P. Thompson might also be said of Du Bois's *Black Reconstruction*: it rejected the separation of literature and truth and challenged those who would "sacrifice history itself to the affirmation of scientistic belief."[114] In this sense, the notion of the book as a literary event (or even of Du Bois's "literary" Marxism) was more significant than his critics recognized. *Black Reconstruction* was an effort to dramatize a social movement of black people into the new symbolic space of democratic history-making. In the attempt to write such an event, Ranciere suggests, "words, whatever the realists might say, are more stubborn than facts." The writing of *Black Reconstruction,* in other words, was itself a symbolic act—a demand for social and civic recognition—through history-writing as the art of "opening a space and time in which those who do not count are counted."[115]

"Can we imagine this spectacular revolution?" Du Bois wrote as if to challenge his erstwhile critics. "Not, of course, unless we think of these people as human beings like ourselves. Not unless, assuming this common humanity, we conceive ourselves in a position where we are chattels and real estate, and then suddenly in a night become 'thenceforward and forever free.'"[116] But how to represent the slave's knowledge of freedom as a condition of black humanity that not only preceded recognition of that humanity by state decree, but also exceeded the truncated legal status that followed?[117] This is where Du Bois's idea that the slaves freed themselves in a "general strike" against slavery before the Emancipation Proclamation is so important. Although condemned by Du Bois's critics, the general strike was a concept improvised to convey the unprecedented situation of slave-freedom. As such, it intimated black collective agency as something that both exceeded and radicalized the master narrative of U.S. history.

Democracy is the defeated hero of Du Bois's text but is also a resource of hope, one linked not to a dead past but to an open future, to the self-determination of black people. Du Bois suggested that the lesson of the Civil War and Reconstruction was neither that capitalism and slavery had been proved incompatible (as many Northerners would have it), nor that blacks were incapable of self-government (as the Southern Redeemers would have it), but the revolutionary power of what Du Bois called the first significant black "attempt to enter democracy."[118] The use of a phrase like "dictatorship of the proletariat" (to describe the early taxation schemes and land-redistribution efforts of black-dominated Reconstruction governments in states like South Carolina) needs to be understood as an effort to convey that the unconditional democratic demand by blacks had a larger significance, one that pointed to the superceding of capitalist property relations in general.[119] In a society in which class division had been recoded as race, race could become a means to contest the class divide.

Du Bois's reading of another great lyric historian, Marx, may have been more faithful than his critics understood.[120] For the young Marx the radicalism of democracy was its "generic constitution," a universal right to politics, unlimited by bourgeois preconditions. For Du Bois, democracy was the political form of an ineluctably differentiated humanity. Democracy was not limited by or grounded in already constituted identity, but promised the generation of new freedoms—new universals—new histories—from the "uncoerced gathering" of heretofore scattered, suppressed, or partial agencies.[121] Du Bois's real point of making the Negro into the proletariat was to say that insurgent struggles for democratic rights by excluded blacks could generate political ideas and social programs that might transcend the class and racial limits of the U.S. state-capitalist order. As C. L. R. James put it in one of the most insightful readings of the book at the time, the import of *Black Reconstruction* was "that Negroes *in particular* had tried to carry out ideas that went beyond the prevailing conceptions of bourgeois democracy."[122]

The reviewers failed to recognize that the "race consciousness" of *Black Reconstruction* was an aspect of its meditation on history-making and the formation of democratic publics. Du Bois's critique of the historiography of the Civil War and Reconstruction, appended as the book's last chapter and entitled, "The Propaganda of History," was overlooked by most of his critics. In it, Du Bois argued that a true history of the Civil War and Reconstruction had not yet been written because "the chief witness in Reconstruction, the emancipated slave himself, has been almost barred from the court."[123] Here, Du Bois made another of his dramatic reversals, describing this exclusion as "an arraignment of American historians and an indictment of their ideas."[124] Du Bois's metaphorical use of the court of law linked the conventions of the historical profession to a legacy of nation-state-sponsored racial exclusion and governmental neglect. In doing so, he recognized that the very appeal to history that underwrote membership within the national community was the monopoly of the privileged—those already deemed to be inside history.[125]

David Levering Lewis has claimed that *Black Reconstruction* was "one of those genuine paradigm shifts periodically experienced in a field of knowledge, one that sunders regnant interpretations into the before-and-after of its sudden, disorienting emergence."[126] Ironically, as later historians came to appropriate many of Du Bois's insights about black agency and political radicalism, his book remained outside the canons of U.S. historiography, partly on its first critics's grounds: a lack of original archival sources, Marxist rhetoric, and excessive or hyperbolic literariness.[127] But Du Bois identified something that is still difficult for those wedded to the rationalist procedures of professional historiography and to the nationalist politics of social inclusion—that the problem of writing "minorities" into the nation-state is more difficult than discovering new archives or producing more inclusive national narratives. Instead, he implied, there might be experiences of the past that both challenge the methods of the discipline of history and strain the nation-form, demonstrating the limits of both.[128]

What, finally, would it mean to enter modern civilization as a black person when the characteristics attributed to blackness were so tied to the absence of modernity and civilized culture: critical reason and the capacity for autonomy and self-governance? This was the most pressing question for Du Bois, and one he believed needed to be posed for the difficult times ahead. While the black freedom struggle was as old as the Atlantic slave trade, and marked by a continuous history of resistance, refusals, revolts, and runaways, Du Bois agreed with his critics that modern freedom had a narrower basis that could only be achieved through collective access to the discourses and instruments of modern politics. That black people entered politics through the social and symbolic exclusion of race meant that black political action had a symbolic burden that exceeded concrete political initiatives such as withholding labor power, boycotting merchants, or voting for legislative representatives. These activities were only partly about reaching practical goals (such as higher wages, greater employment opportunities, or political representation). They were also about demonstrating the democratic significance of racial division and the emergence of an ethical and political standpoint derived from racial subjection, that of a black public.

Du Bois was after a black reconstruction of democracy, something he knew had not yet occurred. History was an arena linked to the nation as a province for securing racially exclusive membership and class privilege. And, like the nation, it required more than amendment; it required wholesale reconstruction. Du Bois believed that this would come, if at all, from the kind of passionate, self-motivated activity black people showed with Emancipation and that had been forestalled by the demise of Reconstruction in 1877. As he summarized the issue (with the kind of flourish that angered his critics), "It was the black man that raised a vision of democracy in America such as neither Americans nor Europeans conceived in the eighteenth century and such as they have not even accepted in the twentieth-century; and yet a conception which every clear-sighted man knows is true and inevitable."[129]

This idea was and still is unthinkable in a historical and political imagination that takes the existing nation-state as its object, privileges its legal categories as markers of social inclusion, and accepts "the state-citizen bind" as the horizon of communal possibility.[130] Because Du Bois's critics could only conceive of black modernity as a movement into normalized, institutionalized forms of national belonging, they failed to see what was most profound about Du Bois's reading of slave emancipation—that it was an event that remade the world, "an upheaval of humanity like the Reformation and the French Revolution."[131] Again, C. L. R. James recognized the import of Du Bois's account where others failed: black struggles for democracy in America represented an unprecedented contribution to the radical imagination of social change. As James wrote in 1948, the "independent Negro movement is able to intervene with terrific force upon the general social and political life of the nation, despite the fact that it is waged under the banner of democratic rights, and is not led necessarily either by the organized labor movement or the Marxist party." In this sense, James concluded, black struggle was "in itself a constituent part of the struggle for socialism."[132]

Had Du Bois delivered the manuscript *A Search for Democracy,* which he had promised to Harcourt Brace in the mid-1930s, he might have spelled these ideas out in detail.[133] It is sometimes forgotten that Du Bois left the NAACP in 1934 because he thought it had become an overly centralized, top-heavy organization devoted to elitist brokerage politics, rather than to direct organizing among a black mass base.[134] Du Bois believed that his young critics made a similar error when they invested all their hopes in the labor movement and argued "that the problem of race" could only "be settled by ignoring it and suppressing all reference to it."[135] Du Bois highlighted his differences with both groups. "The discussion of leadership among Negroes," he concluded, "has not usually been associated with a parallel discussion of democracy. What Negroes have meant by democracy is the right to have their wishes and needs considered in the general social objects of the nation. They have sought to attain this with political power and followed this with a vision of economic power through control of capital. They are now forced to consider the building up of democracy and democratic power among themselves."[136]

In retrospect, it seems Du Bois was onto something. More than a decade later, E. Franklin Frazier would note with alarm that black intellectuals had been so "seduced by the lure of final assimilation" that they had forsaken much of the radicalism and many of the political tasks of the earlier period.[137] Frazier's own experiences during the 1930s may have been instructive for him. His report on the Harlem riot had decried the fact that Harlem had become a "city within a city," cut off from basic civil services and social protections (an idea resonant with the notion that Negroes were a nation within a nation).

Yet, when Frazier turned in his report, it was silently shelved by the New Deal-backed La Guardia administration, fearful of its broad canvas of police abuse, official civic neglect, and economic inequality. In the end, Frazier turned to a primarily black institution—the New York *Amsterdam News*—to publish the report. Perhaps cultural democracy—or the cultivation of a black public sphere—was a precondition to the pursuit of genuine equality.[138]

A similar case can be made for the five-year effort to establish a National Negro Congress. Bunche had once described the organization in glowing terms, claiming that "its equal has never been seen in the history of the American Negro." Its task, he argued, was "to reach the Negro masses with the cogent, realistic message of labor organization."[139] But the demise of the Congress is instructive. It collapsed in 1940 around the issue of its affiliation with the Labor Non-Partisan League. While the contention has been understood as revolving around the issue of communist domination of the Congress and the political fissures that opened after the Nazi-Soviet pact, these controversies were themselves the manifestation of the Congress's inability to decide whether race-organization or interracial class-solidarity would be its primary principle. Randolph, for example, who had been president of the Congress since 1935 (and the single older black leader lionized by Howard's young turks for his pioneering work in the labor movement), quit the Congress in 1940 after it endorsed affiliation with the Labor Non-Partisan League because he believed it meant that the NNC was "no longer truly a Negro Congress" with a "leadership which is uncontrolled and responsible to no one but the Negro people."[140]

Although some see Randolph's use of the race-first argument as politically opportunistic and less a cause of his resignation than his long-standing anticommunism, Randolph justified his departure otherwise. He claimed that, under pressure from the labor movement, the Congress had departed from its initial "principle of minimum demands," which had been designed to bring politically heterogeneous agencies of the struggle for black equality into concert for the first time. By 1930 more than one-third of the Congress delegates were white, a group that significantly overlapped with trade unionists and Communist Party members and effectively controlled Congress proceedings and political orientations. As the Urban League's Lester Granger suggested, control of the Congress by exponents of labor and political ac-

tion had largely eclipsed efforts at "coordinating . . . national programs for the improvement of the Negro population."[141]

With this in mind, it is worth remembering that the wildly popular
successor organization Randolph founded, the March on Washington
Movement, was a black organization that explicitly excluded whites.
The MOWM has been heralded as a model for the modern civil rights
movement for extracting concessions from the Roosevelt administration regarding wartime employment of blacks. At the same time, the
all-black character of the MOWM alarmed everyone from mainstream civil rights leadership to progressive trade unions to the U.S.
president himself. Franklin Roosevelt said that he could "imagine
nothing that will stir up racial hatred and slow progress more than a
march of that kind," a sentiment matched by threats of withdrawal of
support from progressive unions like the United Auto Workers (UAW)
and by belated, ambivalent endorsements from established civil rights
leaders. Both the black and white press captured these sentiments,
claiming that the MOWM had raised the ghosts of Garveyism.[142]

Of course, New Deal black cabineteers like NAACP President Walter White used the threat of a march to broker concessions from the
Roosevelt administration. Yet there is little evidence that he played a
significant role in organizing popular black sentiment for the march.
Even Randolph, the titular head of the MOWM, was not entirely sure
whether the MOWM was in fact a gigantic "hoax or bluff." This
partly explains why the planned march, much to the chagrin of young
rank-and-file organizers like Bayard Rustin, was cancelled in final-
hour negotiations with the Roosevelt administration. If this was the
first victory and "symbolic inauguration" of the modern civil rights
era, as Rustin later claimed, it was a politically ambiguous one that
failed to produce a mass event and collective memory that might have
been a spur for future protests. Yet, at the same time, the very fact that
the threat of thousands of black folk marching on the nation's capital
was credible hints at the deeper source of the movement's intimidating
character: it had galvanized the black public when other efforts had
failed.

As the culmination of the new black activism of the 1930s, the
MOWM was at least a partial vindication of Du Bois's search for
a black public. The black public, as Du Bois recognized and the
MOWM confirmed, was less important as an actual set of persons
than as a point of reference, signifying black capacity for independent

democratic action. In turn, the intensity of the debate between Du Bois and his critics demonstrated that black intellectuals and activists had developed a more profound awareness of their own custodial powers in relation to U.S. black populations, even when arguing against the viability of race organization. In the end, even as austere a critic as Ralph Bunche had to concede the main point. "The charter of the black man's liberties can never be more than our legislatures and, in the final analysis, our courts wish it to be. And what these worthy institutions wish it to be can never be more than what American public opinion wishes it to be," Bunche wrote. "The Negro," thus "finds himself in the uncomfortable position of decrying racial differentiation, while being compelled to demand it when important policies are being formulated in order to hold his ground in an uncongenial milieu."[143]

In his efforts to modernize the race concept in the 1930s, Du Bois presented an intellectual challenge to perfectionist American liberalism that still has not been met. Refusing the modernist teleology of Negro disappearance and the difference transcending historicism of American nationalism, he used the social fact of racial differentiation as a critical instrument with which to widen the imagination of social justice. The race problem as he correctly anticipated was "the central problem of the greatest of the world's democracies, and so the Problem of the future of the world."[144]

Although the radicalism of Du Bois's later years has been judged naïve or rigid, his sense of the recalcitrance and unyielding nature of race within the American social order—not only as a political and economic reality, but a "vaster and more intricate jungle of ideas conditioned on unconscious and subconscious reflexes"—was borne out in the decades to come. In 1940 Du Bois still believed that the best chance for black equality lay within the United States. Seasoned by cycles of racial disappointment, however, he was willing to "frankly face the possibility of eventual emigration from America" if racism continued to truncate black capacities and aspirations. That this was the path he finally chose remains something to be reckoned with.[145]

CHAPTER THREE

Internationalizing Freedom

Constituting the subjective aspect of the change in the social structure was the attitude of the Negro himself. He found the problems of
the Chinese, the Indians, and the Burmese strangely analogous to
his own. In this sense the Negro became more international-minded
than the rest of the population . . . A blow struck for freedom in
Bronzeville finds its echo in Chungking and Moscow, in Paris and
Senegal. A victory for Fascism in the Midwest Metropolis will sound
the knell of doom of the Common Man everywhere.

—ST. CLAIR DRAKE AND HORACE CAYTON, *BLACK METROPOLIS* (1945)

During a speaking tour in 1942, just after the United States's entry
into World War II, NAACP Chairman Walter White described an interesting encounter. At a black college in the South, a friend of White's
was confronted by a student who challenged him with the following
view of the war: "I hope Hitler wins. Things can't be any worse than
they are for Negroes in the South right now. The army Jim-Crows us.
The Navy lets us serve only as messmen. The Red Cross refuses our
blood. Employers and labor unions shut us out. Lynchings continue.
We are disfranchised, Jim-Crowed, spat upon. What more could Hitler do than that?" White recounted the story to a black audience in a
midwestern city, probably Chicago. "I told the story," White recalled
in an article published later that year, "as an illustration of the kind
of dangerous, short-sighted thinking which Negro Americans had to
guard zealously against. To my surprise and dismay, the audience
burst into such applause that it took some thirty or forty seconds to
quiet it. Though I went into as detailed an explanation of the fallacy
of such thinking as I could, I left the meeting with a feeling of depression born of the conviction that I had not convinced my audience that
Hitlerism could and would be worse."[1]

This anecdote is revealing. It shows White, one of the nation's most
prominent black civil rights leaders, enlisted in a quasi-official function, educating blacks about how to interpret World War II. He uses
the "question" of the southern student to make the case against war-

time Jim Crow while insisting that "Hitlerism would be worse." At the same time, White assumed that his urban black audience would see the bigger picture, only to express "surprise and dismay" at their approval of the student's views. Reflecting on the story, White explained what he believed to be its lesson. "We Negroes are faced with a Hobson's choice. But there *is* a choice. If Hitler wins, every single right we now possess and for which we have struggled here in America for three centuries will be instantaneously wiped out. If the Allies win, we shall at least have the right to continue fighting for a share of democracy for ourselves."[2]

But this story offers other lessons about "the attitude of the Negro" during World War II. White's audience may have interpreted the war that had been raging in Europe since 1939 differently. Perhaps what they betrayed was less enthusiasm for Hitlerism than skepticism about what C. L. R. James called "the loud-voiced shrieking of 'democracy,'" especially a democracy allied with British imperialism.[3] Perhaps White's audience distrusted his dual role as a broker of black democratic aspirations and as a pedagogue working to inculcate a sanctioned patriotism. Perhaps their recalcitrance was a sign of what A. Phillip Randolph described when he launched the March on Washington Movement (MOWM) in 1941—how black leadership lagged behind "the followship"—rather than evidence of the "dangerous, short-sighted thinking" of the black masses.

White's parable was a warning to the nation (especially its public officials) about seething black resentment of racial inequality. It may be better understood as a reflection of a dialogue that was taking place within the nationwide, black counter-public sphere, in which black audiences informed their would-be leaders and intellectuals that they refused to make another Hobson's choice. White would have seen this new reluctance first-hand as he sat onstage in Madison Square Garden before 18,000 blacks in June of 1942 at the zenith of the MOWM. Not since the years following World War I, when Marcus Garvey was said to have "rallied millions of Negroes in his nationalistic mass movement, had Madison Square Garden been filled by an all-colored audience."[4]

By the onset of World War II, the militancy of blacks across the country was pushing the NAACP in more radical directions. A resurgent National Negro Congress, and the newly founded Council on African Affairs (CAA) and Congress of Racial Equality (CORE), reflected an increasingly crowded organizational field of black activism. With little effort from the national office, the NAACP itself verged on becoming a mass movement of the kind Du Bois had hoped it would become in the 1930s, as its membership increased dramatically during the war. Secretly, White might have agreed with the assessment of Claude Barnett of the Associated Negro Press, who felt the MOWM would weaken the war effort and "the all-Negro philosophy of the March" was likely to "intensify racial antagonism." But even the figures, movements, and organizations most focused on securing black social and political rights within the normative discourses of U.S. liberal-nationalism took more critical postures during the war years.[5]

The political stakes were high as the imperative to include blacks within the nation was increasingly linked to the struggle to imagine the world-system and the future U.S. role within it—what might be called the international reconstruction of nationhood. The global struggle against fascism "plunged the country into a dramatic contest between conflicting constructions of civilization and the ordering mechanism of race."[6] If New Deal economic reforms helped make the status of blacks a national concern, World War II elevated U.S. racial division to a question of national security, international relations, and global justice. Not only was public recognition and discussion of the consequences of racial difference and inequality heightened; black activists and intellectuals increasingly came to view their own struggles as encapsulating struggles for equality and justice across the globe.

The great promise of World War II (and the hope of civil rights leaders like Walter White) was that black aspirations for justice and the interests of American world-ordering power would coincide. Roosevelt's stated transition from "Dr. New Deal" into "Dr. Win-the-War" in 1943 encapsulated the steady replacement of the stalled New Deal reform agenda with a robust, military Keynesianism that gave new impetus to black claims on equality and democracy. Projected onto the global arena, documents and speeches defining America's war aims such as the *Atlantic Charter* (1941) and Roosevelt's "Four Freedoms" (1942)—"Freedom From Want, Freedom From Fear, Freedom of Worship, and Freedom of Speech"—set out general principles of self-determination, social equality, personal liberty, and economic security now believed to extend from the United States to the entire world. Highlighted by the passage of Roosevelt's Executive

Order 8802, which established a Fair Employment Practices Committee in 1941 (the first Executive Order on racial matters since Reconstruction), the official U.S. response to war and race appeared to be a new political equation between human rights abroad and civil rights at home.[7]

Just as had New Deal reform, the global rationale for fighting World War II upped the ante of the promise of American universalism in ways that had unprecedented implications for blacks in the U.S. No less than the president himself announced in May of 1942 that "the day of the white man's burden is over. Henceforth we must treat all races with respect as equals."[8] The sentiment transcended partisan politics. As Roosevelt's one-time Republican opponent Wendell Willkie argued in his popular book, *One World* (1943), the international sphere was now a social, political, and economic unity, which meant an end to the old politics of isolationism and spheres of influence. It was possible to sustain neither empires abroad, Willkie argued, nor the "mocking paradox" of "our imperialisms at home." The *Atlantic Charter* codified this idea, declaring that the U.S., Britain, and their allies would "respect the rights of all peoples to choose the form of government under which they will live." British Prime Minister Winston Churchill pressed for a narrow application of the charter to those nations "now under the Nazi yoke."[9] But the genie of self-determination had been loosed. From as far as war-torn China, anticolonial nationalists such as Chinese communist leader Mao Zedong hailed the signing of the *Atlantic Charter* as opening "a new stage in the history of the world" favorable to the agency and development of colonized peoples.[10]

The novelty and power of such universalizing rhetoric was unmistakable. Despite signs of racial progress in the 1930s, there was still no self-determination in Mississippi or in any of the states of the old Confederacy. For blacks across the country, World War II intensified the conflicts that had been building around the limits of New Deal reform, casting them on a wider canvas. Black activists, intellectuals, and attentive publics, in other words, warily assessed U.S. claims at home and abroad in relation to their experience of racial exclusion and the relatively autonomous frames of reference it had produced. As Ralph Ellison later reflected, "Most of this nation's conflicts of arms have been—at least for Afro-Americans—wars-within-wars."[11] This was never truer than during World War II, a war in which a discourse of antifascism, freedom, and democracy was counter-poised with clashes along the color-line—allied colonialism, racial segregation, Japanese internment, white hate strikes, race war in the Pacific theater, and race riots on the home front.

Everyday life during wartime raised the heat and pace of racial struggle, conflict, and fear throughout the country, as 1.6 million black migrants streamed into urban centers in search of war work. The Fisk University Sociology Department, under the direction of Charles Johnson, monitored racial conflicts and attitudes on a monthly basis throughout the 1940s. Johnson's pamphlet, *To Stem This Tide: A Survey of Racial Tension Areas of the U.S.* (1943), identified an alarming spread of racial antagonism to cities and regions once thought immune, the result of black labor migrations into arenas that were formerly white labor preserves. Across the South, white sociologist Howard Odum reported, rumors of imminent racial catastrophe were spreading, the kind that had first circulated during Reconstruction, including white fears that black communities, aided by "Negro soldiers," were organizing "shock troop units all over the country" and stock-piling knives, ice-picks, and arms in silent preparation for a coming "race-war" at home.[12]

From Beaumont to Mobile in the South, to Detroit, Harlem, and Philadelphia in the North, to Los Angeles in the West, wartime saw a sharp spike in incidents of racial violence, often involving servicemen, police, and war production workers. In Beaumont, Texas, three black men and one white man died when white shipyard workers terrorized black neighborhoods after hearing a rumor that a black man had raped a white woman. Detroit, the "Arsenal of Democracy," saw a series of escalating racial incidents beginning in 1942, when white picketers opposed black settlement in the newly built Soujourner Truth housing projects. In 1943, 25,000 white workers at Detroit's Packard plant struck in protest of the upgrading of three black workers from janitorial service to assembly-line work. One of the worst civil disturbances in U.S. history erupted in Detroit later that year: blacks and whites fought with bricks, bats, knives, and guns for forty hours, leaving thirty-four dead and hundreds injured. The same year in Belvedere, Los Angeles, roving gangs of white sailors went on a forty-eight-hour spree of violence, targeting Mexican "pachucos," whose richly tailored "zoot suits" had become the sartorial sign of new public confidence among urban youth of color across the country. The deaths of four Mexicans scarcely tempered the glee of the local guardians of public morality, as the Los Angeles Police Department and *Los Angeles Times* heaped praise upon the servicemen for disciplining the young "gangsters." Later that summer in New York City, a white policeman shot a black soldier and Harlem's black residents rioted. Eight thousand national guardsmen were called up to pacify a disturbance that left five more people dead and several hundred wounded. In 1944, President Roosevelt was forced to call up another five thousand national guardsmen to quell a hate strike by Philadelphia's streetcar conductors, who opposed the employment of black motormen.[13]

For the almost one million blacks who served in the military, World War II was, if anything, more racially conflicted than civilian life. The three branches of military service remained rigidly segregated and hostile to appeals for reform. White southerners, who saw black soldiers as a dangerous subject population rather than as citizen-soldiers, dominated the officer corps. Most basic training operations took place in the South, putting black soldiers at additional risk from white civilians who saw blacks in uniform as an affront and a threat to the "southern way of life." The 480,000 blacks sent overseas had the worst labor details and the most dangerous, unrelieved combat operations. Elite black units like the Tuskegee Airmen, created in response to pressure from civil rights groups, were concealed from public view and often unknown even to the other soldiers with whom they served. The U.S. Red Cross's campaign for blood donations segregated the blood of blacks and whites. The black press was banned from military bases and pressured throughout the war to tone down its charge that the U.S. military was fighting a phony war against racism.[14]

Domestically, the upheavals of wartime labor migrations further entrenched patterns of residential segregation. There was no greater strain on black migrants, and no more intense site of racial conflict, than the struggle over urban space, particularly housing. By the early 1940s blacks were already spatially isolated to a degree unprecedented in U.S. history. What Arnold Hirsh has called "the second ghetto" was distinguished by the fact that it "was carried out with ongoing government sanction and support."[15] Despite the success of accumulated legal challenges to racial covenants by the late 1940s, government agencies like the Home Owners Loan Corporation (HOLC) and the Federal Housing Administration (FHA), in cooperation with local real-estate interests, contained the expanding black metropolitan presence to central cities while subsidizing white middle-class flight to the suburbs. Where the selling, credit, and building practices failed to control black overflow of the older racial boundaries, or where class limited white mobility, white residents themselves policed the borders, making housing the site of continuous racial violence in cities like Chicago and Detroit throughout the 1940s and 1950s.[16]

Ghettoization intensified the contradictions of black political life, which was repeatedly forced to invest in the power of a separate black communal existence even as it called for an end to segregation and exclusion. This was the context for Walter White's encounter with a popular black reading of the war that was sharply at odds with official patriotism. As Carey McWilliams, contributing editor to the influential liberal periodical *Common Ground,* warned in his wartime documentation of racial tensions, Axis propaganda about U.S. racism had a ready audience among black populations that had become "extremely—one could say militantly—race conscious." "One young Negro, on being inducted into the service, is supposed to have said: 'Just carve on my tombstone, 'Here lies a black man killed fighting a yellow man for the protection of the white man.'" A similar joke emerged in black communities, in which young men spoke of getting a pair of "slant eyes" so they could "kick a white man in the ass and get away with it." "We don't want to fight Hitler or anyone else," reported the *Baltimore Afro-American* in 1941, "we seem to have too many battles to settle right now."[17]

In the face of black recalcitrance and white violence, prominent liberal commentators were at pains to affirm a sanguine view of the future of race in the United States. Gunnar Myrdal, in his celebrated work of the period, *An American Dilemma: The Negro Problem and Modern Democracy,* argued that New Deal and wartime expansions of the power of the federal state had started to nationalize, and thus to modernize, American political subjectivity beyond the color line. Dubbed "the Keynes of race relations," Myrdal (and the thinkers who followed in his wake) claimed that New Deal liberalism heralded a new governmental logic, one that expanded the scope and enriched the texture of abstract citizenship by successfully embedding it within socially stabilizing networks and institutions of civil society. "Progress, liberty, equality and humanitarianism are not so un-influential on everyday life," Myrdal concluded, "because of the existence in society of huge institutional structures like the church, the school, the foundation, the trade union, the association generally, and of course, the state." Through these institutions, blacks and whites, especially in the South, were being Americanized, shedding parochial attachments to "caste" distinctions and attaining the political intelligence and organizational solidarity of modern political subjects.[18]

Expressing confidence in the United States as the bearer of the ideals of the Enlightenment and Western Civilization in a world facing disaster, *An American Dilemma* transformed conditional hopes for racial equality awakened by the war into teleological certainties. In doing so, it obscured how the wartime dynamics of racial antagonism were seeding a bitter conflict about the meaning of Americanism both at home and abroad. For if America's creed of liberty and equality was being nationalized—even internationalized—by war, then so was white supremacy. As Chester Himes caustically observed, the racial violence that erupted in Los Angeles in 1943, in which white servicemen attacked, stripped, and beat "all dark skinned people who wore zoot suits," showed that the "nazi-minded" values of the South were winning in Los Angeles. "The South's narrow conception of race relations is a national problem," black poet and wartime journalist Langston Hughes agreed in his weekly *Chicago Defender* column. "It affects every citizen from Dallas to Denver, from Washington to Seattle." Making matters worse, Hughes complained, under the banner of the U.S. military, "the South carries its Jim Crow ideas to London, Paris, Melbourne, and Naples."[19]

The majority of black activists and intellectuals—including Hughes and Himes—increasingly supported the Allied cause as the war progressed; few, however, were willing to soft-pedal racial conflict or to compromise the struggle for racial equality in its name. Black journalist Roi Ottley sounded a popular theme when he wrote that victory in war "must bring in its train the liberation of all peoples." This interpretation remained constant even as black thinkers went from skepticism about Allied war aims and rhetoric to embracing the war's potential for intranational, as well as international, transformation. Rather than assume an uncomplicated standpoint of national unity, black activists used racial division as an interpretive lens upon broader problems of nationality and world order. The war thus sharpened the dialectic of race and nation—color and democracy—as U.S. blacks viewed their own struggles, in Himes's words, as "the very essence of the fight for freedom of all the peoples of all the world."[20]

From this point forward, black populations would pose a legitimacy dilemma for the U.S. state, not only as a large, vocal minority clamoring for citizenship rights, but also as a constituency that could be mobilized around anti-imperialism and antiwar sentiment. The juxtaposition of Walter White and his unruly black audience ultimately serves then as a reminder of the political complexity, global vision, ideological heterogeneity, and political radicalism of the modern black freedom movement as it entered an accelerated phase during World War II. Political divisions among blacks were never as absolute, or as simple, as splits between nationalists and integrationists, communists and anticommunists, anti-imperialists, and American patriots. Rather, if there was a great divide in the modern black freedom movement, it was between black activists and intellectuals who gravitated toward an identification with the U.S. state and social policy as the answer to black mass discontent, and those who eyed rhetorical professions of American universality and inclusiveness from the more exacting and worldly standpoint of subjection to racializing power.

A Black Popular Front?

The global reach and rising domestic racial tensions of World War II deepened and widened the political purchase of the forms of black radicalism that had developed during the 1930s, resulting in what some have described as a black popular front.[21] In part, the black popular front was a manifestation of revivals of the leftwing alliance politics of the popular front after the Nazi invasion of the Soviet Union. With it came a partial truce in the on-going competition between liberalism and communism over the formations of black public opinion, as well as a return to the slogans of national unity and cross-class cooperation. What distinguished black versions of popular front politics, however, was that they also reflected a far less compromising, and more broadly informed, commitment to struggles for racial justice at home and abroad within the black public sphere.

What initially gave the "reds" credibility in black communities, St. Clair Drake and Horace Cayton noted in *Black Metropolis* (1945), was that they had "fought for Negroes as Negroes."[22] "Thousands of Negro preachers and doctors and lawyers, as well as quiet housewives, gave their money and verbal support for freeing the Scottsboro boys and for releasing Angelo Herndon. Hundreds, too, voted for

Foster and Ford, Browder and Ford, for what other party since Reconstruction days had ever run a Negro for vice-president of the United States? And who had ever put Negroes in a position where they led white men as well as black?" In the South, associations between communism and black liberation were so deep that many rural blacks called communists "new abolitionists" and envisioned their leader, "Uncle Joe Stalin," as another incarnation of Lincoln, come to free the slaves. Carl Murphy, editor of the *Baltimore Afro-American,* showed that communism had insinuated itself into the urban, black nationalist lexicon as well when he wrote, "the Communists are going our way, for which Allah be praised."[23]

Although the party line on the "Negro Question" fluctuated during the 1930s, communists had long understood blacks to be the most exploited segment of the American proletariat and had given rhetorical support to the view that blacks in the American South comprised a "nation within a nation" and the center of global anti-imperialist struggle. The 1935 black protests against the Italian invasion of Ethiopia represented the high-water mark of the party's engagement with what its Negro section chief, George Padmore, described as an international awakening of "Negro consciousness." The emphasis upon anti-imperialism and black autonomy was downplayed under the first Popular Front from 1935 to 1939, leading Padmore to quit the Communist International in disgust. During the interregnum of the Nazi-Soviet pact from 1939 to 1941, however, the Party reverted to the posture of nonintervention and sectarian condemnation of imperialist war, a viewpoint that retained considerable resonance for blacks, communist and noncommunist alike.[24]

Indeed, even after the CPUSA again reversed itself to support a broad "anti-fascist" front against the Axis powers, the global critique of imperialism continued to inform black understandings of the war's meaning. Reflecting on his tour of duty as a U.S. soldier in French North Africa, Harold Cruse (who was a party member from 1947 to 1953), claimed that World War II continued a longer process of internationalizing black views of the world. This was not because black participation in the war effort opened new pathways to national belonging, but because wartime travels abroad yielded a racially tinctured cosmopolitanism that was rooted in the recognition, for example, that blacks in the United States were not so remote from the Arab and Berber peoples colonized by the French. Cruse's reflections were undoubtedly inspired by the anticolonial ferment of the 1950s and 1960s, but they belie a greater continuity in black social thought and structures of feeling across the long civil rights era than has generally been appreciated. Although the communist, fellow-traveler Ralph Ellison may not have been as extreme (or as jaded) as a young Harlem hustler named Malcolm Little (later known as Malcolm X), who avoided military service by claiming that he was "frantic to join the Japanese Army," Ellison was not alone in the dyspeptic hope he confided to then-party member Richard Wright, in May 1940, that Hitler might "invade England and break the Empire."[25]

It would be a mistake to attribute these sentiments solely to the far-left milieu inhabited by many of these figures.[26] The rigid anticommunist consensus that dominated U.S. politics and historiography after World War II obscured the fact that many important black radicals—including Wright, Ellison, Bayard Rustin, Langston Hughes, and Chester Himes—actually distanced themselves from the CPUSA during World War II, not because they sought the political mainstream, but because they felt the party was not radical enough and believed it had betrayed a consistent and principled commitment to black self-determination and the primacy of struggles against racism and colonialism. The marginality of communism within American political culture, combined with its uncritical and self-effacing relationship to the liberal state during the war years, actually diminished its prestige among blacks. In fact, despite their political differences, Wright, Ellison, and Cruse all came to essentially the same conclusion: black struggles were more important for defining the aims and purposes of an American communism than communism was for defining the meaning and future importance of black struggles.[27]

In part this conclusion was the consequence of the political and intellectual weaknesses of Popular Front nationalism on questions of race. The influence of political discourses and styles of thinking associated with the Popular Front promoted an inclusive discourse of civic nationalism aimed expressly at blacks. At the same time, the liberals and progressives of the New Deal and Popular Front largely collaborated to give national belonging precedence over class and ethnic divisions, but failed to envisage substantive transformation of divisions associated with race. World War II contrasted markedly with World War I in its expansion of an official pluralism, yet the recalcitrant spirit of black protest nurtured in the 1930s meant that fewer blacks were willing to "close ranks" this time, as W. E. B. Du Bois had counseled them to in the Great War.[28]

Notable efforts to reassure, such as Spencer Logan's *A Negro's Faith in America* (1942), were less compelling to black attentive publics (and far less common) than controversial and assertive works like Rayford Logan's collection, *What the Negro Wants* (1944). And, despite the public emphasis on black inclusion within the nation—marked by such events as black singer-activist Paul Robeson's wartime renditions of Earl Robinson's Popular Front "Ballad for Americans," radio programs highlighting black contributions to U.S. history like "Freedom's People," filmmaker Frank Capra's film segment on "The Negro Soldier" (1944) for the Office of War Information's (OWI) "Why We Fight" campaign, or the publication of Myrdal's *An American Dilemma*—the hard facts of racial segregation, particularly in the military, continued to stir black dissent.[29]

Among a liberal-minded punditry swelled by the demand for cultural and symbolic work in the war effort, the intranational heterogeneities of America's immigrant populations—grouped under the newly minted concept "ethnicity"—were increasingly identified as the source of an exceptional universalism that prepared the United States for global leadership.[30] Few did more to popularize this idea than Louis Adamic, founder of the wartime organization called the Common Council for American Unity and author of several books on American diversity, including *A Nation of Nations* (1944). "The fact that our population is an extension of most of the Old World, stemming from about sixty different backgrounds," Adamic wrote, gave the United States an advantage over other nations: an opportunity to create a national culture that was "universal or pan-human and more satisfying to the inner human make-up than any culture that has yet appeared on this earth."[31] Paul Robeson famously gave voice to Adamic's vision of the United States as "the world-in-miniature" in the lines he sang from "Ballad for Americans" that personified the American as an "Irish-Negro-Jewish-Italian-French and English, Spanish Russian, Chinese, Polish, Scotch, Hungarian, Swedish, Finnish, Canadian, Greek and Turk, and Czech and Double Czech American."[32]

The linked emphasis on voluntary migration and self-made origins reinforced the idea of an exceptional and exemplary model of U.S. national identity and discredited still-potent expressions of American nativism. Every American, President Roosevelt had declared, was the "descendent of revolutionaries and immigrants."[33] World War II solidified the idea that the incorporation of immigrant difference was the template for solving the problem of national minorities in general and racial minorities in particular. Yet, if Catholics and Jews, southern and eastern Europeans were finally being reconciled with the normative nationality produced by generations of Anglo-Protestant settlers, the same could not be said of the other "indigenous" U.S. culture, that of southern migrant blacks. Early on in the war, Langston Hughes counseled blacks and immigrants to form "some sort of protective unity" in the face of attacks on them by "pure Americans." At the same time, Hughes reflected on the irony of his advice. "I am pure American," Hughes mused, "though colored, I date way back." Scorned by "that other pure American," Hughes doubted that "the man who spoke the foreign language would help me." This was because foreign-born and second-generation immigrants had managed to lessen their own distance from "pure Americans" by joining in "the American pattern of Jim-Crowing Negroes."[34]

Hughes pinpointed an irony of the black presence in the United States lost even in the most progressive paeans to national unity: it was at once foundational to the American realm and, at the same time, the exclusion that made the fiction of the "pure American" possible. Construing intranational difference on the analogy of immigrant incorporation not only failed to amend this situation, it arguably reinforced the cultural and political legacies of unreconstructed racial hierarchies built upon the involuntary migration and forced labor of Africans, Asian migrants ineligible for naturalization, and the colonization or removal of Indians and Mexicans. In a country supposedly marked by unprecedented diversity and universal tolerance, it was an acute, unresolved question as to whether people of color could be folded into what was cast as a revolutionary drama of ethnic succession in which immigrants became—in a popular phrase from the period—"Americans all."

A directive from OWI guidelines provides a telling example of wartime thinking about the legacies of racial exclusion, especially as it pertained to blacks: "the fact that slavery existed in this country is certainly something which belongs to the past and which we wish to forget at this time when the unity of all races and creeds is important."[35] To forget, however, was the prerogative of a "we" already encased within racial supremacist presumptions. A closer look at Earl

Robinson's Popular Front and wartime unity anthem, "Ballad for Americans," further illustrates the point. For, even as the song used class ("the et ceteras and so forths that do the work") and ethnicity as markers for a more inclusive national identity, it also bewailed the perpetration of "murders and lynchings" in the South that took cover beneath "patriotic spoutings." More ironically, the joke "Czech and Double Czech American" that completes the construction of a pan-ethnic American nationality in the song is a phrase first popularized by radio minstrels Amos 'n' Andy in the 1920s, suggesting that at its most generic, U.S. national identity still depended on antiblack tropes. (That Robeson, the singer most closely associated with the "Ballad," would, in a few years, be so widely vilified and easily discredited for his "un-American activities" during this period compounds the irony.)[36]

Americanism of this sort was an ambivalent cultural production—a contradictory distillation of a powerful new universalizing rhetoric and intensifying racial violence and division. For black publics long attuned to the fissures between the universalism of U.S. political and judicial rhetoric and the exclusionary practices of government institutions, banks, homeowners, employers, schools, trade unions, and cultural representation, the struggle to align the practices of everyday life with American universals was haunted by the constant threat of disillusionment. Indeed, for black writers, activists, and intellectuals, who had already nurtured more effective politics and techniques of racial representation through the late 1930s, the wartime tactics of national unification raised the opportunity to again "play the changes" on the old problem of national belonging. They did so not by joining a mythic consensus that blacks, like immigrants, were being Americanized, but by asserting that black struggles for equality defined the war's most expansive and most global, civic imperatives.

In other words, appeals to neither patriotism nor pragmatism were enough to ensure black assent to the U.S. war effort. In his famous essay, "Blueprint for Negro Writing" (1937), Richard Wright effectively outlined the problem early on. Blacks, Wright wrote, "have been made to feel a sense of difference. So deep has the white-hot iron of exclusion been burnt into their hearts that thousands have lost the desire to become identified with American Civilization."[37] In his unpublished novel, *Lawd Today* (1937), Wright slyly mocked official efforts to write blacks into unifying scripts of U.S. nationhood, interspersing the harsh, disjointed lives of his urban black characters with the crackling sounds of a radio broadcast celebrating Abraham Lincoln's birthday. Metaphorically adjusting the frequency of the official story of black progress from slavery to freedom against contemporary scenes of black, urban abjection, Wright posed a fundamental question about the rhetoric and function of national myths and symbols: Were they illusions irrelevant to the conduct of black lives, or were they, if tuned-in properly, instruments of black social and political progress?[38]

Early in the war years, the answer was definitive and often sharply negative. Few writers expressed the mood of black skepticism and defiance more powerfully than Ralph Ellison in a letter he penned to Wright in May of 1940:

> Well, things are developing rapidly here. I've just heard FDR in a Fireside chat giving the signal for a drive against anyone who opposes his war moves. There is also a bill just through the House preventing the hiring of Reds and Bundists on the WPA. It's a black, nasty picture. Here is the same conjuring with religion, patriotism exploited by Hitler. FDR is oh soreligious these days. And that's no typographical error. Dies has become respectable in his sight and all our other fascists are held up as models of Americanism. The Negro press screams for the indiscriminate rights of Negroes to die in the army . . . But the new men are rising, and this war will bring forward many more. Fellow up from the South tells me that their problem down there is to work rapidly enough to make the Negroes aware of the necessity of discriminating between white folks. He says its dynamite. Consciousness of the necessity for revolt is growing rapidly. It would be interesting to see what'll happen when they are made soldiers and given guns. Hell, you become so impatient in times like these that you could say a good word for anarchy.[39]

Ellison's dissent expressed a militant racialism and radicalism marked by the return of the hard-line sectarian politics of the pre-Popular Front era. Ellison specifically pointed to the specter of an indigenous fascism born of white supremacy, effectively re-coded in more palatable terms of anticommunism and patriotism. Indeed, a vernacular anticommunism—linking white supremacy, xenophobic nationalism, and fears of radical subversion—circulated widely among opponents of New Deal reform in the late 1930s. Antiblack and anticommunist sentiments were difficult to distinguish in the arguments of white Southerners during this period, so thoroughly were the two intertwined in the popular racist imagination. Texas Congressman Martin Dies, who convened the House Un-American Activities Committee (HUAC) in 1938 to investigate "communist penetration of the New Deal," maintained a special interest in links between the organized left and black civil rights agitation. Dies called the communist party "a Trojan Horse for Negroes," an indication that his concerns were as much about subversion of the racial order as they were about leftist influence. The growing power of anticommunism during and after World War II developed at least in part because it provided cover for increasingly discredited racist practice and rhetoric.[40]

Where state-oriented black leaders like Ralph Bunche joined Walter White to complain about the parochialism and short-sightedness of blacks who failed to choose between "America's imperfect buffeted democracy on the one hand, and totalitarianism on the other," Ellison identified with what he believed was a profoundly valuable restiveness and assertiveness in black everyday life.[41] In fact, Ellison reserved his harshest disdain for what he described as a "subsidized Negro leadership" that sought to discipline black opposition to racism in the name of national unity. His prose on the page ("FDR is oh so religious these days") literally allegorized a black vernacular discontent that refused to be made legible in the name of a sanctioned patriotism ("And that's no typographical error"). His sense that blacks in the South were losing the ability to distinguish between whites suggested that the persistence of racial discrimination and rising black consciousness had the potential to fracture U.S. nationality along racial lines.[42]

Finally, Ellison's "good word for anarchy" suggests the wider repudiation among black thinkers of the ethical primacy of a "civilization" bankrupted by racial, colonial, and right-wing politics. Indeed, this was the ideological kernel animating wartime black radicalism: fascism, colonialism, and racism were interrelated phenomena, whose linkages undermined Anglo-American claims to special moral standing among nations. "That the Negro has no stake in this war," Wright stated in a 1941 interview with fellow black communist Angelo Herndon in the *Communist Daily Worker,* "is borne out by the fact that England and France oppress more Negroes and colonial peoples than all the Empires of the world combined."[43] The Caribbean radical and Worker's Party theoretician C. L. R. James, Wright's admirer and confidant during his American sojourn carried the same insight into his keen participation in the U.S. race radicalism of these years: "British imperialism has for years exercised a tyranny comparable only to fascism. Hitler had little to invent in the methods and techniques of fascist oppression."[44]

During World War II, perspectives such as these, well established in the U.S. black metropolis, resulted in a popular black rejection of "American exceptionalism in favor of a global, coalitional politics in which anti-imperialism and anti-racism might be seen to interact if not to fuse."[45] The conviction behind this viewpoint once again cannot be attributed to the communist rejection of the Popular Front against fascism occasioned by the Nazi-Soviet Pact. For while it is true that many black radicals in the orbit of the CPUSA briefly became anti-interventionists during this period, the communists neither created nor monopolized the field of popular black radicalism. Black publics, as Paul Robeson argued in 1943, understood the war in terms of "an awareness born of their yearning for freedom from an oppression which has pre-dated Fascism." The parallel between black interests and "those of oppressed peoples abroad," he added, originated with "the Fascist invasion of Ethiopia in 1935." This perspective, in other words, was organic to modern black political sensibilities, at once preceding and outlasting the periodic disruptions and restorations of the unity politics of the official Popular Front. As the *Chicago Defender* editorialized in 1938, the "age of hate" did not begin with "the triumphal entry of Herr Fuehrer into Vienna. The age of hate began with the slave trade and the intensification of prejudice which followed the liberation of the slaves." As late as the mid-1950s, Martiniquan poet Aimé Césaire would assertively maintain the equation between fascism and colonialism, polemicizing that Naziism was legitimate as long as it was applied to "non-European peoples."[46]

The global vision of the black popular front was distinguished by a connective, transnational sensibility that refused to privilege national boundaries or party lines. One did not need to be a communist, Garveyite, Pan-Africanist, or veteran of the 1930s Ethiopia solidarity movement to recognize that at the center of the war was an explosive, racialized geopolitics. As the anticommunist, trade unionist A. Philip Randolph put it in 1943, there was "no difference between Hitler of Germany, Talmage of Georgia or Tojo of Japan and Bilbo of Mississippi."[47] Similarly, Langston Hughes, an early supporter of U.S. intervention who refused to be associated with far-left positions on the war, also refused a stance of simple, patriotic affirmation. His biographer Arnold Rampersad has argued that this period saw Hughes's movement toward the political mainstream after a decade of association with international communism. But World War II actually renewed Hughes's radical and activist engagement. He thus would share, rather than depart from, the black transnationalist outlook when he characterized black participation in the war as something that could "shake the British Empire to the dust . . . Shake Dixie's teeth loose too, and crack the joints of 'Jim Crow' South Africa."[48]

Black activists and intellectuals from a range of ideological persuasions, regions, and backgrounds joined in what Horace Cayton called a wider political "awakening" in which "the Negro placed his problems in a new and larger frame of reference and related them to world forces."[49] The common ground shared by figures as diverse as the scion of Seattle's black bourgeoisie, Cayton; the lyrical Harlem poet, Hughes; the Caribbean Trotskyite, James; the erudite, East Coast college graduate, Robeson; the hardscrabble, southern communist, Wright; and the aspiring jazzman from Oklahoma and Tuskeegee, Ellison, shows the extent to which the intellectual and political perspectives on anticolonial and minority radicalisms had cohered inside the United States as an independent factor in the struggle over the terms of the global future.

Although it was short-lived, the black popular front emerged at the confluence of a number of important intellectual and political currents, including far-left confrontations with white supremacy, the more inclusive civic culture of New Deal liberalism, and the idealistic internationalism of World War II. Most of all, however, it reflected the on-going development of a black public sphere stimulated by everyday acts of resistance by ordinary black people. As the MOWM demonstrated, black political sensibilities were increasingly forged at the intersection of state-oriented liberalism inclined to ameliorative reform and a relatively autonomous black activism inclined to acts of rebellion. At the same time, the heterogeneous patterns and epistemologies of intranational racial differentiation were recast by the war at new scales of association and influence. Black activists and intellectuals subsequently embraced new national and global conceptions of black struggle with surprising intensity, unanimity, and radicalism. This was not done in the name of an un-reflexive, or "essentialist," belief in racial unity, but in response to a heightened sense of linked fate, or what Ellison would call the "identity of passions" that tied together racialized and colonized peoples around the world.

Black Worldliness

A hallmark of black political and intellectual development in these years was the number of key black intellectuals who felt their attachments to the organized left begin to wane as U.S. communists downplayed racial antagonism in the name of wartime unity after Nazi invasion brought the Soviet Union onto the side of the Allies in late 1941. Black struggles, it seemed, had come to possess a vibrancy that no longer required external mediation. Ellison prefigured his later disenchantment with the party in 1941 when he defended Wright's controversial proto-Marxist works, *Native Son* (1940) and *Twelve Million Black Voices* (1941), for putting forth what he called "Negro truths" ignored by communists and liberals alike. "I hope our political leaders will realize what is here made available for them," Ellison wrote, "here is their statistics given personality . . . All Marx and Engels, Lenin and Stalin won't help unless they understand this part of the theoretical world made flesh."[50]

The wartime dialogues of Wright and Ellison in particular reveal a great deal about the burgeoning self-confidence and worldliness of black intellectuals stimulated by the war as they began to substantially re-envision the old left equation between black social experience, popular struggle, and social transformation. Specifically, they argued that black democratic struggles in the United States were inherently radical, rooted in indigenous, if frustrated, communal understandings of freedom that ultimately exceeded the abstract, programmatic concepts and slogans of the organized left. Reflecting a style of thought similar to that of Du Bois's *Black Reconstruction* (1935), Wright and Ellison, along with key figures within their intellectual milieu, including C. L. R. James, Horace Cayton, Angelo Herndon, and Chester Himes, thus came to view black struggle as an independent frame of reference for making political judgments about the nation, the world, and modern political life in general.

Explaining his own exit from the party, Wright argued that the history of forced dispersal, subjugation, and emancipation experienced by enslaved Africans had obtained a singular and more universal resonance than abstract theories of class struggle and the vanguard party. As he elaborated in his celebrated essay, "I Tried to be a Communist": "It was not the economics of Communism, nor the great power of trade unions, nor the excitement of underground politics that claimed me. My attention was caught by the experiences of workers in other lands, by the possibility of uniting scattered but kindred peoples into a whole. It seemed to me that here at last, in the realm of revolutionary expression, the Negro experience could find a home, a functioning intellectual value and role."[51] Although communism had provided a temporary home for thinking the radicalism of black experience, it had outlived its usefulness. Indeed, Wright recalled being drawn to communism when reading about Soviet policies on national and colonial questions, particularly how Soviet phonetic experts had worked with the peoples of central Asia to develop a written language, newspapers, and means of mass communication from their primarily oral traditions. What Wright found inspiring about these efforts (as he speculated about them) was that they were attempts to improve (or modernize) the everyday life of suppressed and subjugated peoples without erasing cultural difference. "I read how these forgotten folk had been encouraged to keep their old cultures, to see in their ancient customs meanings and satisfactions as deep as those contained in supposedly superior ways of living. And I had exclaimed to myself how different this was from the ways Negroes were sneered at in America."[52]

Although U.S. communists certainly did not sneer at blacks, Wright believed that by viewing blacks stereotypically and sentimentally, they failed to recognize the remarkable transformations of black life under conditions of mass migration, urbanization, and print culture. Specifically, Wright argued, communists were deaf and blind to the richness and tragedy of black life, to the dangers as well as possibilities that inhered in the specifically black experience of modernity. Commenting on time he spent with black youth at the South Side Boys Club in Chicago, Wright contrasted "their talk of planes, women, guns, politics and crime," with the mirthless, unimaginative discourse of his fellow party members: "The communists who doubted my motives did not know these boys, their twisted dreams, their all too clear destinies." In other words, American communists had failed to penetrate black everyday life because they refused to learn its language, the "most forceful and colorful as any ever used by English speaking people."[53] As a consequence, Wright argued, they had abdicated their role as privileged translators of the black social experience into the idioms of a broader politics and struggle.

That role had passed to the activist black intellectual, who, like the black masses, was now in a position to negotiate directly with the nation's political and intellectual establishment. (As Wright slyly put it years later, "Many a black boy has seized upon the rungs of the Red ladder to climb out of his Black Belt.") Wright explicated this in the provocative essay he added to the new edition of *Native Son*, "How Bigger Was Born." Party reviewers had disparaged Bigger Thomas, Wright's infamous black everyman, as an irresponsible and negative portrayal of the noble black proletarian. For Wright, however, Bigger was much more than the proletarian antithesis to capitalism. Rather, Wright saw Bigger as a new kind of revolutionary man who "carried within him the potentialities of either Communism or Fascism." In this sense, Bigger represented the impasse that confronted the regulative ideal of American freedom at home and abroad. Bigger Thomas "was an American, because he was a native son," Wright wrote, "but he was also a Negro nationalist in a vague sense because he was not allowed to live as an American." If America continued to fail to create a "culture which could hold and claim his allegiance or faith," Wright warned, "the Bigger Thomases of the world" would rise up and expose the anarchy beneath the pretense of American civilization.[54]

Irving Howe once mused that American culture changed forever on the day *Native Son* was published. This insight is important. As we recover the challenging, dissenting visions of long-canonized figures like Wright and Ellison, it is important to recognize their novelty. It is particularly crucial not to assimilate them too quickly to the post–World War II dominance of anticommunist liberalism over black social and intellectual life. Neither Wright's nor Ellison's rejection of the Party can be understood simply in terms of their movement away from left-wing radicalism into liberalism and literary celebrity, as some critics have suggested.[55] Wright's prose was certainly anticipatory of the anti-communist, Cold War equation of communism and fascism, yet he also continued to prefer the marxification of Bigger. Indeed, Wright refused to condemn his detractors in the Party, writing, "I'll be for them, even though they are not for me."[56] As late as 1945, a more politically disaffected Ellison still described himself as a believer in the Marxist doctrine of a "classless society" while proclaiming the need to defend the "unity of peoples . . . both Negroes and labor" from the "CP sell-out" of their militant struggles against the no-strike pledge and desegregation of war work.[57] Richard Crossman, who reprinted Wright's essay, "I Tried to be a Communist," in the famous anticommunist anthology *The God that Failed,* noted that Wright was alone among the contributors to the volume who recognized that communism could be "a liberating force among the Colored peoples who make up the great majority of mankind."[58]

The wartime views of both Wright and Ellison were less anticommunist than they were efforts to articulate an independent and indigenous black radicalism—to imagine the ongoing formation of U.S. blacks as modern, political subjects who, although constantly imperiled by the degradations of racism, also frequently possessed practical knowledge ("Negro truths") that might become the basis for achieving a more enduring knowledge and practice of freedom. This was further reflected in their new respect for the vernacular signs and recalcitrant spirit that inhered in urban black popular culture and everyday life. As Ellison put it in a 1943 essay published in *Negro Quarterly,* "perhaps the zoot suit conceals profound political meaning; perhaps the symmetrical frenzy of the Lindy-hop conceals clues to great potential power—if only Negro leaders would solve this riddle."[59] Almost a decade later, Ellison, more beholden to anticommunist orthodoxies, still mused prophetically about the chiseled figure of the zoot-suit favored by young black men cut adrift in urban America as the sign of a burgeoning subaltern creativity within black life that defied both the conventional modernizing narrative of black cultural pathology and left-wing idealizations of "the folk."[60]

For Wright, too, the ordinary struggles and popular expressions of urban blacks had begun to have the unprecedented power to, as he put it, "represent what America is." Wright's own personal odyssey out of the South to become a native son of American letters exemplified this shift. As he noted, "One of the things that made me write is that I realize that I'm a very average Negro . . . and maybe that's what makes me extraordinary."[61] The prospectus Wright formulated with C. L. R. James for a popular magazine called *American Pages,* to counter the racism and xenophobia of the mainstream press, envisioned the broad dissemination of this idea. *American Pages* conceived "the Negro question as an abstract and concrete frame of reference to reflect constructive criticism on the nation as a whole."

Although the magazine did not materialize, this conception behind it reflects the new political and intellectual purposefulness with which black intellectuals challenged the idea that race was a parochial concern. "If America can be brought to understand the nature and meaning of minorities, whether as individuals or groups, she will have taken the first step toward a unified culture."[62]

Virtually every major black intellectual and activist advocated black participation in the war effort after 1942. They did so, however, not by emphasizing an unconditional patriotism, but by arguing that the global stakes and scales of the war had sharpened the dialectic of racial differentiation and national belonging. In *Negro Quarterly,* the short-lived black left periodical he edited with Angelo Herndon, Ellison called for the "critical participation" of blacks "based upon a sharp sense of the Negro people's group personality." Ellison called this position a "manifestation of black nationalism" that existed in tension with the goal "of integrating the large American nation and compelling it untiringly toward true freedom." "The Negro," as James put it in his inimitable style, "is a nationalist to the heart and perfectly right to be so. His racism, his nationalism, is a necessary means of giving him strength, self-respect and organization in order to fight for integration into American society. It is a perfect example of dialectical contradiction."[63]

This idea took concrete political form in the public call, widely advertised in the *Pittsburgh Courier* and throughout the Negro press in 1942, for a "Double-Victory" against fascism abroad and racism at home. Wright succinctly explained the logic of the Double-V: "If this is a war for democracy and freedom, then we fight in it, for democracy and freedom. We shall fight as determinedly against those who deny freedom at home as we shall fight against those who deny it to others abroad."[64] Developing the idea further, Chester Himes called for "a second front for freedom" in the struggle against white supremacy. That Himes's essay, "Now Is the Time! Here Is the Place!" (1942), appeared in *The Crisis,* the premier forum of black intellectual moderation, indicates just how much the war intensified both racial and national consciousness among blacks. Like Ellison, Himes argued that blacks needed to participate in the U.S. war effort, but not within the "boundaries" of an "existing interpretation of freedom" codified by "statute and administration," but through a "contemporaneous, concurrent" fight for "freedom at home." Himes proceeded to ask searching questions about blacks' participation in the war effort that would reverberate long after these years. "What pride will there be to urge us on? What ideal for which to fight? What love of country to inspire us with patriotic ardor? Is not victory abroad without victory at home a sham, empty, and with no meaning, leaving us no more free than before?"[65]

James summarily described the black intellectuals in the Wright circle as "groping pioneers for a native American radicalism."[66] By this he meant that they were attempting to find a way out of the impasse between the critique of allied imperialism and the capitulation to state patriotism demanded by the war. Such a perspective sought to balance the wartime revival of Popular Front–style antifascism with the rejection of political ideas and programs predicated upon black self-erasure or subordination of popular black opposition to racism. It emphasized the critical independence of black social experience and the intranational and supranational forms of imagined community and political struggle that experience had yielded—which applied as equally to emerging anticommunist, liberal perspectives on black life as it did to the organized left, both of which deferred uncritically to official demands for wartime unity.

As James wrote in one of the most insightful and prophetic commentaries on the black intellectual and political agitation of this period, "The Revolutionary Answer to the Negro Question in the US" (1948), "The Negro struggle, the independent Negro struggle has a vitality and validity of its own; it has deep historic roots in the past of America and in present struggles; it has an organic political perspective, along which it is traveling to one degree or another."[67] As "one of the crucial pivots of the American political system," James predicted, blacks would have a decisive role to play on the world stage in the coming period. Future black movements would neither be subsumed into class struggle on the Marxist model nor simply serve as a vindication of existing U.S. national ideals. Rather, they would provide an independent, political standpoint for advancing civic inclusion in the United States and stimulating anticolonial ferment in the world-system.[68]

Finally, James emphasized the singular universalism of black aspirations for freedom and democracy that began to emanate from the United States during the war. If the antifascist declamations of the *Atlantic Charter* and the "Four Freedoms" were initiating a new American epoch in the history of international civilization, James wrote in his key reflections on these years, then "the Negro question in the United States" was "the No. 1 minority problem in the entire world."[69] A measure of the currency of this idea was that it was not necessarily a radical or even an exclusively black viewpoint, but one that attained a wider resonance within a national and international public sphere by the war's end. As Carey McWilliams wrote, "If England is haunted by the problem of India, so are we haunted by the problem of our 12,000,000 Negroes."[70] Announcing the publication of *An American Dilemma,* Carnegie Foundation President Frederick Keppel wrote that "the eyes of men of all races the world over" were turned upon America "to see how the people of the most powerful of the United Nations are dealing at home with a major problem of race relations."[71]

What differentiated the major black activist articulations of this idea was the emphasis they placed on blacks as independent agents of change—their refusal to subsist either as a "problem of race relations" or as "our Negroes." To put it another way, the black search for justice under the sign of U.S. nationalism was inextricable from the idea that blacks in the United States comprised a distinct people entitled to the protections of national sovereignty. Black intellectuals may have disagreed on whether the Negro was a "nation within a nation," but they recognized that the national aspects of colonial and minority questions were of a piece. The world within America had to change, they reasoned, because the world beyond American borders presented the possibility of wider, imagined publics—indeed the majority of the people on the planet—who were similarly restricted with respect to questions of nationality. Articulating a theme that has endured ever since, black activists distinguished both the national and global dimensions of the "Negro problem" in this manner. Harlem journalist Roi Ottley's aptly titled, *A New World-a-Coming* (1943), is just one more example of this new sense of *black worldliness:* "Events abroad have lifted the 'Negro Problem' out of its limited orbit of a strictly domestic issue. Today, more and more, race and color questions are being thrown into the public scene. The Negro's future—and what he thinks it should be—is of great consequence . . . Black men in this country—*a group larger than some nations involved in the war*—are feeling a great resurgence of racial kinship to other colored peoples of the world. And this is acutely the concern of white America."[72]

The central black radical intellectuals of this period, including Wright, James, Himes, Ellison, Hughes, and many others, finally offered something a good deal more complicated than an "aesthetics of integration," as they staked out a middle ground between declarations of black disaffiliation from the nation and an uncritical standpoint of patriotic affirmation.[73] In his weekly *Chicago Defender* column, Hughes excoriated moderate black officials such as the Council for Democracy's Warren Barton, and prominent southern liberals like Virginius Dabney, who supported efforts to "soften and quiet down" black demands for freedom and equality in order to get on with the more important business of winning the war. Hughes challenged the temporizers on matters of racial equality as people who would "dilute the Four Freedoms to the strength of near-beer." By contrast, he conjured a revolutionary nationalist tradition, extending from Patrick Henry to Abraham Lincoln to Franklin Roosevelt, rooted in the unconditional demand for liberty and equality.[74] As Himes wrote, "No American of any race, true to the ideals of Americanism, can refuse to participate in the Negro Americans' fight and on their side, for that for which we fight is the only true Americanism—that of our founders and of our Constitution."[75]

It is tempting to seize upon these statements as evidence of a new and profound identification of black writers with American nationalism. Following in the train of *An American Dilemma,* generations of post–World War II U.S. commentators have argued that the black deployment of American universals in the struggle for American privileges and national belonging is far more significant than the influences of left-wing politics, anti-imperialism, and black nationalism. It is certainly the case that in World War II, as in the past, black thinkers took up liberal and republican ideas about American exceptionalism and exemplarity, adapting them to their own ends. In doing so, not only did they affirm American universalism, but more importantly, they reinvested it with the symbolic power of their own struggles. One thing is true: if the modern internationalist nationalism forged in the United States during World War II retains many of its associations with a far-reaching and progressive universalism and continues to be put forth as a paradigm of good nationalism, it is due to the ways it was grafted onto the struggles of the oppressed.

At the same time, every significant black intellectual activist during World War II noted the disjuncture between the global promise of American universalism, the domestic realities of racial exclusion, and the problems of colonial empires. Unsatisfied by the progressive guise of the *Atlantic Charter,* they remained intent on monitoring the implementation of what was little more than a vague and open-ended guarantee. As black historian L. D. Reddick wrote in *The Crisis* in 1943, "what happens in Africa in the immediate future will reveal to the submerged masses everywhere, and to ourselves, whether our stirring declarations have meaning or whether this is just one more indecent war."[76] Seasoned black radicals fundamentally doubted that America's new global reach would be good for peoples of color at home or abroad. Writing in the *Chicago Defender* in 1942, George Padmore pointedly asked whether the war was being fought "for the security of Europe to enjoy the Four Freedoms," while the people who suffered under the yoke of colonialism subsisted in their "pre-war status."[77]

In the 1960s, Harold Cruse influentially defined the conjunction of decolonization and U.S. black liberation as the fulcrum of radical politics in the post–World War II world. "The revolutionary initiative has passed to the colonial world and in the United States is passing to the Negro," Cruse wrote, "while Western Marxists theorize, temporize and debate."[78] Cruse suggested that mid-century black activist intellectuals had ceded a hard-edged racial politics to bland affirmations of national belonging under the dual pressures of left-wing ideology and liberal-integrationist visions of communal liquidation. He thus believed that they had defaulted on the historic task of producing theoretical and political insights relevant to new conditions of national racial oppression and the cultural and political autonomy of black life these necessitated.

Ironically, Cruse's overestimation of his own originality and vindictiveness toward his more famous predecessors obscured the intellectual and political context that enabled many of his more important insights. As C. L. R. James noted as he criss-crossed the country doing agitprop in the war years, black movements were developing simultaneously on two fronts—as self-constituting feelings of racial pride and as uncompromising political demands for national equality. James viewed these tendencies as inextricable from one and other: "Whereas in Europe the national movements have usually aimed at a separation from the oppressing power, in the U.S. the race consciousness and chauvinism of the Negro represents fundamentally a consolidation of his forces for the purposes of integration into American society."[79]

In contrast to a prior generation of leftists, as well as to a future generation of civil rights liberals for whom racial integration essentially meant the public invisibility of blacks as blacks, activist intellectuals such as James, Wright, and Ellison refused to accept anything that smacked of submission to civic inferiority. They further believed that the shared fact of black oppression had produced not merely a form of negative collective identity, but also affirmative cultures and styles of communal belonging. Black self-identity, James wrote, was "the natural excess of the desire for equality."[80] In this view, integration presumed neither political accommodation nor normative assimilation. Rather, it imagined the independent, democratic, self-mobilization of blacks as one of its prerequisites.

In carving out a position between anticommunist liberalism and communist party lines, the heterodox Marxists of the black popular front, as Cedric Robinson argues, made one of the more significant theoretical efforts to extend the Marxist tradition in the face of the intellectual and political disaster that loomed on the Cold War horizon. In James's description of Richard Wright, they sought to "clear the way to be revolutionary and anti-Stalinist."[81] We might interpret the latter statement in the following way: black movements were beginning to illustrate a crucial political lesson, namely, that the demand for democracy was both irreducible and unpredictable, in "excess" of the deterministic designs and schemas that captivated Marxists and modernizing liberals alike.

It was thus that James concluded his reflections on wartime black politics with a complex affirmation of black autonomy and initiative. "The Marxist support of the Negro struggle for democratic rights is not a concession that Marxists make to the Negroes. In the United States today this struggle is a direct part of the struggle for socialism." Written in 1943, this idea hearkened back to *Black Reconstruction*, just as it anticipated the flexible grafts of Marxism onto struggles for national self-determination that would characterize anticolonial and black movements in years to come. It also correctly foresaw that U.S. black movements were rapidly becoming the most reliable conduits of the radical imagination in capitalist America, able to sustain broad and compelling visions of social justice when other movements and organizations no longer could.[82]

Toward the Peoples' Century

Rather than confirming American universalism, or subsisting as America's dilemma, it would be more accurate to say that black wartime critique viewed America as the site of conflicting political constructions of civilization and race. If black thinkers began to deploy a rhetoric of American universals in their own interests, they also recognized that its appeal was politically ambiguous, multiple, and contradictory. In this way they extended and transformed Popular Front contestations around the figure of America as a global ideological sign with an uncertain meaning and an unclear future.[83]

Few debates of the period illustrated this better than the one between Roosevelt's vice president, Henry Wallace, and Time, Inc. Chairman Henry Luce. In his "Century of the Common Man" address of 1942, Wallace put forth many key terms of the progressive nationalism of the period, in opposition to the frankly imperialist vision Luce outlined in his famous pamphlet, "The American Century" (1941). "Some have spoken of the 'American Century,'" Wallace proclaimed, "I can say that the century on which we are entering—the century which will come out of this war—can and must be the century of the common man." Deploying a historical analogy with obvious resonance for blacks, Wallace called World War II a "fight between a slave world and a free world. Just as the United States in 1862 could not remain half slave and half free, so in 1942, the world must make its decision for complete victory one way or another."[84]

The opposing visions of Wallace and Luce encapsulated an intense, racially inflected struggle over the meaning of American freedom that unfolded during these years. That Luce's phrase "American Century" often gives its name to the era of U.S. global ascendancy since World War II indicates which vision won, even if the phrase is used more often than Luce's essay is read. "The American Century," though, was an argument for restraining what Luce regarded as the excessive reformism of the New Deal at home, while exerting unilateral U.S. military power abroad to ensure the future basis of U.S. economic prosperity and world order.[85] Luce feared that the war heralded a collapse of imperial systems of global rule and called upon the United States "as the most powerful and vital nation in the world . . . to exert upon the world the full impact of our influence, for such purposes as we see fit."[86] Wallace, by contrast, echoed what black radicals like Ellison had called "the people's aspect of the war." "Those that write the peace must think of the whole world," Wallace wrote. After the war he declared, in a phrase taken up by Roosevelt, "There can be no privileged peoples."[87]

The opposition between Wallace's "Century of the Common

Man," or "People's Century," as it came to be known, and Luce's "American Century" demonstrates how claims to American universalism could spur social reform or vindicate the status quo. In fact, Luce's and Wallace's disagreement reflected the fact that American elites at that moment held sharply alternative *readings* of American universalism. Wallace's conception, *ideal* in character, was predicated on the republican demand for the "rights of man" *as citizen,* thus evoking a revolutionary democratic tradition thought to precede and exceed the social institution of modern states. In this view, the open-ended, unconditional demand for freedom and equality—closely identified with questions of racial exclusion—also held the potential to challenge the uncontested primacy of capitalist property relations. Luce's conception of the universal, by contrast, was crafted in *the very name of the American state* as an established political institution and "the sanctuary" of the supranational cultural lineages, class hierarchies, and material advantages of Western Civilization. Thus, if Wallace wanted the United States to promote something like the New Deal on a global scale, Luce called upon the nation "to go with our ships and ocean-going planes, where we wish, when we wish and as we wish," in the effort to conserve existing hierarchies of world order.[88]

In the black public sphere of the early 1940s, it wasn't difficult to identify what was at stake in these conflicting constructions of race and nation. Nor did black thinkers simply endorse Wallace's "People's Century" or follow in the train of assumptions that imagined the world recast through a uniquely *American* revolutionary idiom. With a clever lexical shift, Ralph Ellison and Angelo Herndon transformed the univocal idea of a "People's Century" into a call for "the peoples' century." They argued further that when one looked for "the basic outlines of a democratic vision of life" and "the truly human motivation behind this potentially peoples' war . . . one finds it expressed most intensely among the darker peoples."[89] Most important, Ellison and Herndon alerted their readers to the shifty and deceptive powers of political rhetoric in the moment of crisis:

This war has brought about the greatest upset of human values and assumptions the world has ever known. The plans of Roosevelt and Churchill are mocked by the vision of a world they flirt with but fear to embrace. Liberal Democracy plays Hamlet, while the "great sickness" spreads from within, allowing Fascism at the very moment it begins to lose battles, to win its greatest victories. *For the Four Freedoms is a vision that must be embraced wholly or else it changes its shape to confound us* . . . If minority and colonial peoples are to be convinced that the statements of Wallace rather than those of Churchill embody Allied intentions, and that the action of the Senate does not express the Administration's Negro Policy then let us see convincing action.[90]

It remained to be seen which conception of U.S. world power would triumph—whether the rhetoric of American universals would be approximated in deed, or whether it would be the new face of empire. It was not only the domestic heritage of white supremacy that mocked the idea of the "People's Century." It was equally unclear, as black and anticolonial activists and intellectuals pointed out, whether U.S. world-ordering power could be disentangled from a long history of imperial fantasy and racial supremacy in international relations. The U.S. posture as the defender of freedom, of general human or global interests, was especially difficult to separate from the networks of transnational affiliation, identification, and "special relationships" (particularly U.S. Anglophilia and the British defenses of the "Empire" with which it was linked). Writing in *Common Ground* in 1943, Padmore presciently forecast that the "Anglo-American condominium" in World War II would form the basis of a "new imperialism" after the war, whose flashpoints would be in colonial southeast Asia, the Middle East, and Africa.[91]

These worldly black intellectuals finally went further than Wallace, refusing to locate wartime visions of radical Americanism in "America" as the singular repository of the idea of freedom, but in a world-system convulsing with calls for self-determination, democracy, and equal rights. As Rayford Logan put it in his introduction to *What the Negro Wants* (1944), a book of essays by fourteen prominent black intellectuals: "We want the Four Freedoms to apply to black Americans as well as to the brutalized peoples of Europe and to other underprivileged peoples of the world."[92] "If now is not the time, then there never was a time," Hughes echoed Himes. "Now is when all the conquered nations of Europe are asking for freedom. Now is when the Jews are asking for it. Now is when America is fighting to keep it. Now is when Nehru and Gandhi are sitting in jail silently demanding it for India . . . How can anyone expect American Negroes not to catch the freedom fever, too, is beyond me."[93]

Emphasizing the multiplicity of freedom dreams, black thinkers drew on a long history of efforts to *rearticulate* American freedom—to, in effect, liberate freedom from the material and ethical distortions of the slave past. At the same time, the collective optimism of what Hughes called "the freedom fever" threatened to slide into violent erasures of heterogeneity under the radiating sign of American power. Insofar as black global vision was tied to a broad perception of the symbolic importance of U.S. racial division in the context of the new world-ordering powers arrogated to the American realm, it threatened to collapse the rest of the world into itself. Thus, if Hughes was inspired by anticolonial ferment, Wright boldly claimed that the obverse was now also true: "Today the problem of the world's dispossessed exists with great urgency, and the problem of the Negro in America is a phase of this general problem, containing and telescoping the lives of a billion colored subject colonial people into a symbol."[94]

Such hubris, while perhaps understandable, risked making black advance *within* the United States the first proof of an effective decolonization around the world. Perhaps not accidentally, it was the Caribbean sojourner, James, who sounded the relevant cautions. Although the "Negro Question" may have been a symbol abroad, James wrote, "at home it is not merely a symbol, but a vivid and potent actuality." Second, nothing was more misleading than to understand black struggles as a vector of U.S. nationalism. Rather, the conjuncture of World War II had illuminated the struggle for racial justice within the nation as a part of "a truly international task" tied to unfinished struggles for socialism and to emergent struggles for self-determination among the world's "oppressed peoples."[95]

The stakes of these struggles would only become clearer as they unfolded in the coming decades. Yet, even as black activists pursued their vision of global transformation during World War II by sharpening the dialectic of race and nation at home, increasingly influential and well-funded discourses of U.S. race and ethnic relations sought to fold blacks into a liberal-nationalist narrative of American freedom. The fundamental problem remained (as Ellison and Herndon discerned) the mystifying imprecision of the word *freedom*. By *freedom*, most black activists in World War II meant something beyond individual rights and formal citizenship, but also democracy, equality, and self-determination: the equalization of freedoms both at home and abroad. The background image they embraced—that of a "peoples' century"—was a manifold and insurgent idea of freedom. Pluralizing the traditional referent of nationalism, that is, "the people," this image in a sense re-envisioned freedom as a vector of radical democracy: the uncoerced gathering of heterogeneous social collectivities throughout the world denied the ability to develop their cultural aspirations, political capacities, and economic potentials by racial and colonial violence.

At the same time, the language of freedom most black activists embraced was increasingly difficult to distinguish from a more coercive vision of freedom that animated U.S. conceptions of global power. In this view, best articulated by Henry Luce, American freedoms were to be bequeathed to the world as a dispensation, a model of politics, economy, society, and culture to be followed behind the barrel of a gun if necessary. Luce accurately reflected the anxiety of U.S. global planners, who, despite their stated support of decolonization, were concerned that the collapse of British and French imperialisms would create power vacuums amenable to what Cold War strategists would begin calling "Communist-Soviet penetration."[96] People were stirring throughout the world, demanding the self-determination promised by the *Atlantic Charter* and the development promised by the "Four Freedoms." It was not clear which social system these peoples would choose, but it was clear that their choices would not necessarily comport with U.S. designs.

One of the ideological challenges of American power in the coming period would be to finesse the disjuncture between strategic interests and stated ideals, to contain not only Soviet communism, but also the potentially exorbitant popular demands for democracy and development at home and around the world. Insofar as blacks remained "more international-minded than the rest of the population," they would make the task of papering over the gap between U.S. government practices and promises much more difficult. As Drake and Cayton wrote in their conclusion of their remarkable urban ethnography, *Black Metropolis* (1945), black populations in the United States had "realized more acutely than whites the global significance of a guaranty of democratic rights and privileges to all people of the world." In the coming period, what Richard Wright called their "new worldliness"—one part grassroots recalcitrance and one part global dreaming—challenged the unilateral decree of an "American Century" with the unfinished dialogues of color and democracy.[97]

CHAPTER FOUR

Americanizing the Negro

Most American Negroes of education and property have long since oversimplified their problem and tried to separate it from all other social problems. They conceive that their fight is simply to have the same rights and privileges as other American citizens. They do not for a moment stop to question how . . . America may have fundamental injustices and shortcomings which seriously affect not only Negroes, but the world.

—W. E. B. DU BOIS, "ON THE FUTURE OF THE AMERICAN NEGRO" (1953)

In the aftermath of the Harlem riot of 1935, Carnegie Foundation Trustee Newton Baker conceived of the idea of undertaking a broad study of "the Negro Problem" in America. Baker, former mayor of Cleveland and son of a Confederate officer believed that the Harlem disturbance proved that urban migration was raising new and potentially serious problems with governing Negroes. Although he did not live to see this project to completion, his idea was embraced by foundation President Frederick Keppel two years later. What Keppel set in motion eventually became the work St. Clair Drake described as the "study to end all studies," an unprecedented, multiyear investigation of "the Negro Problem and Modern Democracy." Presided over by Swedish economist Gunnar Myrdal, and published in 1944, *An American Dilemma* would set the respectable parameters for the study of race in the United States for the next quarter-century.

The political thinking that led to the choice of Myrdal to oversee the study is significant. When Keppel first went in search of a director, it apparently never crossed his mind to select a U.S. black scholar. Howard University sociologist E. Franklin Frazier, for example, had already ably studied the causes and consequences of the Harlem riot. And, W. E. B. Du Bois was just then circulating his own ambitious funding proposals for a multivolume "Encyclopedia of the Negro." Given the scope of what the foundation had in mind, however, it was inconceivable that a black intellectual could be in charge. Not only were black intellectuals presumed to be incapable of sufficient objectivity (this was particularly true of Du Bois), but the idea of a black director would surely offend the white South.

Indeed, Keppel first considered having a British colonial administrator preside over the report. The global understanding animating this idea was of a piece with Baker's local concern. Who, after all, better than the British to illuminate the problem of governing an inferior, subject race?[1] In the racial-imperial imagination that enveloped the West in the age of Empire, dark-skinned people—regardless of geographical location or origin—were believed to share a common trait. These were people whom U.S. presidents, British and French prime ministers, and German chancellors alike described as "unpracticed in the habits of freedom," unfit for self-government, and in need of the tutelage and stern discipline of white governors.[2] The United States and Great Britain expressly killed a Japanese proposal that a "racial equality" amendment be added to the Covenant of the League of Nations. For all the talk of democracy and self-determination in the inter-war period, there was little doubt that such things were intended for whites only.[3]

By the mid-1930s, the rise of National Socialism in Germany, the late-colonial adventures of Italy and Japan, and the emergence of anticolonial solidarity movements in the United States and Britain brought racial nationalism into disrepute. Alerted to this fact by his intellectual advisers, Keppel rethought his initial conception. It was still out of the question that a U.S. black could head up a study of such importance. However, in light of the "emotional factor" affecting "the Negroes no less than the whites," he wrote, "the search was limited to countries of high intellectual and scholarly standards but with no background or traditions of imperialism which might lessen the confidence of Negroes in the United States as to the complete impartiality of the study and the validity of its findings."[4]

Myrdal proved a brilliant choice to fulfill this function. The intellectual and political background to his selection illuminates the crucial transition in U.S. discourses about racial equality and national belonging in this period. Under Myrdal's leadership, *An American Dilemma* expressly cast racial equality as the *telos* of American nationhood. At the height of the war, when it was published, moreover, it was not just the confidence of Negroes that was at issue. Rather, as Myrdal astutely discerned, the Negro problem had become the symbolic pivot on which America's proximity to and distance from the colonialist heritage turned. On the one hand, as in the initial plan conceived by Baker and Keppel, it signaled the family of resemblances between U.S. and European traditions of subordinating and civilizing "darkies." On the other hand, the effective incorporation of Negroes into the nation would demonstrate that the United States had succeeded in its civilizing mission where Europe had failed.

Much like Keynes before him, Myrdal argued that the new geopolitical situation made U.S. state power an instrument of the general interests of humankind throughout the world. Against the backdrop of World War II, the study's most important conclusion was that black inclusion in the nation-state was an index of U.S. world-ordering power. This vindicated a major claim of wartime black intellectuals: racial division was not only an internal matter of domestic reform, but also a problem implicated within U.S. public diplomatic commitments to the universalization of national sovereignty. During World War II, the ideological thrust of U.S. diplomacy was strongly anti-imperialist, premised on the dismantling of old colonial empires and extending worldwide what were said to be uniquely American successes in the arts of self-government. Roosevelt resurrected the Wilsonian world vision (mostly shorn of its overt racism) rejected by the U.S. Congress at the end of World War I and institutionalized it in arguably his greatest achievement, the United Nations. Solving the "Negro problem" at home became a corollary of this vision, something that would both affirm the underlying theory of American nationhood and also prove that the United States was the world's greatest democracy, whose ability to harmonize the needs of a heterogeneous population fitted it to be the broker of the world's security concerns and aspirations for social progress.

The status achieved by *An American Dilemma* as a watershed document can be attributed to its use of the Negro problem to underscore the "Janus-faced messianism" of American exceptionalism.[5] The emergence of U.S. internationalism as the dominant internationalism after World War II brought with it a renewal of a core nationalist ideology: the notion of America as a republic at once unique and universal. What was most distinctive about this idea, as it was transferred from its continental and hemispheric dominion to a global scale, was the insistence that the U.S. capacity to mediate the general interests of humanity (in other words, to civilize) derived from America's distinctiveness as a power amicably divorced from old world intrigues of empire and hierarchies of blood and rank. Rather than being antithetical to U.S. nationalism (or to U.S. national interests), America's global reach was represented as an outgrowth of the universalizing force of U.S. national ideals—America, to paraphrase Benjamin Franklin famous words, as the cause of all mankind.

The denial of the historical legacies of racism and empire had long been central to American exceptionalism. From the inception of the slaveholding republic, finessing the contradictions between the racial and imperial parameters of U.S. nationalism and its universalizing claims was one of the more refined exercises of American social thought. The less wholesome racist underpinnings of U.S. society were on display from the beginning—in slavery, Indian removal, and hemispheric and Pacific wars of conquest from the mid-nineteenth to the early twentieth century. Yet, as in the U.S. Civil War, when slave emancipation transformed a war between commercial interests into a war for infinite justice, in World War II the singular evil of Nazi racism and Holocaust became the basis for reasserting a vast American innocence and mission. Here, a different gap was often exposed, as a war fought in Europe in the name of freedom and human rights degenerated in the Pacific into race war (and, eventually, nuclear conflagration). The problem was not only that high-sounding declarations of American universality might be a cover for imperialism (old wine in new bottles, as it were), but also that darker forces might be animating American uniqueness: a domestic legacy of territorial seizure, occupation, and racial domination.[6]

In the more prosaic arena of interests, it is also important to recall that U.S. anti-imperialism during World War II had a more restricted meaning. It meant that the United States wanted to see the dismantling of the only world-imperialism of that time, namely, that of the British. This never stopped U.S. world-planners from envisioning the postwar world unified in "a dominion centered on America."[7] As Henry Luce's popular brief, "An American Century" made clear, most U.S. elites had little doubt that they were to take the place of Great Britain as the hegemonic state within world-capitalism. This project was nominally anticolonialist in that it counted national sovereignty and decolonization in its arsenal of tactics. But it was also quite explicitly a new imperialism in the sense that it conceived of the United States as the leader of a new stage in the development of an international civilization created by the expansion of European capitalism and colonialism. In the words of a U.S. State Department official, Americans were "the heirs of empire" and, as such, committed to "preserving its vital parts."[8]

As suggested in the previous chapter, the political straddling act of many black intellectuals during World War II manifested the tension between a future based on the instruments and advantages of world imperialism and one imagined to stem from the broad dissemination of democracy. Armed with a critique of "imperial-colonialism" as twinned artifacts of white supremacy, black thinkers sought to differentiate what naively celebratory discussions of U.S. global power deliberately left ambiguous. More important, insofar as blacks marked broadly recognized limits of freedom inside the American realm, a black intelligentsia increasingly fluent with mass communication claimed unprecedented symbolic powers to invalidate America's expanded realm of action in the world whenever the latter appeared, in Du Bois's pithy phrase, "weighted toward the side of imperialism."[9]

The elevation of U.S. blackness into what Richard Wright called a global symbol was thus ineluctably tied to the U.S. rise to globalism. In turn, the intensification of the egalitarian struggles within the U.S. black metropolis drew strength from the promise of American universalism, even as they undermined its exceptionalist premise—the idea that U.S. history could be severed from the world-systemic projects of racial and colonial domination. The NAACP's *Declaration of Negro Voters,* signed by all the major black civil rights organizations on the eve of the U.S. presidential election of 1944 (and penned by Du Bois), illustrates both the complexity and critical participation blacks activists tried to sustain.

> We are concerned that this war bring to an end imperialism and colonial exploitation . . . We insist that all parties and candidates unequivocally oppose either the perpetuation or extension of exploitation based upon 'white superiority' or economic or political advantage to 'white' nations at the expense of the two-thirds of the earth who are brown, yellow, or black of skin. The United States must point the way by including Negroes among its diplomatic, technical, and professional experts engaged in international post–war reconstruction.[10]

This statement encapsulates the hopeful confluence of radical and liberal, worldly and patriotic sentiments joined briefly in the black popular front. A carefully moderated appeal, it imagined U.S. blacks as the key diplomatic, technical, and professional intermediaries between U.S. world-ordering ambition and a global, anti-imperialist politics. Such middle ground was rapidly eroding, however, exposing the fragility of and divisions within black coalition politics by the war's end. Mainstream black leaders redoubled longstanding concerns about appearing unpatriotic, leading them to disassociate themselves not only from any left-wing affiliations, but also from positions that might be associated with the left. Meanwhile, black radicals were bracing themselves for a new round of betrayals.

Such divisions were hastened by the fact that from an official point of view, more radical gestures of black critique and disaffiliation were not easy to distinguish from gestures of dissent, even those articulated in the name of a higher "Americanism." Indeed, the latter may have been even more threatening in the context of the national security crisis, as suggested by the government suppression of black newspapers on military bases. Leavening dissent with patriotism did not make the state apparatus any less wary of the potential threat posed by a politically active black citizenry. In 1942, the FBI began its Survey of Racial Conditions (RACON) among blacks, modeled on similar work conducted in Japanese-American communities. As future investigations of the southern civil rights movement in the 1950s and the infamous COINTELPRO program of the 1960s would make clear, racial intelligence work of this sort was not the exception but the rule for the state's policing and security agencies during the long tenure of J. Edgar Hoover, for whom blacks remained at once a subject and a suspect population.[11]

Moderate and pragmatic U.S. black leaders such as Walter White were at pains to establish the credibility of black struggles for equality as a tributary of American global hegemony. This required a complicated, perhaps contradictory, strategy of de-linking questions of black equality from the critique of empire, while at the same time advancing domestic racial reform as a proxy for U.S.-sponsored decolonization in the world at large. Writing in this vein, Charles Johnson tellingly identified the amelioration of racial divisions on the home front with what he called "our new *world conception of* ourselves as a nation." In *To Stem This Tide,* Johnson advanced what would become a virtual corollary of post–World War II liberal-nationalism: progress on issues of racial equality at home were the litmus test of America's claims to global leadership: "If the United States is to take its rightful position on the high moral ground among the nations of the world, it must first take a forthright and honest step to clear its own conscience on the issue of the rights of the common man. It must first free itself from those iniquities which it shall have fought a war to eradicate from the world at large."[12]

In the face of this more sanguine view of U.S. power abroad, issues of left-wing affiliations and longstanding efforts to fuse antiracist and anti-imperialist politics marked a set of important political fault-lines among black activists and intellectuals, which would widen considerably by the onset of the Cold War. Ralph Bunche, for example, had previously joined White in rebuking black activists who had jumped to "the dangerous conclusion that there is little to choose between an imperfect American or English democracy, often abusive to non-white populations, and a Nazi 'new order.'"[13] The increasingly influential Bunche, one of the more strident (noncommunist) left critics of the New Deal in the mid-1930s, had by the 1940s exchanged his pessimistic race-blind Marxism for a more optimistic (though equally race-blind) liberalism. Where his 1936 book *A World View of Race* emphasized racial division as a tool of capitalist exploitation throughout the world and viewed black struggles in the context of international class struggles, in 1941 he celebrated the political philosophy and institutional achievements of Anglo-American liberalism. "It is within this conceptual milieu, inherited from the American Revolution," he concluded, "that the Negro has carried on his struggle for social, political and economic emancipation."[14]

What may seem like a dramatic distance between Bunche's Marxism of 1936 and his defense of the "fertile soil" of American liberalism after 1940 is belied by some important commonalities, including his prior rejection of an autonomous black standpoint on political action and his strong identification with the U.S. national purpose as the object and horizon of political reform. "Unlike the colonial peoples," Bunche asserted in 1945, "the Negro, who is culturally American, has no nationalist or separatist ambitions."[15] Offering himself as the embodiment of this promise, Bunche became the highest-ranking black official at the Office of Strategic Services (OSS) and principle author of a series of "psy-ops" pamphlets for U.S. military campaigns in North and West Africa. Here, he suggested that the "elite African" might be "more sensitive on racial matters than the U.S. Negro," but could be won over by the "legend of America as a liberalizing force in world affairs." In an ironic twist, Bunche was not beyond deploying the idea of race in the national interest. With regard to African campaigns, he concluded, "carefully chosen Negroes could prove more effective than whites, owing to their unique ability to gain more readily the confidence of the Native on the basis of their right to claim a good relationship."[16]

Du Bois would bitterly remark around this time that Bunche was "getting to be a white folks' nigger."[17] Bunche's trajectory, however, cannot merely be understood as the story of individual opportunism, or "Uncle Tomism." Rather, it exemplifies the new opportunities for the black intelligentsia within the expanded governmental milieu of the welfare-warfare state. The state's rhetorical and institutional expansions had, since the mid-1930s, made racial division and inequality a site of intense social and symbolic ferment across the broad front of society. New Deal claims for national integration through the federal state apparatus, followed by wartime claims for U.S. diplomatic and military leadership in world affairs, put tremendous pressure on "race" as a legitimate means of dividing the population for the purposes of political rule.[18]

Much like the market economy, racial difference was the nexus of a fragile process of social and political contest over the formation and dissolution of legitimate governmental powers. More specifically, the changing form and conception of the U.S. state as an instrument for stabilizing the national market and creating general conditions for global security arguably *required* an explicit accommodation with black populations as one of its proofs. In part, this entailed the production of new types of knowledge. During the 1930s, more than 2,500 social scientists worked for the federal government on a range of social reform issues, a trend continued by the government's enlistment of intellectuals in the war effort. It is therefore not surprising that as the status of the black population became an important variable within a calculus of governance, blacks were increasingly constituted as new objects of knowledge, and that black intellectuals attained enhanced prominence through their ability to sanction or discredit state practice.[19]

The Carnegie Foundation study, *An American Dilemma: The Negro Problem and Modern Democracy* (1944), grew directly out of this context. Presided over by Myrdal, closely assisted throughout by

Bunche, this study was an ideological enterprise of the first order. Enlisting the support of hundreds of U.S. academics, including many prominent black academics, it reveals a great deal about the period's overall reformulation of U.S. liberal-nationalism as a world-ordering conception based on claims to ethnic and racial inclusiveness, political democracy, market freedoms, and human rights. The landmark reference work for the long civil rights era, it not only codified almost a decade of liberal reformist thought around racial division, it also established the achievement of black inclusion in the nation-state as the paramount domestic reform question linked to the imperatives of U.S. global leadership.

Most important, *An American Dilemma* exuded fresh optimism about America's democratic mission in the world. "American ideals," Myrdal wrote, "are just humane ideals as they have matured in our common Western Civilization." The still regnant power of white supremacy, however, guaranteed a long period of bitter racial conflict at home. While Myrdal refused to acknowledge that racism, too, was one of the common components of western civilization, he could not fail to see that "the Negro problem" had become "the main divider of opinion in national politics."[20] The challenge within the domestic arena would be remarkably similar to the challenge abroad: to initiate a system-wide reform without upsetting the entrenched patterns of power and privilege that had given the system its order, coherence, and legibility—or more specifically, to produce an official antiracism that could at least partially accommodate the historic claims of white supremacy on the U.S. body politic.

Reading *An American Dilemma*

By the mid-1940s the identification of race with struggles for self-determination around the world posed a clear challenge to U.S. world hegemony. From the end of Reconstruction to World War II, dominant U.S. thinking regarded the "Negro problem" as a parochial, regional concern. During this period, however, black activists asserted with growing influence and cohesiveness that the color-line was an internal border within the country that also had global reach and significance. They not only struggled for full citizenship rights, but also claimed race as a site of communal investment and political action that exceeded U.S. political discourses and boundaries. Disciplining the latter tendency was part of the challenge of recoding the meaning of race in line with U.S. imperatives at the end of World War II. Most immediately, this meant severing black political and intellectual life from its engagements with parties of the left, or with anti-imperialist politics. It was imperative, Myrdal wrote, to demonstrate that "no social utopia can compete with the promises of the American Constitution and the American Creed it embodies. Democracy and lawful government mean so much more to a Negro, because he enjoys comparatively little of it in this country. Merely by giving him the solemn promise of liberty and equality, American society has tied the Negroes' faith to itself."[21]

Closer analysis of the production and interpretive procedures of the massive study sheds light on the racial commonsense of mid-century American liberalism and what might be termed its state's eye view of racial reform. The two published volumes bore the sole name of their Swedish author, even though black intellectuals (often laboring in segregated institutions) provided much of its substantive intellectual content and frequent reviews of the materials produced. Bunche, for example, penned four memoranda, comprising well over one thousand pages of prose, whose major findings were silently incorporated into the final report, while Frazier was entrusted with a final review of the manuscript. After World War II, when Myrdal returned to Sweden, an abridged version of the study was published under the name of another of Myrdal's assistants, the white academician Arnold Rose. Meanwhile, on the black "street" an argument raged as to whether Bunche was in fact the "real" author of the justly famous work.[22]

The debate about authorship might be read as an allegory for an era in which black gains were frequently tied to a demand for faithful forbearance, quiet acquiescence, and even self-erasure. Indeed, though it recognized the ongoing differential treatment of blacks under the New Deal, *An American Dilemma* primarily testified to the powers of liberal-nationalism to recast black life in terms of the normalizing economic, juridical, and intellectual patterns of the nation-state as a whole. As Myrdal wrote with canny precision, "The Negroes' share may be meager in all this new state activity, but he has been given a share. He has been given a broader and more variegated front to defend and from which to push forward. This is the great import of the New Deal to the Negro. For almost the first time in the history of the nation the state has done something substantial in a social way without excluding the Negro."[23]

Like the other new liberals who came of age in the economic crises of the 1930s, Myrdal believed that the New Deal's national-class settlement was the key to solving historic legacies of racial antagonism. "The race issue in these New Deal measures is not an isolated element which can be cut-off," he wrote. "It is always involved in the bigger issue of whether poor people shall be helped or not." This idea, however, should not be construed as an expression of sympathy with Marxist perspectives. Myrdal stamped his own intellectual influence upon the study by *rejecting* an idea that had once been vehemently espoused by such young black radicals as Bunche and Frazier. The idea that there was no race problem, only a class problem, wrote the strongly anti-Marxist thinker, was an "escapism in a new form." Racial divisions among workers in competition with each other, he concluded, had been the norm, not working-class solidarity, which meant that it was frequently the "better" classes of whites who had been the real friends of the Negro.[24]

Myrdal was especially determined to reassure the public that the period of black flirtation with the left was over. This aspect of *An American Dilemma* was particularly important because it prefigured Cold War efforts to establish the uncontested rationality and racially progressive *bona fides* of American liberalism.[25] A quick study, Myrdal understood that his task was at once to reassure a white readership of the normality of black social and political aspirations and to educate blacks into the acceptable forms of political thinking and behavior within the U.S. context. Indeed, Myrdal believed that the blockage of black advance within the civil and political sphere had been the result of the denial to blacks of meaningful forms of affiliation with "recognized national groups." Leftist identification, as well as most black tendencies toward "color-consciousness," he believed, were compensatory responses to this situation, ones that reinforced black marginalization and consigned black politics and social thinking to "a sphere of unreality and futility."[26]

Like most U.S. liberals after the 1930s, Myrdal argued that racial hierarchy had no basis in biology or culture—at least not in American culture. Insofar as racial subordination persisted, he concluded, it was an atavism, the result of a cultural lag that had led to a "vicious" circle in which racial discrimination produced black social pathology, which in turn reinforced racial discrimination. Myrdal and his collaborators were certain that this phenomenon would wither under the pressures of economic modernization and wartime nationalism. Yet, the "dilemma" that Myrdal could not evade—one unintentionally ironized by the title of the famous study—was the conflation of an abstractly liberating process of national belonging with the reality that national ideals were monopolized by the prerogatives of people who still understood themselves as, and were understood to be, *white*. As much as he and his collaborators sought to plot lines of escape, they were caught within a hermeneutic circle as tight as the vicious circle they used to explain racism:

> We assume that it is to the advantage of American Negroes as individuals and as a group to become assimilated into American culture, to acquire traits held in esteem by the dominant white Americans. This will be the value premise here. *We do not imply that white American culture is "higher"* than other cultures in an absolute sense . . . But it does not gainsay our assumption that *here, in America, American culture is "highest"* in the pragmatic sense that adherence to it is practical for any individual or group not strong enough to change it. Also not to be taken in a doctrinal sense is the observation that the peculiarities of the Negro community may be characterized as social pathology.[27]

Similar to the welfare-warfare expansions of the federal state apparatus, which had internalized rather than transcended the everyday practices and networks of the racial segregationism, Myrdallian liberalism (and its many successors) at once failed to fully count the intellectual cost of historical racism and rationalized its ongoing prevalence within its own structures of thought. This problem is much greater than those simply categorized under the rubric of culture, or in relation to questions of cultural difference. Rather, what is laid bare is the larger context of a history of ideas in which the unequal power of naturalized, racial prerogatives has shaped our most powerful thought systems and the standpoint they "assume with respect to other ideas and forms of life."[28] Even though Myrdal posed an unprecedented challenge to the institutions and ideologies of white supremacy and racial discrimination, he implicitly confirmed the rationality of their judgments (about politics, morality, intellect, and economics), transferring whiteness to the threshold of nationality (from "white American culture" to simply "American culture"), and inscribing racism as a negative "effect" that was primarily manifested in black individual and communal behavior ("Negro community" as "social pathology").

Moreover, the Myrdal study gave racial hierarchy an expanded purview within the intellectual field by simply aligning U.S. "national ideals" with the very freedom from interracial context that its principle author was alleged to have brought to the study as a neutral observer. "I was chosen," Myrdal wrote, "because I was a stranger. . . Stripped of all conventional moorings and evaluations, and lacking an orienting system of coordinates." In this context, he confided, "the facts of 'the Negro problem,' were rather dark." Imagining a community with his readers, he concluded: "As it was for me as the writer, the reading of this book is surely an ordeal for the good citizen." Yet, a question arises: just *who* was the good citizen/reader? From the text, it is clear that the good citizen was thought to be someone similarly "free" of race. As Robert Lynd noted in a glowing review of the book, for Myrdal, "the Negro problem is really a white problem . . . a moral problem within us white Americans. . . What the Negro thinks and does and is," Lynd wrote, "is a distorted development of the general American culture, i.e. what we white Americans think and do and are." What is remarkable about this formulation is its rejection of white supremacy simultaneously reinscribed whiteness as the normative basis of U.S. national culture. Moreover, when we read carefully, it becomes clear that so-called distortions of the "general American culture" were once again being *ascribed* to "Negroes."[29]

The white problem notwithstanding, the "general American culture" and "our national ideals" thus emerged as implicitly undistorted and explicitly not Negro. The good citizen, in other words, was imagined to be a white person who was at worst ignorant of racial matters and, at best, burdened with a troubled conscience. As for "Negroes" themselves, they did not fare very well in the account. Indeed, one of the more startling aspects of the Myrdal study to a contemporary reader is the way in which a work dependent on more than a decade of relatively autonomous black social research and extensive black intellectual collaboration could so thoroughly belittle black political and intellectual capacity. Lacking access to the "nation" or national identification, Negroes lived in a provincial world. "Instead of organized popular theories or ideas," Myrdal concluded "there is, in the Negro world, only a fluid mass of all sorts of embryos of thoughts."[30]

The greatest cost of racial discrimination, Myrdal concluded, was that it "denied the Negro a balanced and integrated world-view." As a consequence, both intellectual and popular Negro thought exemplified "derivative," second-order thinking with *little connection with broader American or world problems.*" Picking up on earlier arguments by both Bunche and Frazier, Myrdal singled out Du Bois for special attention, writing that even as fine "a Negro brain" as his took on a "queer touch of unreality as soon as he left his problem, and made a frustrated effort to view it in a wider setting as an ordinary American and a human being." "The tragedy of caste does not spare the integrity of the soul of either the Negro or the white man," Myrdal summarized. "But the difference in degree of distortion of world-view is just as great as the difference in size between the American Negro community and the rest of the world."[31]

In the end, Myrdal denied the autonomous capacity of black people as individuals and as a collectivity (even as humans) to formulate a coherent, public standpoint on the social and political realities of American life. In this he scarcely departed from a European philosophical tradition that had long *racialized* (i.e., dehumanized) peoples according to their supposed inability to exercise the sort of disinterested judgment that was the prerequisite of modern rationality, what Kant had called the "sensus-communis," the public use of reason, or common-sense.[32] It is arguable that modernizing racial liberalism went imperial discourse one better: black thinking was not merely childlike but *fetal*. That mental incapacity was seen as the result of a prior exclusion from the public sphere (the denial to blacks of normative national identities), rather than as the result of inherent capabilities, was not actually a significant advance. Myrdal not only failed to question the rationality of the initial exclusion, but he allowed this exclusion to determine the intellectual grounds of his inquiry and to set the parameters of meaningful, collective, identity-forming discourse.

The study was expressly intended to break the vicious cycle by presenting a moral appeal to whites and a lesson in nationalist pedagogy to blacks. The problem was that its interpretive structure was based on a social formation normatively constructed along racial lines. Negroes, Myrdal seemed to say, could never understand or effectively challenge the "Negro problem," because this was the only thing they could understand; white Americans were capable of more mature and capacious judgment. Even as he elevated racial matters into a position of unprecedented centrality then, Myrdal interpreted their salience as the *difference* between a passive, provincial, and childlike "Negro world" and an active, broad-minded, self-reflexive, and white American one. America (i.e., white America), though beset by a "moral dilemma"—the famous gap Myrdal discerned between the nation's self-image and reality, political theory, and social practice—nonetheless held the capacity for reform *within itself*.

In the final analysis, what made *An American Dilemma* such an influential document was its presentation of "the Negro problem" as the symbolic pivot on which future claims to U.S. global mission rested. In almost perfect symmetry, the counterpart to Negro provincialism was the promise of America's universalism. Carnegie Foundation President Keppel went so far as to trumpet the publication as an event in the incipient constitution of an international civil society. The importance of such a claim should not be underestimated, especially if we recognize the significance of that watchword "publication" (as Keppel apparently did) as not simply a reflection of existing public opinion, but a performative act seeking to bring a new public into existence not just at a local or national scale, but at a transnational scale. Myrdal sounded the same theme as a warning: "The treatment of the Negro is America's greatest and most conspicuous scandal. It is tremendously *publicized* . . . For the colored peoples all over the world, whose rising influence is axiomatic, this scandal is salt in their wounds."[33]

Indeed, the very act of making race relations an object of study was offered as a vindication of the thesis that the United States, despite its failings, was equipped to mediate intranational and supranational claims for social justice and civility. That the very concept of "the West" included problematic racial and imperial practices (that is, "the white man's burden") that excluded most of the world from the economic and political promise of modernity was to be dissolved not by the deconstruction of a western pretension to universality, but by its proper Americanization. Following U.S.-based scholars, the Myrdal study went as far as to delete "race" from the lexicon of relevant historical concepts, substituting instead the imported term "caste" from ethno-histories of the Indian subcontinent. Caste was a serviceable concept because it added to the sense that racial difference was an atavistic prescription alien to modern society. It further implied that racism was aberrant within western modernity, a moral and cultural lag

resulting from failures of capitalist industrialization and class formation. (Indeed, even a highly modern German fascism would soon be
explained as a product of Germany's "late" industrialization.)

When read through this more critical lens, *An American Dilemma*
can be viewed as an ideological resolution to real contradictions of racial division at home and abroad: a massive effort to rationalize an
epochal shift in transnational intellectual life in which reformulations
of American liberalism were becoming the basis for asserting that the
United States had achieved a superior degree of universalization relative to other nation-states, and was therefore the best instrument of
rational change not just in the domestic arena, but within the world-
system as a whole. As a document, it provides important insights into
the transition away from an era of "Atlantic Crossings," in which
U.S. civic experiments and intellectual life had remained in the thrall
of Europe, to an era in which the United States became the radiating
center of the globe. The New Deal reversed the vectors of transatlantic political influence, just as World War II reversed the vectors of military and economic power within the world-system.[34]

An American Dilemma in this sense represents perhaps one of the
last in a long line of European paeans to American exceptionalism
and prophecies about the nation's future world-historical importance.
As Myrdal concluded, "The Negro problem is not only America's
greatest failure, but also America's incomparably great opportunity
for the future. . . The century old dream of American patriots that
America should give to the entire world its own freedoms and its own
faith would come true . . . [if] America can demonstrate that justice,
equality and cooperation are possible between white and colored people."[35] The door to the American future of the world had finally appeared, and the solution to the Negro problem was the key that
would open it.

One of the more salient, although less well-recognized, features of
American exceptionalism is that its organizing contrast between the
European past and an American future highlights the distinctive virtues of American society while also defining the American political
experiment as continuous with, rather than disjoined from, the progressive movement of world history envisaged by the Enlightenment.
Thus, on the one hand, *An American Dilemma* affirmed that America's distinctive promise was an egalitarian ethos that would clear
away the primeval mists of racial division. Even undertaking such a

study, Myrdal and Keppel agreed, was "an idea singularly American" that vindicated "moralism, rationalism and optimism." At the same time, Myrdal's ability to confer civilizational legitimacy derived from his status as a European with "no background of domination of one race over another."[36] In this way, he also embodied a supranational lineage and family of resemblances ("the intrinsic harmony of the Enlightenment and the American Revolution") in which the stain of racial difference was cleansed from the past as well.

In this sense, Myrdal played a kind of intellectual midwife to the American century. Excavating the transatlantic philosophical circuits that he recapitulated is hardly an incidental concern, especially when we consider his status as a modern de Tocqueville, or as the Keynes of race relations. Like Keynes, Myrdal looked to the United States to provide a model for the resolution of the world crisis that promoted "continuity and rational change within the existing framework" of global relations of power and influence. While ostensibly antiracist, even anti-imperialist, this vision reinscribed the notion of primordial racial difference as both anterior to and antithetical to the progressive, historical course of Euro-American modernity. And, in doing so, it ironically reconstituted the logic of white supremacy. For like the New Deal, which transplanted rather than uprooted domestic segregationism, Myrdallian liberalism merely transferred whiteness to the threshold of U.S. nationality. Such an America, at the threshold of globality, would in turn begin to repot much of the philosophical soil of empire.

An American Dilemma can finally be understood as a symptom of a global shift from Eurocentrism to Americocentrism within the world-system—in which America and Europe would gradually collude in disavowing the more pernicious legacies of western colonialism. Myrdal's not insignificant genius was to envision "the Negro problem" as the alibi rather than the obstacle to an era of U.S. global hegemony. In doing so, he helped to consolidate a significant amount of intellectual armature for the long civil rights era, an era when blacks "were fortunate to live in a unique time when their own goals and that of the nation coincided."[37] But complete alignment was elusive, and it came with a price attached. Just as Myrdal's interpretive framework put black agency under erasure within the domestic realm, his transnationalism displaced more challenging counter-narratives of race already at work within the domestic and global arenas in which race had been set against empire, and a context of international divisions of wealth and labor.

The translation of the racial division of humanity into an infinitely solvable dilemma focused on the United States was crystallized in a phrase seized upon by many reviewers of the book: *"the American Negro Problem is a problem in the heart of the American."*[38] In addition to producing a syntax separating Negro and American once again, it is ironic that this work, which set out to challenge the racist maxim of U.S. social science, "stateways can't change folkways," lapsed into a stereotypical discourse of moral sentiments. The metaphor of the heart was in a sense exemplary, as it (along with the related term "soul") had a longstanding salience for thinking about the black presence in the United States. It recalled James Madison's rueful comment that the black man in our bosom was an obstacle to forming a perfect republic. *An American Dilemma* preserved this structure of thinking and feeling—the oppressive interrogative long at the center of U.S. discourse on race: "How does it feel to be a problem?" The difference, of course, was that now "our" national perfection was assured by an ability to reflect upon our flaws and imperfections—even if those flaws and imperfections remained embodied in the Negro.

Against Exceptionalism

When *An American Dilemma* was published, few black intellectuals sounded any sharp criticism. Arguably, so many had been drawn into its material and symbolic nets of funding and prestige that it would have been difficult to criticize. The text's almost universal acclaim is at least one important indicator of the ways in which black intellectual activists, like many labor activists during the period, were being effectively enlisted in the government project. Even Du Bois, who had been snubbed by the Swede in the early stages when memoranda for the study had been solicited, and whose own grand plan for a Negro Encyclopedia had to be scrapped as the funding sources were sucked up by the Myrdal team, recognized *An American Dilemma* as a watershed in the struggle for racial equality.[39]

But as events would demonstrate, the idea that there was a black consensus behind this work was quite misleading. The irascible black nationalist J. A. Rogers, for one, was not ready to applaud and he was not alone. Rogers wrote bitterly in 1944 that "nearly all our scholars are in the grips of the white foundations and philanthropists who use them to keep the Negro in his so-called place . . . [and] discredit, belittle and create mistrust of the few Negroes who dare to have a soul of their own."[40] As one who could never have been accused of lacking a soul of his own, Du Bois offered a different, more telling account of this period, more resonant with Rogers's in his final autobiography, in which he lamented the fact that "the Negro problem," which had been so ably studied by a more or less autonomous coterie of black leftists in the 1930s, had become the provenance of what was now surely a "white" liberalism.[41]

The recalcitrance of these two old men would see its most complete formulation in an unpublished review of Myrdal written at the time by a young black radical named Ralph Ellison. "In order to appreciate it fully and yet protect his own humanity," Ellison wrote, "the Negro must, while joining in the chorus of 'Yeas' which the book so deservedly evoked, utter a lusty and simultaneous, 'Nay.'" Ellison correctly perceived the study as representing the terms of the classic double-bind. On the one hand, it pointed out that Negroes had no proper intellectual orientation of their own; on the other hand, it said that the only proper intellectual orientation for addressing their situation was premised on the idea that Negroes as such could not exist. The cruel irony of the Myrdal study for black people was that their very presence was believed to contradict the "American Creed" of equality and liberty for all, which was in turn the very thing that was supposed to assure their emancipation.[42]

Ellison's critique (which surfaced with great import in the 1960s) challenged the emergence of a conceptual standpoint reflecting the interests of governance and political rule rather than the insurgent aspirations of the oppressed. Like "all great democratic documents," Ellison argued acutely, *An American Dilemma* contained "a strong charge of anti-democratic elements." These, he claimed, "can be easily discerned through the Negro perspective." "For the solution of the problem of the American Negro and democracy lies only partially in the white man's free will. Its full solution will lie in the creation of a democracy in which the Negro will be free to define himself for what he is, and within the large framework of that democracy, for what he desires to be." Ellison was not especially swayed by Myrdal's criticisms of the left, although he perceived a certain complicity shared by leftists and liberals around what might be called the modernizing assumption. "Both, it might be said, went about solving the Negro problem without defining the nature of the problem beyond its economic and narrowly political aspects." In other words, both assumed racial difference would be swept away by the force of progress. And, both failed to recognize how the substantive collective identities of racialized subjects needed to be central to the elaboration of a true practice of democracy. To this end, Ellison posed a simple, devastating question that would reverberate across the long civil rights era: "Men have made a way of life in caves and upon cliffs, why cannot Negroes have made a life on the horns of the white man's dilemma?"[43]

In their celebrated, but often overlooked, study of Chicago's "Bronzeville," *Black Metropolis* (1945), published just one year after *An American Dilemma,* St. Clair Drake and Horace Cayton, for example, noted what might have seemed a curious phenomenon to readers of Myrdal. Here, the black city was in many ways less intellectually isolated than the larger society—the site for the generation of cosmopolitan discourses that often surpassed conventional American views of the world. Observing the budding black campaign for a "double victory" against fascism abroad and racism at home in World War II, Drake and Cayton suggested what was arguably a more faithful rendering of the propensities and potentialities of the emergent forms of black democratic insurgency. Although not a world sufficient unto itself, a black counter-public had developed many of its own *independent* frameworks of normative judgment, lines of debate, and social action—frameworks that the Myrdal study appropriated and re-presented as its own, even as it disparaged their autonomous significance and blunted their increasingly radical implications.

Though relatively unknown at the time, the most strident intellectual critique of Myrdal was penned by the black Marxist thinker Oliver Cromwell Cox. It offered a reflection in theory of much black common sense of this period. Like Ellison, Cox discerned a deep, antiradical animus in the Myrdal brief. Specifically, Cox argued, the "caste" theory of race relations was a form of political displacement that short-circuited recognition of the linkages between the development of racial formation, the emergence of modern class-society, and the moral identity of the "West" itself. In Cox's view, the dual framework of race as caste and racism as a "moral dilemma" obscured how racial hierarchy had been a crucial component of capitalist labor disciplines and central to processes of world trade and accumulation since the sixteenth century. Given the vested economic interests that had been shaped through racial prerogatives, Cox seriously doubted whether any of "the great imperialist democracies, either can or intends to practice its democratic ideals among its subject peoples." By failing to specify the material interests and power relations that had created both investment and profit in racial hierarchy, and by relying on "time as the great corrector of all evil," the Myrdal study obscured these issues and was thus little more than a "powerful piece of propaganda in favor of the status quo."[44]

In the same year that *An American Dilemma* was published, the Trinidadian scholar/activist Eric Williams issued a related challenge to the story of the West as the triumph of moral and civilizing agency over racial domination and pecuniary interest. Williams proposed that capitalism and slavery, rather than being distinct modes of production, had been historically linked economic and ideological projects. Forty years of efforts by American and British historians to kill the "Williams thesis" with empirical refutation (disputing his claims about the "profitability" of slavery and his critique of abolitionist "humanitarianism") have failed to dislodge the core challenge he raised.

Williams argued that slavery had formed the basis of capitalist accumulation in the era preceding the industrial revolution. He further suggested that slavery opposition had become a "convenient foil" for the expansion of freedom defined as submission to a less capricious, but equally subordinating market contract. Together these claims undermined the progressive mythos of liberal historicism that cast racial inequalities as the vestiges of a prior era now embodied in the habits and dispositions of the black poor. Williams recognized that his argument was particularly unsettling in a time that again was seen as a struggle for human freedom against enslavement and domination. "This does not invalidate the arguments for democracy, for freedom now or for freedom after the war," he wrote. "But *mutatis mutandis,* the arguments have a familiar ring."[45] Humanitarian discourse, he suggested, should not become a means of absolving the present from the unequal relations of the past that produced the humanitarian crisis in the first place. Like so many other black intellectuals during this period, Williams thus amplified the caution against taking universalizing rhetoric on face value. "We have to be on our guard," he concluded, "not only against these old prejudices, but also against the new which are being constantly created."[46]

If Cox and Williams emphasized racism as central to the economic and political matrix of global modernity, Ellison emphasized the irreducible importance of black agency to its undoing. "It will take a deeper science than Myrdal's," Ellison wrote, "to analyze what is happening among the masses of Negroes." Myrdal, he suggested, was mistaken in his belief that blacks had put their faith in the meagerness of managed inclusion, as were black intellectuals like Bunche, who privileged the modernizing process over the messiness of democratic insurgency. Just as racist commitments were refusing to wilt in the name of American idealism, black struggles against white supremacy continued to offer visions of freedom in excess of "America" itself.

Characteristically, few sought as comprehensive an alternative in this period as Du Bois. Du Bois inverted the Myrdallian view, warning that the "Negro problem forces the United States to abdicate its natural leadership of democracy in the world."[47] In *Color and Democracy: Colonies and Peace* (1945), his summary overview of the post–World War II geopolitical situation, Du Bois doubted that U.S. global power could reconfigure a world-system defined by a singular history of colonial-racial projects. Lest anyone had forgotten, in the face of American triumph over the discredited and defeated ideals of Aryan superiority, Du Bois reminded readers that it was the moral, intellectual, and legal traditions of race hate in American that inspired the Nazi campaign against the Jews, establishing it on "American lines of caste conditions, disenfranchisement, mob murder, ridicule and public disparagement."[48]

Seasoned by secular cycles of racial disappointment within the United States, Du Bois called on blacks to maintain the posture of critical participation that had been urged by young radicals like Ellison. Agreeing with "one worlders" like Wendell Willkie, he claimed that the world-system itself was the necessary and proper horizon for political and moral judgments about humanity and civilization. Anticipating Hannah Arendt's axiom that only the protections of nationality could secure human rights, he argued that world stability would be assured only when the non-national character of the world's "colonial or quasi-colonial peoples" had been resolved, in other words, when the imperialist, or "master nations," as he called them, "either integrated their colonial subjects into the polity, or allowed them to become independent, free peoples."[49]

This formulation implied that the full extension of the democratic nation-form to all of humanity (that is, its universalization) was the crucial step in resolving inequalities among the world's inhabitants. Like a host of thinkers in this period, including Wallace and Myrdal, Du Bois identified universality (or civilization) with the institutional agency of the democratic nation-state. The crucial difference was that with Cox and Williams, Du Bois refused to accept that the Euro-American seizure of the world established either the legitimate conditions or the cultural or institutional terms under which this process needed to proceed. In other words, Du Bois rejected the notion that self-determination was a dispensation to be bestowed upon "backward" peoples by their historical superiors. Describing his own past fidelity to modernizing discourse as "blithely imperialist in outlook; democratic as democracy was conceived in America," Du Bois declaimed, "Primitive men are not behind us in some swift foot-race. Primitive men have already arrived. They are abreast, and in places ahead of us; in others behind. But all their curving advance line is contemporary not prehistoric."[50]

Du Bois, finally, insisted that the civic erasure of colonial and minority peoples could not be severed from economic questions of unequal material distribution. Recognizing the spatial apartheid that had condensed new forms of urban racial oppression in the United States, Du Bois tied it to the broader sweep of colonial modernity, calling Europe's colonies the "slums of the world."[51] The "colonial status" was "an integral and fundamental part of modern civilization" that exposed the historical contingency of the West's moral, political, and economic achievements.[52] Anticipating a rising generation of black radicals like Malcolm X, Du Bois thus typically reversed the conventional valence of terms like "minority" and "majority." Claims to a universal standpoint on world affairs were bankrupt if they failed to meaningfully represent the voices of 750,000,000 colonized and racialized subjects that together formed a majority of the world's people. More challenging, Du Bois confronted "the dominant majority which calls itself the world" with something that has only recently become visible on a world scale: the enduring centrality of minorities to modern politics and the dissolution of stable, unquestioned majorities.[53]

In a flurry of books, essays, and memoranda, Du Bois took up the call for "human rights" for the world's minorities. Working tirelessly for Negro rights at home, he was adamant that the problem of race would never be resolved until it was treated as global concern. He used his NAACP post, as special adviser on African Affairs, to plan the resuscitation of the Pan-African movement. In this, he collaborated with a wide range of figures, including Robeson and Max Yergan from the Council on African Affairs, Langston Hughes, George Padmore, Amy Jacques Garvey (the widow of Marcus Garvey), and Francis (later Kwame) Nkrumah. These plans once again put him on a collision course with the NAACP Board, and with Walter White in particular, for whom Du Bois's associates were too far to the left, too independent, and too international in their outlook. Nonetheless, for two years Du Bois contributed to a worldwide, anticolonial agenda under the NAACP's auspices, a project that would culminate in the Sixth Pan-African Congress in London in 1945.

That year Du Bois attended the United Nations Conference in San Francisco, along with White and Mary McLeod Bethune as part of an NAACP delegation. Du Bois viewed the United Nations as a chance to leverage world opinion on behalf of black equality by linking it with the issues of colonialism and imperialism. In the process, he pressed an idea that had dominated his thinking since the aftermath World War I, namely, that the social being of relatively autonomous black publics in the United States trumped any deference toward the national interest as long as U.S. officials continued to vacillate on questions of racial equality. For the remainder of 1946 he used his NAACP offices to pour these concerns into a remarkable document: *An Appeal to the World: A Statement on the Denial of Human Rights to Minorities in the Case of Citizens of Negro Descent in the United States of America and an Appeal to the United Nations for Redress.*

Du Bois argued that the national question was only significant as part of the larger issue of extending democracy, at home and abroad: "The United Nations recognizing democracy as the only just way of life for all peoples make it a first statute of international law."[54] This vision still held out slim hope that U.S. hegemony would be weighted toward the interests of the subjects and citizens of all states. With the benefit of a long life that bore witness to the sordid aftermath of two U.S. wars for democracy, however, Du Bois was skeptical that the American universalism that subsumed many of the radical dreams of the 1930s would be true to its word. Although he knew that the logic of the world situation had made the national dimensions of both colonial and minority questions unavoidable, he anxiously viewed U.S. planning statements and documents outlining the post–World

War II world as once again disregarding the status of subject peoples.[55]

Before the ink was dry on the *Atlantic Charter*, the United States had begun qualifying the unconditional promise of freedom and self-determination according to the wishes of its European allies and its strategic, geopolitical interests. Soon the democratic and cosmopolitan ideals of an internationalism of peoples that had inspired the United Nations Conference would be subordinated to the profane goals of commercially integrating the world's leading capitalist nation-states and preventing (or later containing) alternative power centers. This was manifest by 1945, when U.S. merchant marines began transporting 12,000 French combat troops through the South China Sea to Conchin China, now Vietnam. The crew of the *S.S. Winchester* cabled President Harry Truman to protest. The seamen asked a question that still remains largely unanswered within insular discussions of the "Vietnam syndrome." Why, they asked, are "American vessels . . . carrying foreign combat troops to foreign soil for the purpose of engaging in hostilities to further the imperialist policies of foreign governments when there are American soldiers waiting to come home?"[56]

One answer was self-interest; a second was a deep-rooted, racialized contempt for the capacity of nonwhite peoples for self-government. This combination meant that postwar U.S. hegemony would be constructed in accordance with the triumvirate of property, stability, and rule, wherever it appeared to be threatened. Despite internal disagreements among policy-makers, by 1948 U.S. State Department documents were abundantly clear that the nationalist aspirations of the Vietnamese (as well as other colonial subjects) were to be firmly subordinated to "the framework of U.S. security" and to "the interests of maintaining in power" governments friendly to the "furtherance of our aims in Europe." Earnest appeals of the kind sent by Ho Chi Minh to President Truman in early 1946 imploring "the American people to interfere urgently in support of our independence . . . in keeping with the principles of the Atlantic and San Francisco Charters," were thus largely unheeded.[57]

To a person like Du Bois, signs on the domestic front were equally worrying. Blacks and progressive democrats had already lost one of their most reliable allies within the government when Henry Wallace was maneuvered out of the vice presidency by conservative, machine politicians and southern delegates at the 1944 Democratic Convention and replaced by the relatively undistinguished midwestern senator Harry Truman.[58] Liberal democrats like Senator Claude Pepper from Florida expressed mock wonder that Henry Wallace had become too democratic for the Democratic Party. Meanwhile, Du Bois was heading toward his own final confrontation with NAACP insiders, for whom the elevation of a global discourse on "human rights" over a nationalist lexicon of "civil rights" risked courting a perception of black disloyalty. That Du Bois's close associates, like Paul Robeson, were known for their leftist affiliations heightened the alarm. As Myrdal predicted, the time of black radicalism appeared to be over.

Cold War Color Lines

The so-called good war, World War II, has for more than a half-century been the point of historical reference and the source of the ideological and institutional frameworks legitimating the United States as a particular nation-state serving the general interests of all: economic expansion, national sovereignty, global peace, and security—the mantra of freedom, democracy, and human rights. Yet, from the retrospective standpoint of the establishment of U.S. global hegemony in the post–World War II world, and America's self-interested and strategic role as a patron of older imperialisms and an agent of specifically capitalist freedoms, the record looks very different. As historian Michael Hunt has concluded, "The US had begun to backpedal on self-determination even as the Second World War was in progress."[59] Indeed, as early as 1941, U.S. planners at the Council on Foreign Relations were busy designing plans to secure U.S. military and economic control over a "Grand Area," including the "Western Hemisphere, the United Kingdom, the remainder of the British Commonwealth and Empire, and the Dutch East Indies, China and Japan."[60]

By the time Truman ascended to the presidency in 1945, flanked by South Carolinian James Byrnes as his secretary of state, the United States beat a steady retreat from Roosevelt's high-sounding rhetoric and nonantagonistic view of U.S.-Soviet relations. Truman's first decision of import, the detonation of atomic bombs over Hiroshima and Nagasaki, unleashed new fears of apocalyptic weaponry, implicating the United States in the genocidal crimes of its wartime adversaries and signaling the start of a new thirty-years war in Asia. The intervening years would see the United States commit itself both overtly and covertly to supporting Britain, France, and Holland in wars of re-conquest or counter-insurgency to secure lost colonial assets and material advantages.[61]

A small group of holdovers from the Popular Front era continued to emphasize racial equality, democratic reform, and international economic development.[62] With Wallace as their standard-bearer, first as a demoted member of Truman's cabinet, and then as a third-party candidate for president, Robeson and Du Bois emerged as the most prominent and vocal black activists linking struggles for racial equality to the democratic interest in global governance. Out of proportion to their numbers and influence, this nexus posed a sticky challenge to the business and government interests advocating one or another form of U.S. imperial succession through world trade, free markets, and the exercise of preponderant power. America's legitimacy as the leader of a new world order was wired to a delicate balance of military force and moral suasion. Despite being ignored, even disdained, by the bankers, diplomats, and financiers busy designing post–World War II institutions, the bundling of U.S. racial division into the equation invariably tipped the scales within the American calculus of power and legitimacy away from military supremacy and market fundamentalism and toward the development of global standards of justice.

The following few years—perhaps the most consequential in post–World War II history—witnessed a concerted effort to undo the knots of human rights discourse and international law that threatened to constrain the U.S. realm of action in the world. The big business of world finance and world order were simply too important to be held hostage to the concerns of disenfranchised peoples. Thus, New Deal internationalists—economic liberals like Cordell Hull and Henry Morgenthau, who had also been critical of British imperialism during World War II—largely rejected the democratic faithful who coalesced around Wallace. For the scions of elite financial interests, there was no greater threat to the post–World War II world than the possibility of another global economic depression. To prevent one, they believed it was crucial to secure an arena of multilateral global trade relations hospitable to U.S. manufacturers and accessible to U.S. needs for raw materials. They especially feared that the post–World War II prestige of the communist-led, antifascist resistance in Europe might lead to the election of governments in France and Italy that would resist their world-ordering ambitions.[63]

Strongly represented within the State and Treasury Departments, this political tendency pushed for the Marshall Plan for Europe. The rest of the world was another matter. George Kennan, key architect of post–World War II global strategy, was blunt in his assessment of the U.S. situation in the aftermath of the war: "We have 50% of the world wealth but only 6.3% of its population . . . our real task during the coming period is to devise a pattern of relationships that will permit us to maintain this position of disparity without positive detriment to our national security."[64] Kennan's thesis of containment became the guiding concept, providing a language for evaluating and responding to power configurations in the international arena. Kennan argued that the Soviet Union had emerged from World War II bent upon expansion, something that was not only an anathema to U.S. interests in Europe but also a global threat in the social and political context created by the collapse of imperial systems of rule. The United States needed to adopt a policy of containment, Kennan wrote, "to confront the Russians with an unalterable counterforce at every point where they show signs of encroaching upon the interests of a peaceful and stable world."[65]

The doctrine of containment was predicated upon vast simplifications of a world of heterogeneous social conflicts, needs and desires, in which even major communist-dominated insurgencies, many of them underway for a decade or more (for example, in China, Greece, Korea, and Vietnam), occurred with little tactical or material support from the Soviet Union. For U.S. elites who embraced the doctrine of containment, communism itself became an elastic concept whose presence could be deduced from any social project, from local class struggles to anticolonial, nationalist insurgencies that threatened to "destabilize" dispensations of property and power deemed central to stability and order. The equation of any expression of communist "ideology" with the looming menace of "totalitarian" power was highly serviceable. It allowed American planners to make instant strategic judgments about whom to support and how and where to intervene, while at the same time continuing to affirm the idea of the United States as the unique defender and champion of freedom.[66]

The triumph of this vision, not guaranteed during wartime, was established by 1948. As late as 1946, one-world visionaries such as

Wallace advocated strengthening international agreements, particularly over atomic power, and warned of the growing rift with the Soviet Union. At the other end of the political spectrum, old-line isolationists such as Senator Robert Taft worried about threats to U.S. popular sovereignty posed by the uninterrupted wartime growth of the federal state. The Cold War led to the marginalization of these views. In the process, it fostered a new and enduring bipartisanship in foreign affairs, reconciling bellicose, militaristic traditions of America-first nationalism (regionally strong in the South and the West and flush with victory in the Pacific War), with the so-called Eastern establishment interests, oriented towards Europe and preoccupied with the ostensibly peaceful tasks of global free trade, political stabilization, and monetary policy.[67]

Anticommunism was the glue joining these potentially incompatible emphases within U.S. foreign relations. It also emerged as a more or less flexible code for articulating a Cold War consensus on a home front still bitterly divided around the legacies of New Deal reform. The image of insidious, creeping state socialism had long been a weapon that business groups such as the National Association of Manufacturers and the right-wing Hearst press used to attack expansions of the federal power in the 1930s. The mid-1940s saw the resurgence of anticommunism, stalled by the war, as an instrument stigmatizing any non-military extensions of public power.[68] It is unlikely, however, that anticommunism could have attained the subjective hold it did if it didn't also have roots in older anxieties about the subversion of the body politic. Since World War I, red-baiting was well established in American political culture, a ready prism for nativist fears about immigrants and white supremacist opposition to racial equality. Even Kennan's high-minded, rationalist discourse deployed racist tropes about "Oriental secretiveness and conspiracy" to cement its counter-subversive imperative.[69]

As the *sine qua non* of post–World War II U.S. politics, anticommunism arguably gave Cold War liberalism a stability that had always eluded New Deal liberalism. Embraced by the Truman administration after 1947, it became central to the constitution of what Arthur Schlesinger Jr. would famously call "the vital center"—a political space that could override major conflicts of interests and, failing that, discipline or repress recalcitrant elements.[70] An ideological crucible for melding diverse, antagonistic constituencies—business and labor, isolationists and internationalists, white supremacists and ethnic pluralists—anticommunism thus helped to articulate a structure of common differences that could sustain a more or less permanent wartime footing. In the face of ongoing domestic conflicts at home and the uncertain world of international geopolitics opened up by World War II, its simplified morality and common-sense xenophobia thus supplemented, rather than contradicted, elite tactics of global rule.

Cold War discourse celebrated America's pluralism and political exceptionalism at home and tied them to a defense of "West" and the "free world" in the international arena. Wartime conversations about the rights of racial minorities and colonial subjects, and their relationships to the projections of American national power, were in this context subordinated to a generalized anticommunism. American power in the world-system was in turn legitimated in a formula that defined U.S. internal democracy and capitalist dynamism as the twin products of a modernizing western political tradition and cast the Soviet Union as the embodiment of all that was wrong with the world, in a perverse chain that equated social and political revolution with despotism and empire.

The question of the perversion of America's own revolutionary traditions was a real one, but by the Cold War, it could only be projected outward. The perversion within, once unloosened, became the many objects of political demonology that have menaced "normal" Americans ever since. Testifying before Congress in 1949, a livid Du Bois could not restrain himself: "How have we equipped ourselves to rule the world? To teach democracy we chose a Secretary of State trained in the democracy of South Carolina. When we wanted to unravel the worst economic snarl in the modern world, we chose a general trained in military tactics at West Point; when we want to study race relations in our borders we summon a baseball player. . . We who hate niggers and darkies propose to control a world full of colored people. Will they have no say in the matter?"[71]

The message to blacks, however, was that criticism of this sort would no longer be tolerated. In a celebrated essay on the U.S. Communist Party, published in Henry Luce's *Life Magazine*, Schlesinger had already resurrected the racist saw tying communism to black struggles, warning that the CPUSA was "sinking its tentacles into the NAACP."[72] Soon, prominent black radicals who possessed or refused to recant their ties to the left, like Robeson and Du Bois, would become *personas non gratas*. Robeson's assertion at the Paris Peace Conference of 1949 that blacks would not fight in a war against the Soviet Union brought howls of treason and proceedings to block his concert appearances. Barred from traveling abroad for the better part of the 1950s, his fame, wealth, and health declined precipitously (though for many years to come, the FBI continued to test civil servants's loyalty by asking whether they owned any Paul Robeson records). In early 1951, Du Bois, now an activist for nuclear disarmament with the Peace Information Center, was indicted as "an unregistered agent" of a foreign power. Though acquitted, Du Bois's trial proceeded without a squeak of protest from established black leaders. Du Bois too had his passport revoked for a period of eight years.[73] Under the McCarran Internal Security Act of 1950, less well-known black communists and Trotskyites of foreign birth, like C. L. R. James and Claudia Jones, were arrested and eventually deported. Others, like the poet Langston Hughes, faced humiliating loyalty appearances before Senator Joseph McCarthy's House Un-American Activities Committee (HUAC).[74]

For black antiracist theory and practice, the triumph of anticommunism had significant consequences. Most immediately, the moral panic over communist infiltration was a powerful instrument emboldening white supremacy throughout the country. In the South, fifty-six black soldiers had returned home after V-E day, only to be murdered by the resurgent Ku Klux Klan. Within the halls of Congress the defenders of racial segregation proved to be sturdy proponents of anticommunist legislation. Following the rout of New Deal liberalism in the 1946 congressional elections, Georgia Governor Herman Talmage condensed a number of racist tropes into a single image, tarring local CIO and civil rights activists as "Moscow-Harlem zoot-suiters" meddling in the affairs of his state. On a 1948 campaign swing through the South, (unprecedented for its refusal to address segregated audiences), Henry Wallace was ridiculed in the southern press as "the stooge if not the spearhead of those who talked much about democracy as a cloak for their own disloyalty." Buoyed by the claim that black discontent was a product of communist subversion and propaganda, Strom Thurmand's Dixiecrat revolt from the Democratic Party in 1948 revived the age-old *southern strategy* of dressing white supremacy in patriotic robes. Nationally, the CIO's cooperation with an anticommunist purge of progressive unions led to the collapse of fragile, interracial labor coalitions in many localities across the South.[75]

Things were not so different in the North. As early as 1945, Detroit homeowner groups had already begun to shift local politics sharply away from New Deal liberalism with their dire warnings that "communist-inspired Negroes" were being encouraged to "penetrate white residential sections." In a survey conducted in the early 1950s in Detroit by William Kornhauser, 68 percent of all whites and up to 85 percent of poor and working-class whites said they supported some form of racial segregation and pointed to the South as a model.[76] In Peekskill, New York in 1949, organized mobs shouting anti-Semitic and antiblack slogans, backed by local police, attacked interracial crowds attending a union benefit concert by Robeson.[77] Chicago's South Deering Improvement Association (SDIA) helped to dump progressive, New Deal Mayor Edward Kelly in 1947 because he was "too good to the niggers." Their *South Deering Bulletin* routinely tarred the director of the Chicago Housing Authority, Elizabeth Wood, with "communistic connections" for her efforts to further desegregate public housing. Between 1953 and 1955, blacks moving into Chicago's predominantly white ethnic Trumbull Park neighborhood were victims of repeated fire-bombings. Behind the slogan "White People Must Control Their Own Communities," the SDIA achieved Wood's ouster in 1955, the first year of the new reign of Richard J. Daley as Chicago's mayor. For the remainder of the decade, charges of communism and subversion of the racial status quo would be the basis for the FBI's intensifying scrutiny of the emerging civil rights movement and blind eye to resurgence of white supremacist terror.[78]

In the face of attacks of this sort, black leaders found themselves on the defensive. As St. Clair Drake wrote, many black leaders had come to believe that their success depended on "whether or not the espousal of civil rights for Negroes . . . [was] separated in the popular mind from Communist agitation."[79] Thus, Walter White, Roy Wilkins, and Philip Randolph, the leaders of the most important black civil rights and black labor organizations, threw their political capital behind what they believed to be the achievable goal of developing a strong civil rights plank within the Democratic Party platform, including support for fair housing legislation, voting rights, and employment protections, and the desegregation of the armed forces. This meant shoring up northern black support for the Truman administration—

including its foreign policy—against the expected defections of southern Democrats. It also meant sacrificing the black left and elevating anticommunism to an unprecedented centrality within antiracist politics.[80]

Black moderates had no illusions about the specter of communism providing new cover for Jim Crow. They believed, however, that it could also be a basis for attacking the South as antidemocratic and pressing demands for black equality. Typical was Randolph's suggestion that segregation was "the greatest single propaganda and political weapon in the hands of Russia and international communism today."[81] Randolph knew this charge had teeth because so many prominent legislators associated anticommunism with nativism and used Red scare tactics as a weapon in aid of white supremacy. By aligning civil rights with Cold War imperatives, Randolph held out the tacit promise that appeased blacks would help thwart challenges from the left represented most immediately by Henry Wallace's third-party candidacy for president. This tactic was rewarded in no uncertain terms by the Truman administration's Committee on Civil Rights, which publicly announced its opposition to segregation in October of 1947 with the publication of *To Secure These Rights,* the most comprehensive official statement in support of black citizenship rights since the Fourteenth Amendment.

Truman won the election of 1948, securing 69 percent of the black vote, and a new era of Cold War civil rights war born.[82] During these years, black leadership took a calculated risk, agreeing to bargain away the more expansive demands and critiques of black radicalisms, and to publicly testify to the Myrdallian faith that the gap between American ideals and American realities was closing. An unsigned editorial in *The Crisis,* penned by its new chairman, Roy Wilkins, belittled Robeson as little more than an armchair radical and self-involved celebrity, aloof from black struggles.[83] Visionary documents like Du Bois's *An Appeal to the World,* that viewed racial division as both an "internal and national question" and an "international question," were scrapped as black leaders accepted the *domestication* of the meaning of race to the dominant discourse of liberal, anticommunist nationalism.[84] Margaret Just Butcher encapsulated the ascendancy of the normative viewpoint some years later in *The Negro in American Culture* (1956): "In basic attitude and alliance with over-all American concepts and ideals the Negro is a conformist. He believes implicitly in the promise and heritage of basic American documents, and he has applied the principles of self-reliance, personal dignity and individual human worth to the long, rewarding fight to achieve full and unequivocal first-class citizenship. The American Negro's values, ideals and objectives, are integrally and unreservedly American."[85]

There was some cause for optimism. After all, black gains were immediately registered in 1948 in Truman's desegregation of the military and Jackie Robinson's cracking of the color bar in Major League Baseball. In an appearance arranged by the Urban League's Lester Granger, Robinson himself agreed to rebuke Paul Robeson in front of HUAC, and respected black leaders lined up behind him affirming that Negroes would not succumb to "any siren song sung in bass."[86] Yet, hopeful rhetoric of black national belonging quickly sped far away from the real world of racial conflict, division, and disagreement. As Franklin Frazier wryly commented, would-be race leaders were becoming "exaggerated Americans" in their service to the status quo. In a devastating critique of black capitulation to the Cold War, the hard-headed Frazier described middle-class black life in *The Black Bourgeoisie* (1955) as a world of make-believe, discerning that upholding correct images would be easier than changing the dispensations of the political will.[87] Frazier was one of the few prominent black intellectuals who publicly stood by Du Bois throughout the 1950s. By the end of the decade, after the nonagenarian radical had quit the United States for Ghana and renounced his citizenship, Frazier donated his own personal library to the University of Accra. In what can be seen as a sharp turnabout from his stated position in the 1930s, Frazier bitterly condemned his generation of black intellectuals for having been "seduced by dreams of final assimilation."[88]

Another progressive holdover from the earlier period, Carey McWilliams, noted with foresight that without a broad-based social movement to push for the enforcement of its recommendations, the findings of Truman's civil rights commission were likely to remain just a report. Indeed, just the year before the publication of *To Secure These Rights,* Congress finally succeeded in *abolishing* Roosevelt's FEPC. A few years later, as the U.S. Information Agency was distributing to embassies around the world its celebratory pamphlet "The Negro in American Life" (1951), depicting happy scenes of black-and-white togetherness at a neighborhood cook-out, neighborhoods like Trumbull Park in Chicago were engulfed by racial terrorism.[89]

Ralph Bunche's success as a United Nations mediator and Nobel Peace Prize winner was similarly trumpeted as evidence of the "progress of the American Negro," proof that American democracy was superior to Soviet communism. Yet even Bunche was not above being hauled before the International Employees Loyalty Board to answer charges about his past associations with the left.[90] While the well-connected diplomat was able to clear his good name, activists like Du Bois, Robeson, and Wright, who had done so much to advance the theory and practice of racial equality in these years, were subject to show trials or hounded into seclusion, silence, and exile.

That the strategy of Cold War civil rights spurred a spate of successful legal challenges to segregation is undeniable and must be deemed a partial achievement of wartime black radicalism. The Justice Department's amicus brief in *Brown vs. Board of Education* (1954) unmistakably recognized the public currency of domestic racial reform in the world at large: "the United States is trying to prove to the people of the world, of every nationality, race and color, that a free democracy is the most civilized and secure form of government devised by man."[91] By accepting a vision predicated on the subordination of racial equality to national security imperatives, however, mainstream black civil rights leaders acquiesced to the state-sanctioned thinning of the field of robust and independent black public interaction that had been developing since the 1930s. Perhaps more damaging, by tying racial progress at home to U.S. prerogatives within the world-system, they began to squander critical resources developed from decades of confronting the accumulated history of racial inequality.[92]

Although less easy to measure, the costs to the wider world were similarly great. The Cold War strengthened the hand of repressive national security doctrines at home and abroad, overriding many of the more hopeful political openings of the early war years. It was harder and harder after the mid-1940s to distinguish the promise of a "People's Century" from the bluster and threat of the "American Century"—the global promise of American universalism from a new form of American imperialism. The rigid East-West architecture of the Cold War recoded the struggle of freedom against slavery exclusively in terms of the tyranny of communist dictatorship, making it increasingly difficult to maintain public focus and pressure on the interlinked North-South questions of racial and colonial injustice that preoccupied U.S. blacks throughout World War II.[93] By the time Eisenhower's secretary of state, John Foster Dulles, announced that the United

States would not be a party to binding human rights covenants for fear of having "socialistic conceptions" foisted on America, it was difficult to calculate what had been lost.[94]

In the mid-1950s, blacks at home faced a new president who gave succor to a rising movement of massive resistance in the South by proclaiming that laws could never change what was in the hearts of men. After he left office (and despite sending federal troops into Little Rock), Dwight Eisenhower would publicly rue his appointment of Earl Warren, the Chief Justice of the Supreme Court who penned the *Brown* decision. Yet, in a sense, the two men may not have been as far apart as it seems. For the *Brown* decision was effectively undone by its famous temporizing formula calling for integration "with all deliberate speed." This vague mandate, lacking clear enforcement provisions, has left public school desegregation essentially unfulfilled to this day.[95]

Progress under the prevailing terms of Cold War nationalism, in other words, went hand in hand with a tendency to update the exclusions of the past in different names and guises. Thus, even as increasingly vocal black, ex-leftists like Ralph Ellison and Ralph Bunche rose to prominence within the post–World War II cultural and state apparatuses, the silencing of giants like Du Bois and Robeson, along with the voluntary and involuntary exile of anti-Stalinist leftists like Richard Wright, Chester Himes, C. L. R. James, E. Franklin Frazier, and others, completed a purge of the black activist intelligentsia that had come of age a little more than a decade prior.

Some, like poet Langston Hughes, struggled vainly to cleave the middle ground of patriotic opposition. Hughes's 1953 testimony before the House Un-American Activities Committee showed how difficult it now was to resist ritualistic, uncritical validations of American exceptionalism. Beginning with a repudiation of his own "outdated . . . out of print" poems that had used leftist slogans, Hughes mounted a modest defense of black struggles for social justice, freedom, and equality that had dovetailed with his own attraction to communism in the 1920s and 1930s. "Our country has many problems still to resolve," Hughes stated, "and we are trying very hard to be, as the flag says, 'one nation, indivisible, with liberty and justice for all.'" He concluded by testifying to the Myrdallian faith that progress in race relations was helping to make "our country the most wonderful country in the world."[96]

A final illustration of the bitter fall-out from this period was the public split between wartime comrades Ellison and Wright, as the former became the most influential and compelling black defender of anticommunist, American universalism, while the latter left for Paris, taking up a life of worldly exile and travel amid heady discussions about decolonization taking place throughout Europe, Asia, and Africa. The specific importance of Wright and Ellison as figures that gave voice to new styles of radical thought and sensibility among blacks cannot be overstated. Both writers gained a fame and influence unprecedented for black writers of any previous era. Their aesthetic disagreements, including Ellison's stunning novelistic success and retreat from political action and Wright's political disenchantment with the United States and exile into relative obscurity, became yet another index of the normalization of black political subjectivity after World War II and vindication of an America capable of transcending racial difference and inequality.

The conventional account preferring Ellison to Wright tends to gloss over the wartime dialogues between the two men that illuminate a profound if unsuccessful effort on their part to imagine an independent black radicalism beyond the emerging antinomies that defined the Cold War period: liberalism versus Marxism, anticommunist patriotism versus international solidarity, civil rights at home versus human rights around the world. Although Wright cast his move abroad as a break, it was also a continuation of his efforts to hold onto a critical, worldly perspective on the meaning and possibilities of black struggle. As he told his friend and fellow exile, black novelist William Gardner Smith: "My break from the U.S. was more than a geographical change. It was a break with my former attitudes as a Negro and a Communist—an attempt to think over and re-define my attitudes and my thinking. I was trying to grapple with the big problem—the meaning of western civilization as a whole and the relation of Negroes and other minority groups to it."[97]

Wright's self-imposed exile was a symptom of the decomposition of the more optimistic black radicalism of the war years. Yet, the times were such that Wright bore the brunt of the criticism. The rising Negro novelists, James Baldwin and Ellison, accused Wright of having lost his creativity and his political judgment, and Henry Luce's communications empire made sure that the meaning of this division resonated for U.S. publics. "Native Son Doesn't Live Here," read the headline of the 1953 article that appeared in *Time* magazine: "While

Wright sits out the threat of totalitarianism in Paris, an abler Negro Novelist sees the problem of race differently. Says Ralph (Invisible Man) Ellison, 'After all, my people have been here for a long time . . . It's a big wonderful country."[98] Writing in the C.I.A.-funded *Encounter* magazine, a young James Baldwin staked his own claim upon the public discussion of race in the United States with a final rebuke to Wright, entitling his celebrated account of his own Paris sojourn, "The Discovery of What it Means to be an American."[99]

Wright explained his move abroad differently. In "I Choose Exile," Wright aligned himself with the domestic victims of U.S. Cold War policies, particularly his friend C. L. R. James, insisting that he was not "anti-American," but un-American. "My un-Americanism," he wrote, "consists of the fact that I want the right to hold without fear of punitive measures, an opinion with which my neighbor does not agree; the right to travel wherever and whenever I please even though my ideas might not coincide with those of whatever Federal Administration might be in power in Washington."[100] Both *Ebony* magazine (which had initially commissioned the essay in 1950) and the *Atlantic Monthly* refused to publish it. As Wright surmised at the end of his life, this had little to do with the issue of communism. "So far as the Americans are concerned," he wrote, "I'm worse than a communist, for my work falls like a shadow across their policy in Asia and Africa. That's the problem, they've asked me time and again to work for them: but I'd die first."[101]

If wartime black activists had attempted to expand the definitions of freedom—joining liberty and equality—nationalism and internationalism—these definitions were often the most difficult to institutionalize, in part because of the very inequalities to which blacks were subjected in the first place. More worrisome was that the meaning of freedom had been distorted in its subordination to patriotic cant and fear. Astounded by his brutal mistreatment on Ellis Island on the eve of his deportation in 1952, C. L. R. James wondered how the Island's officers had not attained "some elementary consciousness, however primitive, that a Department of Justice, stands for justice." "The loudest shouters for the war against Communism in defense of democracy," James added, "no more believe in democracy than the Communists do." A short ten years later, a rising young black radical named Leroi Jones would amplify the point, describing the period as one when "the term *democracy* was blackened by ambitious, but hideously limited men, who thought it simply meant anticommunism."[102]

In its lustrous phase, World War II had extended the rhetorical application of American freedom to the struggles of colonial and minority subjects. But such rhetoric began to confound struggles for freedom and democracy, as it became a mask of power in geopolitical struggles to shape the post–World War II world at home and abroad. In defiant reflections on his own internal exile, Robeson characterized these years in broad strokes that reflected the stillborn dreams of the black popular front: "The upholders of 'state's rights' against the Negro's rights are at the same time supporters of the so-called 'right to work' laws against the rights of trade unions. The reactionary laws which have undermined the gains of Roosevelt's New Deal—the anti-labor Taft-Hartley Act, the anti-foreign born Walter-McCarran Act, the thought-control Smith Act—all were strongly backed by the Dixiecrats in Congress. Until their political power is broken there can be no real social or economic progress for common people anywhere, North or South."[103]

It is important, however, not to simply yield to a narrative of declension. Robeson didn't, and neither did many less well-known and ordinary participants within everyday black struggles. Beneath the radar of the epochal ideological rigidities of the Cold War, and against the swings of reaction and accommodation that so preoccupied the established black leadership, returning black veterans, such as Robert Williams and Medgar Evers and NAACP field operatives like Ella Baker, had already brought the fierce mood of wartime insurgency home to the South. Enabled by perhaps the most important wartime legal victory, the Supreme Court decision in *Smith vs. Allright* (1944) outlawing the "white primary," men and women like Williams and Baker started to map the post–World War II trajectories of black politics a full decade before the *Brown* decision. These struggles would carry forth the almost century-long, citizenly practice to develop black political power through the instruments of U.S. democracy. The resistance they encountered virtually ensured that grassroots insurgency would again meet up with global dreams of black liberation in the decades to come.[104]

Indeed, the problem of empire had not been forgotten, even if it had been rendered more obscure and remote within U.S. public discussion. As the pressing southern question of black enfranchisement asserted itself against the domestic strictures of Cold War politics in the 1950s, the questions of decolonization, self-determination, and injustice in the global South that spurred the black version of the greatest generation would gradually begin to reassert their prominence as well. It would not be long before the logic of Cold War civil rights collapsed under the weight of its own inner contradictions, as black ghettos exploded across the nation, and the U.S. experienced defeat on the battlefields of Vietnam. Black power would expose the limits of contained racial liberalism when confronted with the vicious defense and accumulated history of racial inequality. (As Stokely Carmichael put it facetiously, "You can't eat Ralph Bunche for lunch.") In Vietnam, the discourse of containment could no longer sustain the contradictions between democratic professions of U.S. anti-imperialism, U.S. defense of the colonialist-racialist legacy of France, and the unleashing of a U.S. military steeped in the traditions of expansionist nationalism (Vietnam as "Indian Country").

Considered from this vantage point, the capitulation of selected black leaders to the discourse of the Cold War might appear as the aberration. From Martin Luther King's embrace of Gandhi's principles of nonviolence *(satayagraha)* to the revolutionary nationalism of Malcolm X, Robert Williams, Harold Cruse, and Huey Newton that looked toward Cuba, Africa, China, and Vietnam, antiracism and anti-imperialism remained powerfully fused within the black political imagination. Upon his return to the United States in 1970, for the first time since his deportation in 1952, C. L. R. James encountered something that was surely familiar to him. Black people, James wrote, were again recognizing "the opportunities that history placed in their hands, not only in regard to the advancement of their own situation but in regard to the ideas and activities of oppressed people the world over."[105] The silences and failures of the intervening years meant that new assertions of black power and black anti-imperialism would be far less easy to reconcile with the promise of American universalism. At this point, "other types of racial classification, of a local, urban, or even international nature," would emerge as potentially "more significant than the overdue chance to be American."[106] Perhaps the lasting legacy of the American Century was a racialized conflict over the meaning of America as a global sign that persists to this day.

CHAPTER FIVE

Decolonizing America

All problems today, particularly the emancipation of the underdeveloped countries, are matters in which the world in general is involved; and at the center . . . particularly in the development of ideas and international strategy are the urban blacks of America.

—C. L. R. JAMES, "BLACK PEOPLE IN THE URBAN AREAS OF THE U.S." (1970)

At the first Congress of Black Artists and Writers in Paris in 1956, the Martinquan poet Aimé Césaire put forth a statement that would have been commonplace to many U.S. blacks during World War II. "Even our American brothers," Césaire told the international gathering, "as a result of racial discrimination, find themselves within a great modern nation in an artificial situation that can only be understood in reference to colonialism."[1] For members of the official U.S. delegation in attendance at the meeting, these comments set off alarm bells. Mercer Cook (soon to be U.S. Ambassador to Haiti in the Kennedy administration) expressed exasperation that the ostensibly nonpolitical subject of black culture had become the pretext for making strident statements against colonialism. Feigning ignorance, John A. Davis, president of the American Society of African Culture, argued that Negroes as a different race were more akin to a religious minority living in a pluralistic society than a colonized people. "What American Negroes want," Davis stated, was "equal status as citizens; and since 1936 we have been making tremendous progress in this regard." James Ivy of the NAACP was categorical: "The problem of integration is not a colonial problem."[2]

Césaire had made every effort in his lecture to construe questions of colonialism as broadly as possible, perhaps to avoid this type of dispute. His definition included what he called "colonial, semi-colonial and para-colonial situations" and encompassed independent nation-states like Haiti, racial minority populations like U.S. blacks, as well as peoples suffering under colonial rule. The American delegates, however, were unwilling to accept any inferences of this kind. They sought to make clear in no uncertain terms where their sense of solidarity and status lay. "American Negroes have a tremendous sympathy for and a working interest in freeing Negroes everywhere in the world," Davis offered magnanimously, "both as Americans *and* as Negroes." Testifying to a traditional benchmark of American exceptionalism, Davis continued, "America has always taken an anticolonial position from George Washington down to Dwight Eisenhower."[3]

Such statements no doubt rang hollow. Césaire, who had come of age in the Caribbean, was likely to have witnessed close at hand the nearly twenty-year U.S. occupation of Haiti after World War I and its brutal aftermath, not to mention successive U.S. Marine invasions across the region. In *Discourse on Colonialism* (1955), Césaire explicitly warned against viewing the United States "as a possible liberator." More likely was "American domination—the only domination from which one never recovers."[4] Recent world events in Iran and Guatemala, where the United States backed the overthrow of democratically elected governments, supported this view. As conference gadfly James Baldwin noted in his reportage on the event for *Encounter* magazine, whatever stature and credibility the U.S. delegation maintained was lost when a telegram from W. E. B. Du Bois, barred from traveling outside the country at that time, was read into the proceedings: "Any Negro-American who travels abroad," Du Bois wrote, "must either not discuss race conditions in the United States, or say the sort of thing which our State Department wishes the world to believe."[5]

Richard Wright made a concerted, if hasty effort to mediate a situation that had become uncomfortable. Not a full-fledged member of the U.S. delegation due to his self-declared exile status, but the only American member of the Paris-based Society of African Culture's conference organizing committee, Wright was a perfect person to hew a middle ground. As he had throughout his career, Wright—a self-professed "man of the west"—attempted to weigh the value of cultural differentiations created under oppressive racial conditions against what he believed to be the unmitigated virtues of Euro-American modernity.[6] Coming as they did from a "different national background," it was understandable that American Negroes viewed the world differently, he said. Nonetheless, as a group, Negroes had been forced to build autonomous institutions in a hostile environment, thus attaining the kind of training and experience necessary to build "black sovereignties in Africa, durable, study, hard, resilient institutions . . . that will resist the shattering of your cultures."[7]

Wright was less sanguine than his compatriots from back home that the United States would provide the keys to a modernization without domination (just as he, unlike Du Bois, was no longer convinced by the Soviet model). While he was silent on the debate about colonial status, Wright concluded his prepared talk for the conference with the hopeful declaration that "freedom is indivisible." With George Padmore, he suggested that U.S. blacks and colonized peoples shared an interest in pursuing what many of the new African and Asian nations that had met in Bandung, Indonesia, the year prior had been calling a neutral, nonaligned path—or "third way"—between the "monopoly capitalism of the West" and the "political and cultural totalitarianism of the East."[8] It is unlikely that the members of the U.S. delegation would have been satisfied with this compromise. The Negro lawyers, scientists, technicians, and writers whom Wright praised for going to Nkrumah's Ghana did far more than "sympathize" with anticolonial nation-building projects; they saw themselves as active participants in struggles for black sovereignty. Like Du Bois and Padmore (each of whom spent their final years in Ghana), they were much more likely to embrace as indivisible the fate of American Negroes, Africans, and other colonized peoples.

Wright himself had suggested as much in his provocatively titled *Black Power* (1954), which recorded his brief sojourn in the pre-independence Gold Coast. "Here in Africa 'freedom' was more than a word," Wright argued. "At a time when the Western world grew embarrassed at the sound of the word 'freedom,' these people knew that it meant the right to shape their own destiny as they wished."[9] It took the capacious mind of C. L. R. James to draw out the full radical democratic implications of this example. Describing an illuminating conversation he had with Martin Luther King and Coretta Scott King after Ghanaian independence celebrations, James suggested that there were clear parallels between the rising movements of ordinary people against forces of governmental repression throughout the world. "The achievement of the Gold Coast masses, of the people in Montgomery, Alabama, in the Hungarian revolution (as different as they were in their spheres)," James suggested, showed "the readiness of modern people everywhere to overthrow the old regime."[10]

Few could have attained such a transcendent perspective on democratic agency across the doctrinaire divides of the Cold War. The new and powerful ideological sluices shaping and constraining flows of information made much of this world increasingly opaque to U.S. publics, including blacks. (The Eisenhower administration may have railed about eastern Europe but had little to say about apartheid South Africa, let alone Mississippi.) Baldwin observed a yawning gulf "between the American Negroes and all other men of color" in attendance at the conference. A measure of Baldwin's own relative youth and inexperience was that he was unable to discern its root causes. While he knew that "there had been a rather sharp exchange between Cesaire and the American delegation," the terms of this debate were a mystery to him. Baldwin was similarly puzzled by Du Bois's telegram, which he described as "extremely ill-considered" and yet also "incontestable fact." Perhaps reflecting his confusion, he misquoted Du Bois in his article as saying that those Americans sanctioned to travel abroad care "nothing about Negroes," when Du Bois had merely predicted that they would be unable to speak frankly about racial conditions within America.[11]

Perhaps the gulf most in need of explanation was the one that had opened between Du Bois, an emblem of racial protest past, and Baldwin, the voice of its present and future. Such a gulf was arguably a conscious creation of Cold War policies, whose effects were being registered on both sides of the divide. For, although Baldwin may have been naïve about the nature of U.S. foreign policy and world events, Du Bois had become jaded in his latter-day conversion to communism, which compelled bitter disavowals of the United States and willful blindness to Stalin's crimes. The fact was that many American Negroes were traveling and speaking about U.S. racial conditions without the imprimatur of the U.S. State Department during these years. As early as 1948, Baldwin's contemporary, Bayard Rustin, had gone to India in the months after independence for the first World Pacifist Convention. In spare bureaucratic prose, the FBI field agent assigned to trail Rustin recommended that a "prominent Negro tour India to counteract unfavorable impression made by Rustin during his trip."[12]

In the following years, a stable of rebuttal witnesses were directly and indirectly enlisted by the United States Information Agency (USIA) to testify to racial progress in the United States, including jazz musicians Dizzy Gillespie and Louis Armstrong, academician J. Saunders Redding, and journalist Carl Rowan. Among the most notable was Rowan, who traveled to India in 1954. Recounting the visit in his memoir, he wrote, "I was not a State Department lackey. I simply went from Darjeeling to Patna to Cuttack to Madras, saying good things about my country because I believed that the society that had given me a break was in the process of taking great strides for racial justice."[13] The unpredictable Harlem congressman Adam Clayton Powell took a similar position when he traveled to observe the Bandung Conference in 1955. What Powell said shocked the delegates and foreign journalists in Jakarta, who expected Harlem's champion to offer more lurid tales of American racial atrocities. Powell instead used his platform to declare that "racism in the United States is on the way out. . . Today it is a mark of distinction in the U.S. to be a Negro." Even Washington, D.C., had become "a place of complete racial equality."[14]

Undoubtedly voluntary witnesses—even those as hyperbolic and unbelievable as Powell—were that much more powerful.[15] Yet it is important to proceed with caution when assessing the depth of black assent to the Cold War. The U.S. Cold War project had the complexities of its truly hegemonic ambition, which meant that it relied on force and suasion, sanctions as well as affirmations. Rowan, for example, was richly rewarded for his loyalty, first with an ambassadorial post to Finland and later with an appointment as assistant secretary of state for public affairs in the Kennedy administration. Powell, though, was playing a trickier hand and therefore had more mixed results. Given a standing ovation in the halls of Congress upon his return from Bandung, Powell was first denied a private meeting with President Eisenhower until he threatened to go public with his report on Bandung. The irony is that Powell—ever a thorny figure for the race-evasive Eisenhower administration—inverted the strategy of black exiles like Du Bois. Instead of using an international platform to condemn the United States in compensation for loss of power at home, Powell gambled that sugary words abroad would enhance his bargaining power at home. He would never have made such sanguine statements in front of his Harlem constituents, but he already had their trust; they were not his primary audience.[16]

All of this activity nonetheless amounted to an engagement in the Cold War on the ideological and geopolitical terms of the U.S. state. These conditions were numerously relayed in cautionary tales of the misbehaving Paul Robeson. Rowan wrote one such piece for *Ebony* as late as 1957, entitled "Has Paul Robeson Betrayed the American Negro?" In the year before his passport was restored by U.S. Supreme Court order, Robeson conducted a concert over long-distance telephone lines to London to dramatize his internal exile. This had only deluded him as to his growing irrelevance, argued Rowan. Robeson was convinced "that the day will come when American Negroes will find that 'black power' holds the key to their freedom," Rowan scoffed unbelievingly.[17] Reflecting upon these years, when as A. Philip Randolph's chief lieutenant he mobilized the black leadership establishment's repudiation of Robeson, the older, savvier political operator Rustin was more candid: "There's sort of an unwritten law that if you want to criticize the United States you do it at home. . . We have to prove that we're patriotic. . . Here is a man who is making some other country better than ours, and we've got to sit here and take the gaff, while he is important enough to traipse all over the country, to be lionized by all these white people, saying things for which he will not take any responsibility."[18]

Such statements were not entirely truthful, however. In fact, Robeson had become a site across which black public opinion was refracted and shaped. By no means was it all negative toward him. As one writer put it in a letter to the *New York Age* in 1949, "As a vet who put in nearly five years in our Jim Crow Army, I say Paul Robeson speaks more for the real colored people than the Walter Whites and Adam Powells. . . I saw the U.S. bring democracy to Italy, while white officers kept informing the Italians that the [black] 92nd Infantry men were rapists and apes."[19] Indeed, to many, Robeson's resistance at the price of fame and fortune made him a figure of assertive black manhood to be admired, if not emulated. Just over a decade later, when the national office of the NAACP warned him not to repeat "the example of Paul Robeson," another black veteran, Robert Williams, just gaining fame mobilizing the local NAACP chapter in Monroe, Georgia, for armed self-defense against resurgent Klan attacks, replied that Robeson showed "that all black men are not for sale for thirty pieces of silver. He has lit a candle that many of the new generation will follow."[20]

A problem for someone like Rustin was that much official racial discourse that came out of the Eisenhower and Kennedy administrations demanded not only that blacks be patient about the slow pace of change at home, but also that they testify to American racial progress abroad. As perhaps the single most important strategist of the non-violent, civil rights insurgency that began in Montgomery, Alabama, Rustin of course did not follow these prescriptions. Yet his "mature" political sensibility, which saw uncompromising protest yielding to political give-and-take, also manifested a disciplinary force ("an unwritten law") aimed at blacks en masse.[21] Rustin identified as dangerous and utopian any performance of black autonomy not tied to responsible black leadership, beholden to a realistic and attainable politics of black citizenship, and deferring to U.S. systemic prerogatives in the world at large. In an effort to counter a long-standing racism linking blacks with political subversion, he repeated the gamble of black reformers like Frazier and Bunche in the 1930s: that white supremacy was being dislodged both from its stranglehold on political power and its monopoly on national norms.

Although deeply considered, Rustin's position divorced admittedly serious questions about political organization to advance black collective interests from wider moral, ethical, and political questions about what those interests might finally be. Someone whose career had followed the full arc of the Second Reconstruction, E. Franklin Frazier believed that the price had gotten too high: "If [Negro intellectuals] show any independence in their thinking they may be hounded by the F.B.I. and find it difficult to make a living. At the present time, many of them find themselves in the humiliating position of running around the world telling Africans and others how well-off Negroes are in the United States and how well they are treated . . . Thus, it appears that the price of the slow integration which Negroes are experiencing must be bought at the price of abject conformity in their thinking."[22] Integration on abject terms, Frazier argued, amounted to a retrogression in the struggle for full equality. It essentially conceded that black people had no independent capacity to assess, let alone to shape a wide array of policies, norms, and values apart from dominant public opinion, except perhaps on the single issue of segregation. And even here it had become necessary to qualify criticism from a black point of view with pious assurances that racial progress was rendering such perspectives outmoded and unnecessary.

It is ironic that Frazier—the longtime opponent of arguments for black cultural and political autonomy—would raise these objections. His influential essay from 1962, "The Failure of the Negro Intellectual," was an expression of his accumulated sense of the bad faith of liberal antiracism, its subtle and not-so-subtle investments in white supremacy, its paternalistic conception of black gains as necessarily ancillary to ostensibly "broader" visions of social reform, and its willingness to compromise in the name of national unity, even when blacks, particularly those at the bottom of society, were made to bear the costs of unity. Resisting the equation of integration and assimilation, Frazier suggested that there was a growing gap between middle-class black leaders and black youth and working poor directly related to the leadership's failure to think through specific problems of black economy, politics, culture, and selfhood beyond the vacant horizon of raceless universalism: "The philosophy implicit in the folklore of the Negro folk is infinitely superior in wisdom and intellectual candor to the empty repetition of platitudes concerning brotherly love and human dignity of Negro intellectuals."[23]

Frazier pushed the argument still further. The African and Caribbean intellectuals gathered in Paris in 1956, who started from "the fact of the colonial experience," were asking the more penetrating and pertinent questions. Until U.S. black intellectuals and middle-class leaders could begin to "dig down into the experience of the Negro, and bring about a transvaluation of that experience so that the Negro could have a new self-image or new conception of himself," they would fail to understand the militant disillusionment that was leading many to turn to groups like the Nation of Islam. Although Frazier would never develop this position into an articulated defense of black nationalism, he foresaw that a sharp turn toward separatist, racialist themes in black life would be in direct proportion to the extent that civil rights leadership traded attainments of American status for a sector of the black population for the development of a vibrant, cross-class, transregional, and multigenerational black public sphere.[24]

In the 1960s, few would do more to develop these fragmentary ideas into a full-blown political perspective than Harold Cruse. "Afro-Americans," Cruse wrote, using the new designation, "are out of step with the rest of the colonial world. They are seeking their identity while we are endeavoring to lose ours in exchange for a brand of freedom in a never-never-land of assimilated racial differences."[25]

The intellectual trajectory that brought Cruse to this conclusion is telling. Himself a World War II veteran, Cruse joined the Communist Party from 1947 to 1953. After leaving the party he drifted toward the American Society of African Culture (AMSAC). Appalled by AMSAC's failure to take up the questions of culture and colonization in the late 1950s, Cruse set out on his own to theorize the cultural dimension of black struggle, publishing in key early periodicals of the civil rights movement and the New Left, including *Freedomways, Liberator,* and *Studies on the Left.* By the late 1960s, Cruse's *Crisis of the Negro Intellectual* (1967) would establish him as the foremost theorist of black nationalism in the United States.

What is most interesting about Cruse's perspective is that it expressly sought to bridge the theoretical and political divide between the black radicals of the 1930s and 1940s and the rising radical generation of the 1960s. He did so by identifying a single, continuous strand of thought—integrationism—and subjecting it to merciless criticism. "Despite the furor over party labels," Cruse wrote, "Negro integrationism is the same thing whether it emanates from the NAACP, the Urban League, SNCC, CORE, SCLC, the Communist Party, Howard University, or . . . the American Society of African Culture."[26] Inverting past arguments of Frazier, Bunche, and others, Cruse argued that integrationism was the philosophy of the black middle-class, one that had served their economic self-interest and pursuit of establishment credentials. Black nationalism, by contrast, was the perspective that arose from the historical position of the Negro "as a colonial being . . . the American problem of underdevelopment."[27] Popularized by the messianic figure of Garvey, bungled and hijacked by the Communist Party, the task, according to Cruse, was to reclaim black nationalism from its escapist legacy and left-wing distortion.

Many black intellectuals had been willing to use the anticolonial revolution to make "shallow propaganda," Cruse wrote, but most were unwilling to logically pursue its true implications at home. These began with the premise that "the Negro is not really an integral part of the American nation . . . not related to the 'we,' the Negro is the 'they.'" The dilemma was there was no longer any question of actual black separation from the United States. "The peculiar position of Negro nationalists in the United States requires them to set themselves against the dominance of whites and still manage to live in the same country."[28] The method for accomplishing this, Cruse believed, was cultural production. By cultivating both black cultural distinctiveness and institutional autonomy (particularly in the cultural sphere), it would be possible to usher in a revolution in U.S. national public culture in which blacks would no longer be forced to choose between autonomy without power and equality without dignity.

While these formulations were maddeningly short on programmatic specificity, Cruse was proposing what might be called a program of black public sphere development not so far removed from moderate prescriptions of contemporary multiculturalism. Cruse sought to persuade black writers and artists in particular to seize control of the means of representation and insist on the right to "the unrestricted expression" of black self-identity. Unfortunately, Cruse concentrated less on thinking through the complexities of this project than on engaging in a narrow politics of ideological regulation. Indeed, few black intellectuals escaped the smear of Cruse's broad brush. An intellectual project that could no longer effectively distinguish the "integrationism" of a Robeson, a Rustin, or a Robert Williams, for example, defaulted on its own promise to provide a political road map across the Cold War divides. Cruse's particular obsession with left-wing (at times, Jewish) control over black media and expression, moreover, led him to recode any authentic black radicalism within an unhelpful racial Manicheanism, a style of thought that would strongly inform the sectarian devolutions of black power politics and aesthetics later in the decade.[29]

At the same time, it is possible to read Cruse against the grain of his sometime paranoid and reductive tendencies. Cruse argued that black movements needed to recognize the integral relationship between black autonomy and the democratization of U.S. public culture. Black separateness in both programmatic and institutional terms was the necessary corollary of America's unfinished democratic revolution. Citizenship rights, understood in liberal-individualist terms, would be an inadequate solution to historic problems of racial inequality. This suggested the hidden cost of instrumental activity focused exclusively on reforming the state. Captive to a pattern of elite brokerage politics first established with the MOWM in 1941, black leadership possessed too limited an understanding of the value rationality of black civic organization and thus tended to bargain away black mass unrest too cheaply.

Cruse's work finally is most useful for its reprise of the varied idioms and political repertoires handed down from the era of the black popular front. Yet, rather than conforming to an invariant and weak model of "integrationism," black activism was actually strengthened by its increasing heterogeneity in these years. It is not clear, moreover, how far down the social scale the disciplinary imperatives of the Cold War actually traveled. As in previous decades, anonymous organizers and the local black people they served would often prove to be possessed of both a worldliness and a recalcitrance that outstripped national black leaders and ideologues. What Timothy Tyson has called an "indigenous current of black militancy" formed the enduring substrate for the shifting formations of black protest. Perhaps the one constant in this period, then, was not the failure and crisis to which Cruse and Frazier alluded, but a passion for justice that was sometimes called Marxist, sometimes black nationalist, and sometimes anticolonial, and was sometimes waged in the name of democratic rights.[30]

By the mid-1960s, black militancy was encapsulated in the slogan popularized by young SNCC militants Stokely Carmichael and Willie Ricks during James Meredith's "March Against Fear" from Memphis, Tennessee, to Jackson, Mississippi, in 1966. Very soon black power would migrate North, where the Black Panther Party, armed with shotguns and incendiary rhetoric about black ghettos as internal colonies, emerged as its most extreme avatar. The Panthers would claim to bring the anticolonial revolt home to urban America. As Cruse observed, the fact they took their cues from anticolonial theorist Frantz Fanon was proof that "the young generation" fundamentally rejected the normative pieties of U.S. liberal-democracy.[31] Once again, Cruse may have overstated the case. In the tradition of militant abolitionism and Christian pacificism, Martin Luther King had looked to India for inspiration. Invoking a right to bear arms and the specter of radical republicanism, the Panthers looked to Vietnam. Both manifested the indigenous militancy and worldliness of a black struggle that unfolded within and against the American grain.

The Global Front of Black Power

The emergence of forty new nation-states between 1945 and 1960 in the former colonial world ushered in "a new world for America's Negroes."[32] Defining the Negro's "new mood" in 1960, James Baldwin put the matter pointedly: "The American Negro can no longer, nor will he ever again be controlled by white America's image of him. This fact has everything to do with the rise of Africa in world affairs."[33] Baldwin, whose political trajectory through the decade led him to increasing militancy, national disaffiliation, and a poetic identification with the Panthers and figures such as Angela Davis, chose his words carefully.[34] A defining characteristic of the 1960s was the geopolitics of images that linked decolonization and the struggles against U.S. racism. As a black veteran of World War II, the autoworker turned radical theorist James Boggs put it, "Revolutions have never depended upon sheer numbers, but rather upon the relationship of forces in the existing political arena. Today when the existing political arena is a world arena, the Negro's relationship is to the world."[35]

Insofar as the U.S. realm of action had become the entire world, it was difficult to prevent the migration of racial meanings between the foreign and the domestic spheres, either as matters of representation or as matters of politics. As early as 1959 on his first trip to India, Martin Luther King recounted that "the strongest bond of fraternity was the common cause of minority and colonial peoples in America, Africa and Asia struggling to throw off racism and imperialism."[36] This gesture presented a vague threat to the formula of Cold War civil rights, although as a former British colony and noncommunist, India was relatively less problematic as a global analogue to U.S. black struggles. This would change dramatically, however, with the emergence of national liberation struggles with a distinctively socialist trajectory in Cuba, Congo, Vietnam, and elsewhere.[37]

By 1960 the question was emerging about a new form of imperialism not limited to passing legacies of European colonialism, but perpetuated through the establishment of global patterns of unequal power and uneven development among formally independent nation-states. The political logic of colonialism, which had allowed nations to become empires over non-nations, was fatally weakened. Yet even as independent nationhood was being normalized throughout the world, nationalist leaders like Mossadegh in Iran, Arbenz in Guatemala, Lumumba in Congo, Castro in Cuba, and Ho Chi Minh in Vietnam discovered that they were to be monitored, policed, and, if necessary, punished, depending on whether what they advocated was viewed as favorable to the stabilization of a U.S.-centered, multilateral state-system geared to the resource needs and expansion of multi-national capitalism.

In these years, usually remembered for the escalation of the nonviolent civil rights movement inside the United States, anti-imperialism steadily gained adherents among a wide range of black activists and intellectuals. In 1960, cultural theorist Harold Cruse, self-defense advocate Robert Williams, Ghana ex-patriot Julian Mayfield, black bohemian Leroi Jones, Harlem nationalist John Henrik Clarke, and poet and CORE member Sonya Sanchez all made the arduous trek to the Sierra Maestra to hear Fidel Castro describe the recent successes of the Cuban Revolution. The delegation, organized by the Fair Play for Cuba Committee, a solidarity group initiated by New Left forebears like C. Wright Mills, suggests that the convergence between the predominantly white New Left and black power politics, thought to mark the implosive radicalism of the late 1960s, was present at the inception.[38]

The Cuba trip stimulated Cruse's seminal essay, "Revolutionary Nationalism and the Afro-American," published by *Studies on the Left*. In the next few years, Cruse would become the first black writer to suggest a properly postcolonial frame for U.S. black politics. "The racial crisis in America," Cruse wrote, "is the internal reflection of this contemporary world-wide problem of the readjustment between ex-colonial masters and ex-colonial subjects."[39] Cruse correctly anticipated that political momentum in the coming years would arise from efforts to bind the fates of U.S. blacks with a new and more radical wave of decolonization struggles. (Fidel Castro appeared to affirm this view: thumbing his nose at U.S. officialdom he made the reverse pilgrimage to stay in Harlem's Theresa Hotel.) Cruse also served notice to potential allies in what was "loosely called the New Left" that they would have to contend with black political initiatives and sensibilities that no longer prioritized alliances with sympathetic whites or the "pragmatic practicalities" of the political mainstream.[40]

If the Cuban Revolution, ninety miles off U.S. shores, was the apposite case for developing an argument about U.S. "domestic colonialism," the Congo crisis cemented the popular pan-Africanist reading of U.S. neocolonialism. Only days after Congolese independence, public disorder prompted a series of alarmist and disparaging accounts in the western press about the dangers to white property owners (white womanhood) and, more forebodingly, questions about the sanity and political trustworthiness of the new prime minister of Congo, the radical pan-Africanist Patrice Lumumba. Two weeks later the resource-rich Katanga Province seceded at Belgium's behest, and Belgian paratroopers (with tacit U.S. backing) entered Congo. Months later as news filtered through the word-of-mouth networks on the streets of Harlem of Lumumba's murder, hundreds of black people gathered in protest outside the United Nations. Several dozen, including Daniel Watts, editor of *Liberator* magazine, and the young poet Maya Angelou, scuffled with guards inside the gallery during a speech by U.S. ambassador Adlai Stevenson. It would eventually be learned that the CIA had played a central role in Lumumba's murder and had backed the installation of army colonel Joseph Mobutu as prime minister. Over two hundred black people marched through Times Square that night, where they echoed the slogan of the Cuban revolution, "Congo, yes! Yankee, no!"[41]

The U.S. press and established black leadership characteristically condemned the United Nations demonstrations as the actions of an irresponsible fringe group, perhaps motivated by communist sympathies. This was a gross distortion, however. Historically, the Belgian Congo was a symbol of the worst rapacity of European colonialism. The contemporary drama—which included typically racist media portrayals of African "cannibalism," rumors of U.S. covert operations, and the division of Africa's largest country—only confirmed mounting black skepticism about U.S. anticolonial pretensions.[42] Even the once-timid American Society for African Culture could not fail to learn its lessons. At AMSAC's Fourth Annual Conference in 1961, St. Clair Drake made the controversy the centerpiece of his lecture. Responding to Harold Isaacs's charges in *The New Yorker* magazine that Negroes were confused by recent events in Africa, Drake asserted that forms of "pan-African identification" were beginning to "inject new meanings into the word 'Negro,'" expanding the "fronts" of black struggle.[43]

In the next few years, Harlem's resident black nationalist and Muslim minister, Malcolm X, missed few opportunities to intersperse references to Lumumba and the Congo in his speeches. Indeed, Malcolm precipitated his censure and eventual break with the Nation of Islam in 1963 in an infamous response to a reporter's question about the group's reaction to the assassination of President John Kennedy. Implying that Kennedy's murder was blowback from the Cold War,

Malcolm said that the United States was reaping the violence it had sown in Congo, that "the chickens were coming home to roost."[44] The next year, following Malcolm's major tour of Africa and the Middle East, Congo was the subject of a rally for his new Organization for Afro-American Unity (OAAU) (modeled on the Organization of African Unity). In a remarkable address, Malcolm linked U.S. support for Lumumba's killer, Katanga secessionist Moise Tshombe, to the U.S. Information Service's overseas myth making about racial progress at home. "When I speak of some action for the Congo," he said, "that action also includes Congo, Mississippi."[45]

It is arguable that Malcolm X had learned the lesson of Cold War civil rights well; he had simply inverted it. He believed that blacks could significantly leverage political struggle in the United States by aligning themselves with anti-imperialist forces in the world arena. This was the context for his new assertions of pan-Africanism. The case for pan-Africanism was often advanced in terms of historical claims to African "cultural retentions" by new-world blacks.[46] While Malcolm certainly gave a nod to the spiritual, cultural, and psychic unity of blacks and Africans extending back in time, this was not what galvanized him. Rather, Malcolm's sensibility combined political and religious universalism within a thoroughly contemporary geopolitical imagination linking U.S. blacks and Africans, as well as peoples of the Islamic world, in what he called "the overall international struggle." He would soon begin to advance the important proposition that the concerns of U.S. blacks could not be met within the framework of American law and civil rights, but required United Nations intervention under the banner of human rights.[47]

It is ultimately difficult to separate cultural from political pan-Africanism. The distinction, however, is consequential because it suggests that the new interest in Africa among U.S. blacks in the 1960s did not simply derive from a psychic quest for positive self-images or genealogical lineages—that is, from racial imputations of shared biophysical essences—but that such psychic and cultural assertions (when they were made) followed from claims about ethical commonality, global relatedness, and political responsibility. This argument was carefully elaborated in these years in relation to the African context as well. In a controversial address at the follow-up conference to the first Congress of Black Artists and Writers in Rome in 1959, Frantz Fanon warned that understandable interests in precolonial, cultural origins ran the risk of being "cut off from the events of the day." Culturally oriented concepts like Aimé Césaire's "negritude" were limited by the historical specificity of social formations. Arguments for African unity, then, had to be advanced on political, rather than cultural grounds—attentive to both African historical diversities and the negative unifying force of colonial rule.[48]

In *Wretched of the Earth* (1961), the most important theoretical influence on such late 1960s radicals as the Black Panthers, Fanon went on to argue that overcoming the colonial condition required a complex double gesture. Hopelessly fragmented colonized peoples would have to violently assert existential claims to the subjugated particularities of ethnic and racial identity, while at the same time upholding a broad struggle toward nationalist and internationalist coordinations of an indivisibly human aspiration for justice.[49] In this regard, it is significant that Fanon was from the embittered, militant generation of World War II, "all those niggers, all those wogs who fought to defend the liberty of France or for British Civilization" only to find the bulwarks of colonialism rising on the other side. In other words, like some of his U.S. counterparts, Fanon held a sharply dialectical view, in which race and nation—as manifestations of the particular and universal—could only be harmonized through an agonistic transvaluation of the local and global hierarchies in which they were embedded.[50]

Adding to the betrayals of World War II was the dimension of the U.S.-Soviet Cold War, which, rather than delivering on its promises of self-determination, had everywhere begun to produce its simulacrum. Remarkably from his different context and vantage point, Fanon was proposing a strikingly similar, if more detailed, analysis to Malcolm's vernacular quip. Fanon is frequently misread simply as an advocate of counterviolence by dominated peoples. Yet, in a text that was pointedly a critique of the Cold War, Fanon accused the United States of having transformed "international political life" into a kind of "universal violence." "It is not by chance, that in consequence Negro extremists in the United States organize a militia and arm themselves." The fact that minority groups living within the borders of the world's superpower no longer hesitated "to preach violent methods for resolving their problems" suggested that the global conflicts peripheralized by the Cold War had reemerged at the center. The chickens had indeed come home to roost.[51]

Fanon recognized that anticolonial struggles had thus far achieved only partial victories. Yet he grasped that a new political logic had begun to redefine international relations based on the universalization of formal nationhood within a sphere of international commodity relations dominated by the United States. "Colonialism and imperialism have not paid their score when they withdraw their flags and their police forces from our territory," he wrote.[52] This suggested that in order to produce liberatory outcomes, decolonization struggles would need to think beyond the horizons of national independence. Fanon's passing references to "the American Negro's new emphasis on violence" and the emerging problem of "minorities" were related to a series of issues, including the global context of local conflicts, the implications of neocolonialism for populations across the world, and the necessity of internationalizing and thus extending struggles against empire.[53]

When Fanon referred to the arming of the civil rights movement in the American South in the 1950s, he was of course pointing to Robert Williams. An ex-marine, Williams was an NAACP organizer in Monroe County, North Carolina, who in early 1959 challenged the national office by organizing local blacks into rifle clubs for the purposes of self-defense. The following year, in an event crucial to broadening the implications of his local efforts, Williams joined the well-publicized delegation that visited Cuba in support of the new revolutionary government. After a series of confrontations with NAACP leadership, as well as the local Ku Klux Klan and law enforcement agencies, Williams was forced to flee the county. Soon he had the distinction of being the first black radical of the 1960s to become the focal point of a nationwide FBI manhunt. Escaping first to Canada, Williams eventually made his way back to Cuba, where he was granted political asylum.[54]

Williams's Cuban exile soon elevated him within the geopolitics of pride and shame so central in these years, as he joined an emerging pantheon of anticolonial heroes. In his newsletter, *The Crusader,* which he began publishing from Cuba, he referred to the island as "liberated territory of the Americas."[55] Cognizant of the unique nature of his sudden celebrity, Williams remarked, "When the racists forced me into exile, they unwittingly led me onto a greater field of battle."[56] Williams's greater field of battle, of course, was the figure he cut in his own movements through space and across national borders, signifying successful resistance to an American geography of apartheid and informal empire. His baldly titled book *Negroes with Guns* (comprised of press clippings and earlier speeches) was a relatively mild, prointegrationist critique of the limits of nonviolent tactics. For young black power militants, however, Williams's confrontation with the U.S. government was a rehearsal for their own brand of liberation politics. His exile and notoriety demonstrated the incontrovertible power of what the Black Panthers would later call "picking up the gun."[57]

The respective journeys of Robert Williams and Malcolm X out of the old southern black belt, and black millennial sectarianism into the geopolitical ambit of decolonization, signaled a return to an earlier emphasis on racialized geopolitics. Williams and Malcolm X not only redrew the coordinates of the intranational struggles of black Americans in light of events within the decolonizing world, but they also popularized forms of revolutionary practice and symbolism that strained the borders of U.S. liberal-nationalist discourse. Thus, while the nonviolent civil rights movement linked the failure to enfranchise black people in the American South with forces that would mock the moral and political claims of American democracy and Christian universalism, Williams and Malcolm X joined in the mockery, criticizing America's democratic pretensions and severing their links with the nation. With struggles for decolonization accelerating, these gestures of public disaffiliation opened up new routes for radical activism at home by the latter half of the 1960s.[58]

Finally, Williams, Malcolm X, and Fanon in different ways argued that the relationship between violence and racism was inextricable. They understood that for the victims of racism, concrete acts of violence preceded the ideational and institutional forms of racism and had to be met with a credible response.[59] By advocating organized counterviolence by dominated peoples, Malcolm X and Williams suggested that the U.S. government, as the holder of the monopoly on the legitimate uses of violence, was either incapable of preventing or complicit in sanctioning racist violence exercised upon black bodies.[60] This was a *de facto* repudiation of the state as the entity safeguarding a sphere of public civility and order for black people. Regardless of the particular programmatic vision to which it was attached, it thus constituted an assertion of the necessary autonomy of black life in America.

For better and for worse, this was brought home by the violent up-heavals that rocked Birmingham in 1963, Harlem in 1964, and Los Angeles in 1965. In the long history of so-called race riots, the 1960s were when black people were perhaps for the first time on the offensive, attacking the physical emblems of the state (and private property). It is thus not surprising that supporters of black aspirations described these riots as revolts or uprisings and that they became a rallying point for a black power imaginary. As Dan Watts of *Liberator* put it, "You're going along thinking all the brothers in these riots are old winos. Nothing could be further from the truth. These cats are ready to die for something. And they know why. They all read. Read a lot. Not one of them hasn't read the Bible . . . Fanon . . . You'd better get this book. Every brother on the rooftop can quote Fanon."[61] Such hyperbole notwithstanding, the riots suddenly made the geopolitics of black power a very local affair. Eldridge Cleaver wrote that although "Watts [had been] a place of shame . . . an epithet," after the riot "all the blacks in Folsom are saying, 'I'm from Watts baby'! and proud of it."[62] As another future Black Panther, David Hilliard, recalled, it was when the afterglow and "excitement of Watts was beginning to fade" that, a few hundred miles to the north, the Panthers were founded.[63]

Rioting in northern urban centers congealed seamlessly with declarations of black power emanating from the South, occasioning new programmatic visions of black liberation. In an important essay, two original radical theorists (and former associates of C. L. R. James), James and Grace Lee Boggs, called "the city . . . the Black Man's Land."[64] Using urban population projections, the Boggses proposed a clever rewriting of an older theory of black liberation, the Communist Party's "black belt thesis." An artifact of a brief rapprochement between communism and black nationalism in the late 1920s and early 1930s, it held that the contiguous counties holding a black majority population within the southern "black belt" states comprised an internal colony, an incipient black nation with the right to self-determination. The CPUSA argued that black out-migration from the South had nullified this position, and abandoned it in 1958, embracing instead the NAACP's integrationist slogan, "Free by '63." The Boggses remobilized the "black belt" argument in light of black urbanity.[65]

Drawing upon the idea of the civil war as America's "unfinished revolution," the Boggses argued that the Watts riot, like the Birmingham and Harlem riots the years before, was an initial skirmish in a "second civil war" that would be played out in America's cities. Vice President Hubert Humphrey seemed to confirm this view when he claimed "the biggest battle we're fighting today is not in South Vietnam; the toughest battle is in our cities."[66] The use of national guardsmen alongside police in quelling the riots, and the descriptions of escalating U.S. forces in Vietnam as "police actions," sealed the association of intra- and outernational conflict and struggle. As Black Panther Party leader Huey Newton would write, "*The police* are *everywhere* and use the same tools, and have the same purpose: the protection of the ruling circle here in North America."[67]

These and other arguments and experiments that came on the heels of urban revolt embraced the black urban space as the basis of a renewed and very different kind of radical vision: the site of a radically dispersed black nation and the model of the internal colonization of America's black people. Black liberation politics valorized the ghetto as a location from which to finally overturn centuries of racial stigma. As a racial space and a zone of underdevelopment and routine violence, the ghetto was seen as inherently recalcitrant to the reassuring teleological narrative of black uplift through citizenship.[68] Its denizens, particularly black men of the streetcorner society, society's degraded, least hopeful elements, were cast as potential heroes and liberators. Once again it was Fanon who provided the conceptual linchpin in his poetic descriptions of the "lumpen-proletariat . . . the pimps, the hooligans, the unemployed and the petty criminals" of the colonial slums. "These workless less-than-men," he wrote, had the most to gain from a revolution, the chance to be "rehabilitated in their own eyes, and in the eyes of humanity." "All the hopeless dregs of humanity, all who turn in circles between suicide and madness," Fanon exclaimed, "will recover their balance." In these images, the Black Panthers would discover themselves.[69]

Internal Colonies

Founded in Oakland in 1966, the Black Panther Party for Self Defense was one of many black power groupings that sprang up in American cities during the latter half of the 1960s. Returning to "black America" in 1968 after almost twenty years of self-imposed exile in Europe and Africa, black novelist William Gardner Smith was astounded by the rising political militancy around the country and the black radicalism that was its center. The riots, he argued, were the result of the collision of the southern freedom movement and the northern urban crisis. This, he argued, had "marked the entry of the tough ghetto youths into the race battle, and the existing organizations, led by intellectuals or the middle-class, could not cope with them—the Panthers had to be born."[70]

The late 1960s produced a qualitative expansion of the black counterpublic sphere. Groups like the Panthers were a manifestation of the new organizational forms and articulate expressions of the indigenous militancy and frustrations of black cities. Indeed, the Panthers begin doing something largely unprecedented in black movements of the day: mobilizing the thwarted, undisciplined, and sometimes ingenious black men born from rural out-migration from the South into a state of permanent ghettoization and underemployment in the North. Perhaps most worth reengaging in a discussion of the Panthers is the dramatic story of their effort to reshape often episodic and disjointed lives of urban, black subalterns, replacing the everyday violence and temporary fulfillments of hustling and surviving with purposeful political action.[71]

Party cofounder Bobby Seale described how he and Huey Newton first began raising money for the Panthers by hawking copies of Mao Tse Tung's *Red Book* in nearby Berkeley. According to Seale, Newton came up with the plan to sell the books at the university, believing that the idea of "Negroes with Red Books" would pique the curiosity of campus radicals and get them interested in supporting (and financing) the Panther Party. The more important agenda was to use the money to buy guns; guns, Newton believed, would give the Panthers street credibility and allow them to capture the imagination of their primary audience: black youth in the ghettos of Oakland and Richmond. This formula of revolutionary self-learning and armed resistance (bridging the campus and the ghetto) would be central to the future career of the organization.[72]

As news of the first armed confrontations between Newton and the police started to spread through word-of-mouth networks in the local black communities, the Panthers were immediately hailed as a leading black militant organization, and their membership quickly grew. Within three years there were thirty Panther chapters—one in every major city—and a membership numbering in the thousands.[73] In the next three years most major black radicals came into substantial contact with or took membership in the party, including the celebrated ex-convict-turned-writer Eldridge Cleaver; SNCC leaders Stokely Carmichael, H. Rap Brown, and James Forman; radical black intellectual Angela Davis; and prison-movement intellectual George Jackson. In addition, the Panthers made symbolic alliances with like-minded organizations, such as the Dodge Revolutionary Union Movement, Chicano nationalist Brown Berets, the American Indian Movement, the Puerto Rican Young Lords, Students for a Democratic Society (SDS), and women's and gay liberation organizations. Combining flair for dramatic actions with a creative synthesis of many of the central radical ideas and revolutionary postures of the time, the Panthers by 1968 were considered by many to be the exemplary revolutionary organization in the country and the one most closely identified with anti-imperialism and internationalism.[74]

It was neither the simple fact of public disorder nor the sheer power of allusion that allowed the urban presence of black people to assume these new meanings. Once the civil rights movement moved northward by the mid-1960s, it no longer encountered racism as a legally enshrined system of segregation and voting restrictions. In fact, even as the legal edifice of segregation was being dismantled by government decree, the more enduring structure of the second ghetto—built upon diminishing housing stocks hemmed in by freeways and tramlines—was continuing to be inscribed into the urban landscape and built environment.[75] Panther ideologues reasoned that the reformist logic of the civil rights era that culminated with the passage of the Civil Rights Act and Voting Rights Act in 1964 and 1965 had reached its terminus, all the while failing to address diminishing life-chances faced by rising numbers of the black urban poor.[76]

With unequal access to basic city services, employment, and tax revenues, and subjected to concentrations of pollutants from highways and incinerators, segregated black urban populations, it seemed, had the least to gain from a civil rights movement and the most in common with the subjects of colonial rule. Indeed, Fanon had argued that reform under colonial conditions would fail to procure "for the colonized peoples the material conditions which might make them forget their concern for dignity." The Panthers reasoned along similar lines. The realities of spatial apartheid not only would prove resistant to civil legislation at the national level, but urban blacks would bear the brunt of this failure. "Once colonialism has realized where its tactics of reform are leading," Fanon predicted, "we see it falling back on old reflexes, reinforcing police effectives, bringing up troops, setting a reign of terror which is better adapted to its interests and psychology.[77]

This suggested a new strategy of confrontation. The Panthers started from the premise that policing provided the basic grammar for what Fanon called the "language of pure force" arrayed against colonized peoples. In contrast to the forms of hegemonic address by which the modern state secures civil society and its public spheres, in other words, urban law and order mostly dispensed with seeking consent through ideological suasion.[78] Staging confrontations with a notoriously racist Oakland police force, Newton and Seale wanted to dramatize how a form of colonial power had been deployed against black people in urban areas. Flamboyantly displaying their own lawful and disciplined resistance to violent policing, they further implied that urban blacks were inured to reformist overtures from the government as a result of their familiarity with the forceful and violent face of the state.

From this initial emphasis on urban policing and self-defense, the Black Panther Party began to project a more utopian sense of hope and mission. This led them to develop a critique of the limits of nationalism—both the American nationalism of the mainstream civil rights movement, and the black separatism and cultural nationalism espoused by many of their rivals for the hearts and minds of the people on the block, including the Nation of Islam, Ron Karenga, and Amiri Baraka.[79] The Panthers argued that all the prevailing options presented to America's black people were inadequate. From the dead-end choice between low-wage work and crime, to the hollow promises of middle-class integration and uplift, to the fanciful notions of a separate black economy or culture, the Panthers believed that no one had faced the central problem: the sustained reproduction of racism within the exploitative field of capitalist social and economic relations.[80]

This viewpoint would appear to have augured a return to Marxism. Like most of their black nationalist rivals, however, the Panthers believed racism was such a deep and defining contradiction in American life that the probability of blacks and whites united in class struggle toward a socialist revolution was poor. The political challenge, as they understood it, was to define black political subjectivity and a revolutionary sense of black peoplehood in the context of the failure of middle-class and working-class struggles for integration, and of the impossibility of a fully separatist program. In the end, this dualism, which had structured black American politics since Reconstruction, was one they straddled, uneasily. They did so by blurring two positions: emphasizing separation and black difference not in terms of racially defined notions of black nationhood, but in terms of spatially defined communal autonomy built upon local infrastructures of self-help; and redefining integration and equality not as a moment of entry into the American mainstream, but as a commitment of solidarity with all those who defined America's margins and all the victims of Americanism at home and around the world.

The Panthers argued that civil rights leadership had missed the main lesson of anti-imperialism, that the United States was not a nation into which black people could successfully integrate, but an empire they needed to oppose—not a beloved community of shared traditions and aspirations, but a coercive state to be overthrown. The ease with which the black nationalists' emphasis on black culture and black business had been taken up by governing elites showcased its inadequacy as well. "We cannot be nationalists, when our country is not a nation, but an empire," Huey Newton declared. "We have the historical obligation to take the concept of internationalism to its final conclusion—destruction of statehood itself."[81]

Such rhetoric could sound outlandish. But in many ways, the Panthers were simply being faithful to the brilliant utopianism of the black vernacular: they were in search of *the way out of no way*. Taking up the old language of U.S. blacks as "a nation within a nation," they were not deluded that that theirs was a struggle to overthrow territorial colonialism. But they were attempting something no less challenging: to imagine how ordinary black people could make a life on the horns of the American dilemma. As Bobby Seale put it: "We don't see ourselves as a national unit for racist reasons but as a necessity for us to progress as human beings. . . All of us are laboring people—employed or unemployed, and our unity has got to be based on the practical necessities of life, liberty and the pursuit of happiness. It's got to be based on the practical things like the survival of people and people's right to self-determination, to iron out their problems by themselves without the interference of the police or CIA or armed forces of the USA."[82]

Defining themselves as revolutionary nationalists, the Panthers supported national liberation struggles abroad, "while dismissing all forms of nationalism within the US context as necessarily bound up with American oppression."[83] This stance placed them as the black radical group at the center of the broad opposition to the war in Vietnam. Indeed, as one of the few black nationalist formations willing to work closely with white radicals, the Panthers became the domestic relay station for a decolonization that was now imagined not only in geographical terms, but also as a set of common exploitative relationships. Indeed, Newton argued that shifts in the spatial scales of world capitalism had disrupted the organization of nations as integral territorial and ideological units. Defining the United States as an imperial state, the Panthers linked the communal fates of Vietnam and Oakland as different local instances in a struggle against it. What united the peoples of the world—"the black people of Oakland and the Vietnamese"—he wrote, was the "desire to run their own communities."[84]

Intercommunalism was the concept Newton developed to describe an imperialism no longer reliant upon territorial possessions, as well as a deterritorialized conception of liberation, in which small groups like the Panthers could participate with other oppressed "communities," like the Cubans or the Vietnamese. This idea contained a number of implicit, but important, ideas. First, it foresaw the waning of the epochal struggle between capitalism and socialism and the emergence of problems of economic growth and uneven development in the global order.[85] It identified what is now often simply called "globalization" as the universalization of an American model of global governance built upon formal nationhood, free trade, open markets, internal colonization, and international monopolies on the legitimate use of violence. Finally, it proposed a new language of popular struggle at a world scale, translating the old Marxist opposition between the proletariat and the bourgeoisie into an open-ended confrontation between "the people" and the "power bloc."[86]

The Panthers' signature phrase, "All power to the people," and their identification with the Viet Cong emerged from this context, and neither can be dismissed as the product of faulty analogies between U.S. blacks and subjects of colonialism. The local strategy commensurate with this vision was the mobilization of the people of the ghetto, the black youth gangs, ex-convicts, welfare recipients, and the growing populations of black prisoners. The Panthers approached these groups armed with their own form of radical pedagogy, one addressed to the denizens of a myriad of subnational, institutional spaces—the housing project, the school, the community center, and the prison. The Panthers metaphorically tore these spaces out of the nation-state and claimed them as their own, organizing their own schools, asserting the *de facto* autonomy of community organizations, and, most importantly, embracing the prison—already a place of black anti-citizenship—as the exemplary site and source of counter-nationalist theory and practice.[87]

Across the United States, Panther chapters emerged, drawing together community organizers, ex-convicts, juvenile delinquents, and intellectual activists into a tenuous and volatile coalition. In Los Angeles, "Bunchy" Carter, a leader of the Slausons, one of the most feared street gangs, along with John Huggins formed one of the most important Party chapters outside of Oakland. In Chicago, innovative community organizer Fred Hampton established a "rainbow coalition," joining together the Blackstone Rangers, the Young Patriots, and the Young Lords, the city's largest black, white, and Puerto Rican youth gangs. In New York, a young ex-convict, Richard Moore (Dhoruba Bin Wahad), helped to build a Panther chapter with well-organized breakfast programs, tenants' rights projects, and other community-based organizations. Finally, in Soledad, Attica, and several other major prisons, the Panthers developed a widespread following within existing prisoners' organizations and especially within prisoners' rights groups, attracting the gifted and charismatic leader of the prison movement, George Jackson. As Mike Davis has put it, "For a time at least, it looked as if the Panthers might become the nation's largest revolutionary gang."[88]

Soon Los Angeles, Chicago, Soledad, and Attica would be the scenes of the most infamous and bloody confrontations between Party members and sympathizers and federal and local police. In Los Angeles, the FBI worked steadily to foment the already existing antagonism between the Panthers and Ron Karenga's U.S. organization, leading to the shoot-out on the University of California–Los Angeles campus where Carter and Huggins were killed. Fred Hampton and Mark Clark were executed in their bedroom by a squad of Chicago detectives responding to an informant's tip about a weapons cache on the premises. In New York, the infamous Panther 21 were framed on conspiracy charges and eventually acquitted after a costly series of trials. Meanwhile, Moore, one of the initial 21, was convicted for shooting two New York City police officers, a conviction overturned eighteen years later because of false testimony and fabricated evidence. Finally, George Jackson was killed in Soledad prison under suspicious circumstances, several days after his brother, Jonathan Jackson, and two hostages died in a botched escape attempt. Two weeks later, forty-three men were massacred when Attica's prison rebellion (partly inspired by Jackson's death) was crushed by state police forces sent in by New York governor Nelson Rockefeller.[89]

These events demonstrate the depth of state-sanctioned violence against black power radicals. What cannot be overlooked, however, is that in many cases the Panthers hastened their own demise. Throughout their brief history, more responsible Panther leaders were engaged in an ongoing struggle to ensure self-discipline and accountability within the group and to curtail tendencies toward spontaneous, violent confrontation. Although the Panthers correctly understood criminality and violence as socially produced, even quasi-rebellious activities structured by conditions of oppression, this often became a rationalization for continuing covert, market-driven, criminal activities in the name of politics and resistance. The party was subject to violent dissension and conflict within its own ranks that not only left it open to infiltration by police agents and provocateurs, but also destroyed the solidarity and cohesion that was absolutely necessary for survival. Perhaps most important, the Panthers failed the challenge of transforming the criminal consciousness and workless, lumpen-existence into a political organization capable of sustained struggle. In the end, they lost even more in saber-rattling, brinkmanship, and what Fred Hampton termed the "adventuristic, Custeristic" confrontations with the force and violence of the state.[90]

This is not where they had started, however. The Panthers' trademark actions of "picking up the gun" and "patrolling the police" were not initially conceived as preludes to armed revolt. Rather, these were strategic choices and carefully posed challenges to the so-called legitimate forms of state violence that had been all too regularly used within black communities. In particular, Newton and Seale understood the ways that the police had become the primary agents of an official, state-sanctioned racism that had receded from public view. Asserting their own right to organized violence, the Panthers policed the police, emphasizing their adherence to California statute. Invoking the constitutional right to bear arms, employing a logic of policing and the law *against* the police and the law, they sought nothing less than a transvaluation of conventional racist imagery about rampant black crime, turning the police instead into the "symbols of uniformed and armed lawlessness."[91]

The violent demise of the Panthers is best understood when viewed in the context of these initial acts of subversion, namely, the threats they posed to the legitimate violence of the state. Those who wield police power invariably prefer disorganized "criminal" violence to the exemplary, potentially organized violence of political militants. In this sense, the police's hounding, infiltration, and provocation of the Panthers sought out and exposed their weakest tendency: their familiarity with and expectation of violent confrontation with the force of law. As the holders of the monopoly on the legitimate uses of violence, government policing agencies set out to prove that the Panthers were nothing more than street thugs and criminals and that their politics was little more than sham and pretense. Although many contemporary writers seem to take this for granted, J. Edgar Hoover himself knew better, labeling the Party "the greatest threat to the internal security of the country" and directing his COINTELPRO agents to *"destroy what the BPP stands for."*[92] This would only be accomplished when the status quo was restored—in other words, when the "legitimate" violence of the state was once again pitted against the disorganized, avaricious, and self-destructive violence of the street.

Since the 1989 drug-related murder of Huey P. Newton, co-founder of the Black Panther Party, the case of the Panthers has been used to condense prevailing assumptions about the failures of black liberation politics in the late 1960s. Ironically, this is an extension of the way the predominantly white student left, along with the national media, embraced and elevated the Black Panther Party during that time. Both accepted at face value the idea that the Black Panthers were the signifiers for black militancy writ large, along with all of its feared or longed-for radical and subversive energies. The Black Panther was a kind of political crossover artist who came to mediate both official and oppositional relationships to the cultures of black liberation, even as the more complex history and significance of black radical traditions in the United States were left unwritten and unexplored. In this way, the revolutionary synthesis that the Panthers embodied, although now the subject of conservative abuse and radical nostalgia, remains caught in inflated, although essentially superficial, terms.[93]

Groups like the Panthers did not simply arise *ex nihilo* out of the general madness of 1968; they were products of an older and wider black radical and revolutionary imagination.[94] In his introduction to his biography of Huey Newton and the Panther Party, Bobby Seale boiled down the complex of influences that created the Panthers in a story about the naming of his son. "The nigger's name is Malik Nkrumah Stagolee Seale," Malik for Malcolm X, Nkrumah to commemorate the first successful African revolutionary, and Stagolee for the hustler, bad man, and outsider of black folklore.[95] The Panther, too, it should be recalled, was originally the symbol of the drive of the Lowndes County Freedom organization for southern black voting power. To make sense of the Panthers, they must be situated within an intellectual and political history of Afro-America's abject negotiations at the alters of American nationality and citizenship. Like black activists past, what made them special was their ability to bring their claims to a world stage and their abiding mistrust of attempts to domesticate their radicalism.[96]

Projections of Sovereignty

There is a subtler dimension to the Panthers' challenge to state authority, one that may better explain why it engendered such a massive retaliatory response from federal and local police agencies. Clearly, with only a few shotguns and only a handful of members in many Party chapters across the country, the Panthers were not a "real" threat to the organized violence of the state. Yet by the end of the decade at least twenty-four Panthers had been killed by police, with untold numbers dead from internecine violence stoked by the FBI's covert operations, and hundreds jailed in the nationwide campaign to destroy the Party.[97] As Jean Genet, one of the most astute observers of the Panthers during the 1960s, put it, "Wherever they went, the Americans were the masters, so the Panthers would do their best to terrorize the masters by the only means available to them. Spectacle."[98] Although the Panthers may have embraced the Maoist slogan "All power comes from the end of a gun," Genet wrote, they also knew that sometimes "power is at the end of the shadow or image of a gun."[99]

The "shadow of the gun" was more important for the Panthers than actual guns could ever be. This was nowhere better demonstrated than in their famous Sacramento action, where a group of armed Panthers marched on the state legislature to protest the pending passage of a bill that would have outlawed the open carrying of firearms, a bill explicitly aimed at stopping the Panthers' armed patrols. This action, perhaps more than any other, put the party in the national spotlight, with headlines reading "Armed Panthers in the State Capitol." Yet, rather than fleeing in terror or running for cover, the reporters and spectators stopped, looked, and asked questions. The question on everyone's lips was, "Are those guns real?" And "If so, then are they loaded?"[100]

Rather than seeing the Panthers as the vanguard of a visible, guerilla insurgency in the country, they might be better understood as practitioners of an insurgent form of visibility, a literal-minded and deadly serious kind of guerrilla theater, in which militant sloganeering, bodily display, and spectacular actions simultaneously signified their possession and yet real lack of power. The Panthers' emphasis upon self-presentation, in this sense, provided a visual vocabulary that was a key component of their politics. The leather, the clothing, the celebration of black skin and "natural" hair, and, above all, the obtrusively displayed guns were all part of a repertoire of styles, gestures, and rhetorical equations like "black is beautiful" and "power to the people" that at once revalued blackness positively, while at the same time drawing on its threatening powers within the dominant U.S. racial imagination.

In the end, the Panther spectacle was arrayed both against and within the realm of what Harold Cruse called "America's race psychosis," and it is here where it may have registered its deepest, most lasting, and most confusing effects. The immediate power of the Panthers' spectacle was that, for a time at least, it revealed the state's own spectacular and performative dimensions. Indeed, one way to understand the Panthers' performance is to recognize how they literally made a spectacle of governmental authority. The excessive, escalating rhetoric and imagery the Panthers invented or popularized ("off the pig," "the sky's the limit," "fuck Reagan," "two, three, many Vietnams") continuously heightened the anxiety of those charged with the duty of securing the state. Verbally attacked and legally outmaneuvered, the police often found their only recourse was to show that their own power was backed by more than words and empty guns. The bind the Panthers presented to the forces of the state was that if their threats went unanswered, they might be proved right. The emperor would be seen to have no clothes, and America would be revealed as little more than a mask of power—Mao's proverbial paper tiger.

Given the fact that black skin has historically demarcated and condensed what lies outside the protection of the nation-state and its cultures of citizenship and civility, the Panthers' ability to capture the imagination of a broad radical coalition was no mean feat. If the nation is secured through forms of representation, then the definitional struggle waged over its contours by black militants was a serious undertaking, grounded in the historic sense of the separateness of black life in America and a plausible reading of the contemporary world situation. Most important, by challenging the police and aligning themselves with the Vietnamese, the Panthers did not so much challenge the government's monopoly on physical violence as disrupt its ability to nominate and designate normative, national subjects—in other words, its monopoly on legitimate symbolic violence.[101]

If we consider more specifically the sites of government power—the police, border control agencies, diplomatic corps, the military, the public schools, and the other state agencies that "prove" the existence of the state in daily life—each depends in the first instance on the population's belief that there is a legitimate state. The performance of the state, then, is in no way contradicted by its material functions. On the contrary, the very sense that the state is something that actually exists requires the more or less continuous activity of heterogeneous institutions and discourses of state in order to assure us, in Gertrude Stein's phrase, that "there is a there there." This formulation also helps explain why violence is at once liminal to the state and at the same time its most important rhetorical instrument. The constantly reiterated threat of violence—from within and from without—is ultimately what institutes the state as a social relation and form of social meaning we inhabit. Violence threatens to undo the state, but it is also its very condition of possibility.

The Panthers were a threat to the state not simply because they were violent, but because they abused the state's own reality principle. Patrolling the police armed with guns and law books, the Panthers undermined the very notion of policing by performing it, and in effect deforming it, themselves. They recognized that the police were among the most important of the state's "actors," whose repeated performance of their own function was crucial to the institution of the everyday notion of being subject to a national, social state. By refusing to recognize the status of policing as it operated within black communities, the Panthers effectively nullified police power and substituted themselves as its alternative. Policing the police, in other words, the Panthers signaled something far more dangerous than is generally acknowledged: the eruption of a non-state identity into the everyday life of the state. That such a small and relatively poorly trained and equipped band of urban black youth could demand so much attention from federal and local police attests to the tenuousness of the insertion of the state itself and to the degree to which it depends on silencing those who would take its name in vain.

The Panthers were finally engaged in a broad series of acts aimed at subverting the state's official performance of itself, far beyond shadowing the police. Enabled by the multiplication of revolutionary centers around the world, they even pursued their own foreign relations, challenging the state in what is perhaps the most sacred of its constitutive monopolies. Thus, "Minister of Defense" Huey Newton boasted that the Panthers were the only Americans who actually had a foreign policy toward Vietnam and concluded his autobiography by describing how he visited China before President Richard Nixon—the world's reputed master of affairs of state. Pursuing a political strategy made famous by Du Bois, Robert Williams, and Malcolm X, the Panthers went to China, Algeria, Mozambique, Guinea-Bissau, Cuba, and North Korea seeking the authority and authenticity of revolutionaries with states through the internationalist rituals of delegation and diplomacy.[102]

Black power in its revolutionary instance was what Eldridge Cleaver tellingly called "a projection of sovereignty"—a set of oppositional discourses and practices that exposed the hegemony of Americanism as incomplete, challenged its universality, and imagined carving up its spaces differently.[103] The use of the idioms of nationalism and anticolonialism by black power militants was not then precisely analytical. Rather, it suggested a practical deconstruction of the pretensions of nationality and state power (policing, waging war, schooling, diplomacy, and so on) and the ideological and cultural production of black people as an outside that was also inside the nation.

Indeed, in their dramatic performance of black anti-citizenship, the Panthers necessarily constituted wholly different regions of identification.

It must be said, though, that the Panthers were effective in producing themselves in this way because they refused the terms of black inclusion and citizenship in the American polity at precisely the point of their greatest augmentation and reform since the Civil War and Reconstruction, as a result of the Civil Rights Act of 1964, the Voting Rights Act of 1965, and Johnson's War on Poverty programs. It may have been the offer of state-aided integration into civil society and the public sphere that gave such a powerful charge to the Panthers' refusals and contestations.[104] More than anything else, the Panthers resignified blackness in all its geopolitical and intrapsychic density. Their much-discussed and oft-repudiated emphasis on violence may actually have more to do with their repudiation of the imperative of black assimilation itself, namely, the internalization of the frontiers of the nation and the recognition of the United States as the place where black people "have always been—and will always be at home."[105] The Panthers saw integration posed in these terms as a ruse and a trap; they consciously refused its internally hegemonizing logic by remapping the frontiers of their own subjectivity in local and global terms.

Perhaps this turn should not be surprising. The Panthers, no less than the marchers and freedom riders of the early sixties, were engaged in a war of conscience aimed at transfiguring a historical system of black shame into one of pride and empowerment. Both shared a new, global, image-centered stage for insurgent politics. In terms of their spectacular logic, then, the nonviolent protest strategy of the civil rights movement was not exactly the opposite of the explicitly confrontational Panther strategy of "picking up the gun" and patrolling the police. Both attempted to expose the exertions of racist violence on black bodies, and both were attuned to the geopolitics of pride and shame, governing the visual transmission, reception, and interpretation of their spectacular performances.

The civil rights movement was not without its own global analogue and appeal as it engaged the force and violence of the state under the international sign of militant pacifism secured by the successes of Gandhi's nonviolent movement in India. In this context, as Harold Isaacs suggested, "Little Rock" entered a global vernacular and mediascape as the term for American racism and racial strife, with "images of armed soldiers, screaming mobs and Negro children, circulating around the world."[106] Yet, while the absorption of violence by civil rights protesters was predicated on an appeal to the world's conscience, it primarily evoked the desire for national redemption and reconciliation. Finally sending federal troops into Little Rock, Arkansas, in 1957, the previously quiescent Eisenhower indicated that he realized just how potent this logic and imagery had become, justifying his action as one that would reestablish the nation "in the eyes of the world . . . [and] restore the image of America, and all its parts as one nation indivisible."[107]

By contrast, the black liberationists of the late sixties were buoyed by the fact that America's racial fissures had been opened for the world to see. In the midst of dramatic antisystemic movements emanating from Cuba, Algeria, China, and Vietnam, they seized every opportunity to demonstrate that America itself was neither united nor secure. Projecting violence back on the nation, groups like the Panthers fashioned themselves as the avatars of James Baldwin's doomsaying prophecy "the fire next time."[108] Reversing the civil narrative of rights and redemption, they threatened to carve up the nation, defined the black ghetto as a territory to be liberated, and, in a final, brutal mockery, cast the most visible representatives of the state—the police—as "pigs."[109]

Revolts against the established order invariably possess a theatrical dimension. Lacking a significant purchase upon the "real," they can often appear unanchored, self-referential, unintelligible, even immature initially. In retrospect, this may be viewed as a consequence of weakness and even failure, although it is impossible to fully calculate this in advance. This is particularly true when relatively powerless people make utopian demands. For it is precisely the exposure of the enormity of the gap between the rhetoric of freedom, liberation, justice, and equality they embrace, and the rooted realities of economic exploitation, racial domination, and institutional compromise, that establishes creative tension and, in favorable conjunctures, momentum for social change.

In this regard it is not an accident that the explicit turn to black power in the mid-1960s followed the defeat of the initiative by the Mississippi Freedom Democratic Party (MFDP) to gain full recognition at the 1964 Democratic Convention. Challenging the representative credentials of the slate of all-white delegates, the MFDP staked itself upon the audacious, violent campaigns for black voter registration in the previous years to demand nothing less than the full and immediate representation of the black majority in Mississippi, the heartland of American apartheid. Bayard Rustin had urged the MFDP to be mature, accept the compromise of two seats, and claim the token as a victory. Black sharecropper Fanie Lou Hamer's famous complaint, "We didn't come all this way for no two seats," was the refusal to allow a popular radical demand to be transformed into a simulacrum of inclusion.[110]

In a violent, racist society, the struggle for black voting rights exposed the limits of the formal mechanisms of liberal-democracy. Yet, as Ella Baker observed, the question of rights, or "the external barriers to the Negro people's freedom," was not necessarily paramount. Rather, the goal was to get ordinary black people acting "on their own initiative and own decision."[111] At its most prosaic and eloquent, this was the meaning of black power: the refusal to concede the right of black people to take the initiative even under the most unfavorable circumstances. Rather than beginning the decline of the movement, it suggested the deepening of its democratic challenge. Finally, echoing Douglass, Du Bois, King, and countless others, the movement, Baker wrote, was never simply about securing black civil and political rights, but about "the implications of racial discrimination for the whole world."[112]

During his 1984 Rainbow Coalition campaign, Jesse Jackson remarked that black struggles had been the "trigger struggles" for an overall egalitarian expansion of the public sphere in the United States that reached its apogee in the 1960s and 1970s.[113] The Black Panthers never learned key lessons about organizing and decentralized democratic authority that Baker taught in the South. Northern black power frequently foundered upon its internalization and even valorization of harsh, male-centered trials by violence. Yet the Panthers, no less than the MFDP, strained at the coercive boundaries of liberal-democracy with something like the demand for "freedom-democracy." They too asked a broader set of questions about whether American institutions could work for the majority of black people. As the primary relay station for the absorption of the liberatory impulses of decolonization, finally, they were no less powerful or important in extending the chain of black democratic initiative to more and more groups, including

Chicanos, Native Americans, students, and women's and gay liberationists.[114]

This perspective points across the ideological limits and generational divides that have too easily stood in for analysis and interpretation of the long civil rights era. The antithesis of civil rights and black power, integration and separatism, nonviolence and violence, of course, are chief among these. As Harold Cruse clearly recognized, black power was always the question in these years, both how to define its meaning and how to achieve it. Indeed, when we consider the career trajectories of less popularly known figures in the struggle, we see how the conventional labels typically fail us. E. D. Nixon, president of the local NAACP chapter and one of the architects of the 1955 Montgomery bus boycott, began as a Garveyite before joining Randolph's sleeping car porters in the late 1920s. Baker, the master builder of SNCC in the 1960s, began her career in the nationalistic Young Negroes' Cooperative League of the 1930s before she attempted to bring grassroots mobilization to the NAACP as their influential, behind-the-scenes field secretary in the 1940s.[115]

These lessons carried forward as well. The coercive hand of the Cold War could be discerned in early pronouncements of Martin Luther King Jr. about the "amazing universalism" of the American dream and paeans to national unity through shared Judeo-Christian religiosity. The early King liked to list black individuals who had made it in America, from Booker T. Washington to Ralph Bunche, invariably avoiding those identified with collective struggle or political controversy. Precious few years later, though, a King armed with what he called "deeper understanding of . . . laws and lines of development" not only reclaimed Du Bois as a spiritual heir, but also asserted the need for black ideological, economic, and political power to bridge the regional divides of North and South and the gap between "white civilization and the non-white nations of the world."[116]

King's example suggests the difficulty of separating yearnings for black power from the fight for black civil and political rights. The convergence, moreover, could happen from the other side as well. As Malcolm X noted in his famous speech, "The Ballot or the Bullet," questions about the constitutional morality of racial integration or separation had obscured the more important issue of gaining civic recognition and equalizing material distribution. "We'll work with anybody, anywhere, at anytime, who is genuinely interested in tackling the problem head on," Malcolm declared. "We're against a segregated school system. A segregated school system produces children who, when they graduate, graduate with crippled minds. But this does not mean that a school is segregated because it's all black. A segregated school means a school that is controlled by people who have no real interest in it whatsoever."[117]

Even the Black Panther Party, which seized the national and international stage with its ringing declamations about racist police and internal colonies in California's East Bay, were engaged in more prosaic, local initiatives along these lines. Less remarked upon in lore about the Panthers are their "survival programs," which were an attempt to develop a self-sufficient infrastructure of community service and learning, including breakfast programs, sickle-cell anemia testing, and political education classes. By the early 1970s, Panther Party leaders Bobby Seale and Elaine Brown sought effective black public input into metropolitan resource distribution in a credible, grassroots political campaign for Oakland City Council. Once again, even in its most self-consciously revolutionary idiom, black power unfolded both within and against the American grain.

Finally, perhaps most remarkably, an aged Ralph Bunche defended black power. Bunche discerned a new "hesitation about acclaiming the country or even identifying with it" among black urban youth, adding that "even true believers in integration like myself . . . are assailed by unavoidable doubts these days." What Bunche called the new "blackism" had fatefully exposed the "credibility gap" between American ideals and practices, as well as the tokenism of much racial integration. He who had so faithfully mediated this gap and played the part of the token for the better part of his career was now taking sides, describing himself as a "partisan in the black revolution." "Black power," Bunche wrote, coming full circle, "is not a new concept. The need for unity of aim and effort by black Americans is as old as the black man's struggle. The National Negro Congress of the 1930s was, in this sense, a 'Black power movement'." Anticipating a future phase, Bunche pushed younger black activists to cast their global vision even wider and to propel "the tragic plight of many millions of black people in the Union of South Africa under Apartheid" into the court of world opinion.[118]

Few were listening to Bunche by this point, just as few remembered those such as Du Bois and Robeson with whom he had once clashed.

Casting the plumb line of black radicalism across the long civil rights era is not to gainsay the extraordinary complexity of negotiating the internal divides within black movements, the powerful obstacles posed by entrenched white supremacy, and the manipulations of the national security state. Much of the radical past was shrouded in these years and needed to be relearned or reinvented from whole cloth. Younger black activists and intellectuals faced a steep learning curve. The dilemmas of generational reproduction of activist agendas were heightened considerably by unplanned, intensifying protest, domestic countersubversion, assassination, and the overall pace of social change around the world. The more radical aspirations for African American unity voiced by both Malcolm X and King at the end of their lives was undermined from both within and without by violent clashes with police, internal conflicts, and rivalries. The FBI played a particularly nefarious role, exploiting and exacerbating existing tensions in the interest of ensuring that no broadly unifying black leaders or organizations would emerge.

If the cautious, integrationist approach of organizations like the NAACP and the SCLC tended to be caught in restrictive nets of political accommodation, self-styled heirs of Malcolm X like the Black Panthers may have learned too late and at too high a price the political lessons of patience, forbearance, and compromise. Yet the fact that policy elites noted with alarm the excessively egalitarian assertions of democracy, and the fact that the "black movement had as surprising a resonance abroad as at home," points to an obvious question.[119] How could a relatively small band of revolutionary black youth like the Panthers assume national and global importance in the first place? In contrast to much written on the subject, the efforts of late 1960s black power radicals to enlarge a narrow vision of civil rights into an expansive, if ultimately more ambiguous, struggle for internal decolonization was resonant because it kept faith with unfinished struggles of the past and raised questions about the future that are still being reckoned and have yet to be settled.

Conclusion: Racial Justice beyond Civil Rights

Their public, which was formerly scattered, became compact.

—FRANTZ FANON, "ON NATIONAL CULTURE" (1959)

At the dawn of the twentieth century, in the shadow of the failure of Reconstruction in the United States, W. E. B. Du Bois stood before the first Pan-African Congress held in London and presented the then-revelatory formulation that racial hierarchy and colonial domination were aspects of the same historical condition. "The problem of the twentieth century," he stated, "is the problem of the color line."[1] A few years earlier, in front of the American Negro Academy, Du Bois delivered his widely known paper "The Conservation of Races" (1897). Addressing his audience in black nationalist tones, Du Bois spoke for "his people" with whom he was "bone of the bone and flesh of the flesh"—those he would later describe as living within the Veil.[2] Without attacking the global problems of racism and empire directly, Du Bois emphasized that "the Negro people as a race, have a contribution to make to civilization and humanity which no other race can make."[3]

As he composed his most famous work, *The Souls of Black Folk* (1903), a few years later, Du Bois deftly combined these two distinct appeals in his searching examination of the racial condition of the United States in the post-Emancipation era. Advocating neither assimilation and its consequent erasure of "Negro" distinctiveness, nor the preservation of an absolutist and damaging conception of black difference, he doggedly attacked the color line while refusing to denigrate those who had lived their lives within it and had been defined by it. Subtly blending the civilizationist appeals of nineteenth-century black nationalism with an insistence on what Albert Murray has called the "incontestably mulatto" character of American culture, Du Bois effectively negotiated the double-bind presented by American racism at the turn of the century.[4] Resisting both segregationist *and* assimilationist tendencies, he instead asked that the nation and the world recognize the freed slave as a "co-worker in the kingdom of culture."[5]

This work of a century ago marks the beginning of one man's immense discursive labor of racial reconstruction, spanning the decades of postemancipation disfranchisement and imperial conquest, the subsequent era of decolonization, and the modern civil rights movement.

In the intervening years, Du Bois deepened and broadened his activist intellectual challenge to imperialism and racism. First, he saw that the symbolic struggles for black rights and recognition within the nation-state could not be separated from material struggles over distribution. This led him to progressivism and eventually to socialism. At the same time, Du Bois soon recognized that American socialists failed to address the interconnected problems of democracy and racism. Understanding nationalism only in terms of class oppression made them underestimate the importance of the struggle for democracy on the part of the disfranchised. Underestimating the power of racism led them to a *de facto* acceptance of the national purpose when it appeared consistent with working-class aspirations.

As Du Bois understood it, the problem was that in the United States, nationalism was captive to a racial pattern. This was clearer once the labor question was viewed from the perspective of the wider world. Capitalism had led not to a leveling among working people as Marxism predicted, but to uneven development within the global economy. Global economic expansion and upward mobility for a sector of the European and American labor force had been purchased at the price of their class-consciousness and their (both knowing and unwitting) enlistment in exploitation elsewhere—what he referred to as "the miserable modern subjugation of over half the world."[6] Emerging from the crucible of southern underdevelopment, international labor migration, imperial scramble, world war, and revolution, Du Bois believed that the post-Emancipation struggles of blacks afforded a unique angle of vision on this problem. In "the philosophy of life and action which slavery bred," as he described it in *Black Reconstruction,* Du Bois saw not the deficiencies typically counted by the sociologist cum pathologist, but the outlines of a radical democratic vision that confronted national capitalism with "the real modern labor problem," the struggle of a racialized world.[7]

Du Bois never lost his early sense that blacks had a contribution to make *as a race.* This has led some contemporary thinkers to suggest that he was a committed racialist to the end of his life.[8] This is a distorting view. Du Bois retained a commitment to race as the dialectical challenge to modern racism, just as Marxists retained class as the dialectical challenge to modern capitalism. He never conceded his faith in radical Enlightenment universals of human freedom and equality. However, he recognized that these universals had been elaborated *within* and not against the European and American racialization of the world. Du Bois embraced freedom and equality not as shibboleths, but as unattained ideals disconnected from human lives lived under racist conditions. Finally, he perceived that those subjected to racism had—against the very negativity and limits of their experience—elaborated self-sustaining, positive styles of being that held within them a truer apprehension of the meaning of freedom.

Du Bois's writings from the 1930s, in their unfamiliar, Marxian patois, are rarely read seriously today. Yet they contain a worldly and radical vision that would remain stubbornly central to the long civil rights era. From the 1930s to the 1970s, blacks developed broad and coherent challenges to the racist limitations of U.S. democracy. In doing so, they consistently found themselves straining at both the borders of the U.S. nation-state and the boundaries of its liberal creed. This interpretation directly challenges conventional wisdom about the (short) civil rights era, which tells us that the mid-1960s were the moment when black people emerged (at long last) as individual subjects of capitalist-liberalism and as formal participants in democratic-nationalism. It is not that the latter story is untrue. It is simply that it cannot provide a full picture of the genuine creativity and political gravity of black movements during this period, nor of the ultimate defeat of their most profound, animating visions.

What may be most remarkable about the long civil rights era is the emergence of black people as a distinct people and a public—and the concomitant development of race as a political space.[9] There was no precedent for this in the liberal-democratic narrative of nationhood that explained how they needed to progress. Segregation, it must be remembered, envisioned the preservation of race precisely as a depoliticized space. Racial integration, which emerged to prominence in the era of reform that began under the New Deal, envisioned the disappearance of race as a meaningful political category. Social struggles born of black communal existence gave the lie to such an easy dichotomy. In doing so, they not only mounted a definitive challenge to white supremacy at home, but also established race as a framework from which to enlarge upon the public meanings of words like "freedom" and "democracy" within the wider world.

The extraordinary sense of shared circumstance and common fate that scattered black populations mobilized during this period was of course constantly fragmenting along class, region, and ideological lines, and by the 1960s, along gender lines as well. Their expansive expressions of affiliation with peoples around the world from Ethiopia to Congo to Cuba and Vietnam were routinely ignored or actively discouraged by the players with significant power. And their achievements, when they were recorded, quickly became a tributary of American largesse and magnanimity. There is nothing new about this phenomenon. The unity and initiative of subaltern and stateless peoples have always been imperiled, from within by the unexamined exclusions and aspirations for higher status that sunder solidaristic connections inside the group, and from without by those for whom democratic mobilizations are an irritant to social stability and existing patterns of privilege.[10]

Yet from the contemporary standpoint the loss of broader imperatives, expansive visions, and communal initiative of the black counterpublic is palpable. Standing in the denouement of the Second Reconstruction in the United States, successful black individuals like Colin Powell who have so definitively made it in America rise before us (once again) as proof of the end of America's tortured racial dialectic.[11] Many historical supporters of black struggles now argue that liberals and leftists must put aside the obsessions with race questions, since by aligning themselves with antiracist reform, they have done little more than alienate a silent majority of Americans and initiate a backlash that has pushed this country on a more or less continuous rightward course since the late 1960s.[12] Meanwhile, on the ascendant right, it is imagined that the legacies of antiracism (that is, antipoverty programs, affirmative action, minority set-aside programs, and voting rights legislation) are the real obstacles to achieving a truly color-blind America as well the crutches that continue to hinder black boot-strap self-discipline and progress.[13]

Such arguments represent the appropriation and dissolution of many of the political and intellectual gains of black struggles over the past century. Indeed, Harold Cruse may have been close to the truth when he predicted in 1968 "that when the legal redress in civil rights reaches the point of saturation *de jure,* the civil righters will then be disarmed and naked in the spotlight of adverse power."[14] Cruse argued that liberal individualistic conceptions of racial integration underestimated the extent to which racially defined collectivity was part of the American life-world. Rather than withering away, it was constantly being redefined by state institutions, market forces, and the everyday practices of racialized subjects. At the same time, the civil rights view overestimated the universalizing propensities of the nation-state and thus failed to grasp how antiblack racism was always a latent force in the nationalization of the individual and the creation of the citizen-subject. Proof of this, he argued, was that the dismantling of the formal vestiges of apartheid was routinely twinned with disciplinary accounts ascribing black deviation from national norms to the poverty of black culture and inherent pathologies of black socialization.

It is important to acknowledge that the central achievement of the civil rights movement, namely, the formal conquest of citizenship rights by African Americans, appears in retrospect as a less than partial victory. This was recognized by civil rights activists working in the South surprisingly early as nonviolent efforts to expand black voting power were thwarted in Birmingham; Albany, Georgia; and by the national Democratic Party machine.[15] This became even more apparent when the movement faced the durable obstacles of *de facto* apartheid in northern cities and suburbs. It has become even clearer today, as whatever value accrues to formal citizenship depreciates under the pressures of inegalitarian distribution and is remanded under the auspices of excessive policing and punishment. Perhaps the most disturbing fact of the current period is the structural and political reconstitution of racial alterity with the decimation of urban aid programs and the concomitant expansion of a prison-industrial complex. The latter processes have been ideologically mirrored and justified by the replenishing of age-old national fantasies about the black anticitizenry, today populated by criminals, drug users, predatory youth, teen mothers, and welfare queens.[16]

One does not need to follow Cruse into a doctrinaire black nationalism to recognize that the political demand for color-blindness, heard from all quarters of American public opinion today, is a product of the steady erasure of the legacy of unfinished struggles against white supremacy. It is also inadvertently an apt description of how racism itself persists in many of its forms, but in ways we now have great difficulty seeing. Overall indices of black political representation and economic prosperity have undoubtedly risen since the 1960s. Yet, when we scratch the surface, it still bleeds. Despite the growth of a black middle-class, three decades after the passage of the civil rights act, the median net worth of whites—which includes inherited assets as well as income—is a staggering twelve times that of blacks. Black unemployment rates during this period have remained in double-digits and have not fallen to less than twice the rate among whites since 1976. Even with the decline in the overall number of blacks living beneath the poverty line, the black urban poor comprise approximately one-quarter of the black population, and one million black people are in jails and prisons. Three decades after the passage of the Voting Rights Act, one in seven black men is barred from voting due to felony disenfranchisement laws, many of which date from the high era of southern white supremacy. Blacks are 12.5 percent of the population and yet 40 percent of inmates on death row. Blacks are seven times more likely to be murdered than whites, yet of the last 840 people executed in America, 80 percent have been executed for killing a white person. Admission to college and professional schools, one of the few places where black gains have steadily registered with the aid of affirmative action, is now under sustained attack. Black life, in short, remains simply less valuable than white life.[17]

An important response to the perils of poverty and prison facing a significant sector of the black population today asserts that deepening economic inequality has yielded patterns of intra-racial class polarization.[18] This suggests the broader point that there is no longer a black counter-public as such: the gains made by middle-class blacks have eroded the significance and salience of race as a political category. In an influential body of work, William Julius Wilson (taking a cue from 1930s radicals such as Franklin Frazier and Ralph Bunche) argues that the best way forward is to renew a national-social compact around the fight for economic justice and economic democracy. Such a campaign should be based on a thorough demonstration of the fact that the vast majority of U.S. citizens experience stagnant wages, more job insecurity, and longer working hours than preceding generations of American workers. In stark contrast to the putative "golden age" of the U.S. welfare-state following World War II, the last quarter-century of job growth and economic expansion in the United States has been accompanied by rising inequality, lower rates of unionization, and declining wages.[19]

In an argument that has become commonplace among leftists and progressives, Wilson claims that "the focus on racial differences" obscures "the common economic problems" that the vast majority of Americans face in a globalizing economy.[20] The revival of a political impetus toward reformist, liberal social and economic policies will help African Americans, but it can only win broad public assent if it is framed as a universal appeal to the economic needs and interests of a multiracial, national majority. Wilson, in other words, calls for the resuscitation of the reformist liberal project that was arrayed under the banner of Keynesianism (i.e., partially redistributive economics), in which capitalist practice (in the developed zones of the world economy) was in some measure accountable to the social needs of laboring populations defined in national-popular terms. He suggests that success renewing this project in the United States will entirely depend on the strength that a progressive social movement possesses to impose its political will at the level of the nation-state. Because economics defines his concept of social needs, and the nation-state defines his frame and horizon of effective reform politics, he argues, such a movement can succeed only if it rejects divisive and impractical vocabularies of race.

The partial liberation of transnational corporations from the limited regulatory regimes (taxation, environmental, and labor standards) imposed by the world's most powerful nation-state raises difficult questions about how such frankly nationalist social policies and economic development strategies might be instituted in the current context. Setting this aside for the moment, what if Wilson's argument is exactly backwards? What if the political lesson of the long civil rights era is that we advance equality only by continually passing through a politics of race and by refusing the notion of a definitive "beyond" race? Indeed, across U.S. history the promise of economic and political democracy has been limited precisely by what might be called racist uses of race. The historic denial of black voting rights, like today's racially coded withdrawals of social welfare provision and carceral solutions to social problems, have disenfranchised and disempowered numerically far greater numbers of nonblack citizens and residents. Conversely, protections granted under the Civil Rights Act of 1964 and affirmative action programs have protected and enhanced the life chances of broad majorities within the society, including women, the elderly, and the disabled.

Throughout the post–World War II period, blacks have been the single group in the United States whose politics have regularly gone beyond narrow self-interest and aimed at broad expansions of social as well as civil rights.[21] In the early 1940s, C. L. R. James argued that black struggles for "bourgeois" civil and political rights should not be viewed as a concession that the left made to Negroes, but as a direct part of the struggle for socialism. James, like Du Bois, recognized that not only could racism *not* be separated from accumulated patterns of material inequality, but also that by virtue of the experience of chattel slavery and the struggle against Jim Crow, black people had deepened the participatory basis and radicalized the intellectual connotations of democracy beyond its typical "liberal" qualifications.

Chicago congressman Jesse Jackson Jr. recently amplified this point: "When we see history through the lens of race, when we understand how the Constitution and our whole political system evolved to maintain the power of white slaveholders, then we are finally freed to speak to the American people in the language of economy."[22] Indeed, it is worth remembering that the 1863 Emancipation Proclamation that freed the slaves was also the largest uncompensated appropriation of private property in United States history. It is arguable that a politics of race has been at the center of every major invention and reinvention of American radicalism, from abolitionism, feminism, and populism to the rise of the CIO, the Popular Front, and the New Left and the struggles for multicultural democracy in our own time.[23]

The argument becomes more and not less powerful when the global dimension is taken into account. From an immanent critique of American claims to universality, and the implicit and explicit forms of racism it has routinely upheld, black activists and intellectuals have cast their understanding of justice in terms of the global reach of the color-line. Colonies were "the slums of the world," Du Bois wrote in 1945, just as black power radicals two decades later declared black slums to be America's "internal colonies." From the vision of a peoples' century during World War II to the revolutionary intercommunalism of the sixties, the one consistency of the black political imagination across its ideological and generational divides has been its combination of grassroots insurgency and global dreams. Perhaps it will only be by again inventing forms of politics, solidarity, and identification linking the local and global scales of human oppression that we will be able to address the increasingly obvious inadequacies of the modern nation-state as a vehicle of democratic transformation and egalitarian distribution for the world's peoples.

The failure to recognize the theoretical depth, the political stakes, and the significance of black radical theorizing across the long civil rights era testifies to the triumph of New Deal and Cold War racial liberalism. In *An American Dilemma*, Gunnar Myrdal gave the fullest exposition of this view. In assuming its proper role as world leader, Myrdal argued, the United States was finally completing "the main trend in its history . . . the gradual realization of the American Creed."[24] From this perspective, black leaders were to be afforded symbolic recognition within a system of elite brokerage politics aimed at the eventual disappearance of so-called race relations within "normal" civic structures of class, party, and nation. This further entailed the channeling of black democratic demands into institutionalized forms of national belonging and, barring that, into instituted zones of social marginality. Indeed, it is not an accident that the military and the prison emerged from this period as the most racially integrated institutions in contemporary America. What this suggests (among other things) is that the ineluctable connection between racism and state violence remains alive and well, and that black bodies continue to bear the brunt of this association.

From inside the early Cold War, such key black intellectuals as Richard Wright and Ralph Ellison challenged the Myrdallian view. As Ellison pointed out, Myrdal and others who proposed that the American Creed held all the solutions to racism and racial subjection operated under the arrogant delusions of their universal visions. As a result, they could scarcely apprehend the fact that black people, in Ellison's words, had "made a life on the horns of the white man's dilemma."[25] "Isn't it clear to you," Richard Wright asked defiantly from his own, self-imposed exile in France during the Cold War, "that the American Negro is the only group in our nation that consistently and passionately raises the question of freedom?"[26] In an ironic formulation, Wright inverted the emphasis of *An American Dilemma* to cast the problem of American universalism from the vantage point of the black, the oppressed, and the unfree. "The history of the Negro in America is the history of America written in vivid and bloody terms . . . the history of Western Man writ small . . . The Negro is America's metaphor."[27]

Wright and Ellison were the intellectual products of black mass recalcitrance during World War II. Indeed, even against the fear and conservatism of the Cold War, Ellison prophetically mused about whether the angry and severe young black men and women, barely a generation removed from the South, cut loose in the city with their "swinging shoulders in too hot for summer suits" might not be "the saviors, the true leaders, the bearers of something precious" that even they did not yet fully understand.[28] By the 1960s, such youth were in revolt against the normative staging of race within American culture. As Wright anticipated, the extension of black struggles beyond the United States had strained the nation-form and with it, the self-assurance that American self-identity transcended and subsumed racial difference. The "violence" of the 1960s stemmed from the frontal challenges blacks posed to the consensus of Cold War civil rights. For a time at least, it seemed as though black people refused racial abjection and seized control of their racial assets. From James Brown's galvanizing "Say It Loud, I'm Black and I'm Proud" to the redolent phrase "Black Is Beautiful," from the startling imagery of bare feet and black fists raised in protest at the Mexico City Olympic Games to the oxymoronic saliency of the black power concept itself, the cultural politics of the 1960s were centered around a series of dramatic transvaluations of blackness.[29]

The most far-seeing theoreticians of black power understood that the symbolic equality enshrined in citizenship would provide little genuine sustenance for working-class racial migrants and do little to counteract the ravages of racial capitalism that had systematically underdeveloped black America.[30] They recognized that even as the legal edifice of segregation was being dismantled by government decree, a much more enduring and pervasive structure of spatial apartheid had been inscribed into the social landscape as the divide between urban ghettos and suburban idyll. For just as Jim Crow subjugated blacks in the South, the black migrants who came North between World War I and the 1960s had their life chances curtailed and confined by racial separation violently enforced by riot, pogrom, hate strike, restrictive covenants, urban renewal, red-lining, and block-busting.[31] Thus, the most radical instances of black power rhetoric—declarations like "the city is the black man's land," or variations on the idea of the black ghetto as an "internal colony"—might actually be seen as reflections upon the fact that few social groups in human history have experienced the depth and duration of residential segregation that has been imposed upon black internal migrants within the United States.

If there was a flaw in the idea of the ghetto as an internal colony, it is that its prospects for liberation were always slim. Today, the options are fewer: a lucky escape, low-wage austerity, premature death, and prison. The ghettoization of racial migrants in the United States might in this sense be more fruitfully compared to neocolonialism. Just as the formal rights of statehood and self-government have provided few, if any, answers to enduring global patterns of inequality, exploitation, and oppression that plague the peoples of many of the world's former colonies, formal citizenship rights have not delivered economic opportunity and political empowerment for a significant proportion of U.S. blacks. For the people of the ghetto, the internalization of neocolonialism reveals that the substance, if not the very notion, of common citizenship no longer holds sway (if indeed it ever did). As South Central Los Angeles community activist Lillian Mobely put it more succinctly: "No one is prepared for them to live, but they are prepared for them to die."[32]

The visionary tactician of the civil rights movement, Bayard Rustin, argued that the essentially revolutionary character of black struggle was manifested by the fact that it had done more to "democratize life for whites than for Negroes" in the United States. Rustin believed this assured its future success, since "economic interests were more fundamental than prejudice" and poor whites realized the "loss of social security" was not worth "a slap at the Negro." He chastised the "new militants" and advocates of black power for being hyperbolic moralists rather than political realists. Reflecting on Lyndon Johnson's landslide defeat of Barry Goldwater in 1964, Rustin argued that the political turning point was at hand, that time was ripe for complete victory. He went on to envision a future in which the majority of blacks and poor whites would reconstitute the Democratic Party (especially in the South), leaving the Republican Party as the "party of economic conservatives and refugee racists."[33]

There is something to be said for Rustin's argument, particularly about the overall democratizing impact of the movement. It would be difficult, however, to imagine an analysis that was more breathtakingly wrong in its conclusions. By fantasizing that the U.S. political economy could simply be lifted out of its racial matrix, Rustin underestimated the cultural and economic investment in white supremacy, for example, among middle- and lower-middle-class homeowners, police, firefighters, and construction workers, as well as rural Southerners, gated-community dwellers, and others whose very market or social locations were quite precisely defined against black encroachment. He therefore did not foresee (or refused to see) the ease with which race (and its codes) could (and would) be used once again to drive a wedge between people at, or near, the bottom of society. Appeals to "law and order," promised crackdowns on criminals and welfare cheats, and moral panics about black teen pregnancy, wilding, gang violence, racial quotas, and falling standards have from the 1968 election onward been part of a concerted (and highly successful) strategy of making the Republican Party the majority party in the United States, refugee racists and all.

Equally significant, Rustin underestimated how the imperial and neocolonial dimensions of U.S. capitalism, so powerfully on display in the war in Vietnam in the late 1960s (and in the war in Iraq today), both relied upon and began to reconstitute the very logic of an antagonistic, racialized world that was supposedly being dismantled. This was not simply an issue of "guns or butter." Rather, it was an issue, to paraphrase Lillian Mobely, of who was being prepared to live and who was being prepared to die (both at home and abroad). The racialization of the world in this sense needs to be understood as one of the supreme, constituent acts of modern power. It has helped to create and re-create "caesuras" in human populations at both national and global scales that have been crucial to the political management of populations by nation-states ever since. To understand this, we need to recognize the technology of race as something more than skin color or biophysical essence, but precisely as those historic repertoires and cultural, spatial, and signifying systems that stigmatize and depreciate one form of humanity for the purposes of another's health, development, safety, profit, and pleasure.[34]

In the face of something so big and powerful, how does one begin to respond? The proliferation of cultural and identity politics since the 1970s is often understood today to be a symptom of the profound disorganization of progressive political forces at the nation-scale. In another sense, however, the disavowal of the nation-form of boundary drawing might be the necessary beginning for any future dismantling of invidious uses of race, especially since race and nation have never been very far apart. The history of the long civil rights era has much to teach us on this score. The black intellectual activists of this subaltern counterpublic left behind a rich legacy of radical visions for imagining coalitions and thinking and feeling beyond the nation-state. Although many of the most representative among them were male and middle-class, invested at times in their own politics of regulation and reputation, the movements they tried to voice were not. The struggles that blacks advanced during this period were not defined by the closure of an essential identity, cultural or national; they were worldly, heterogeneous, insurgent, participatory, and disorderly in ways we desperately need once more. Against the exclusions of the United States as both a nation and an empire, they remind us of the radical threshold of true democracy: the needs and aspirations of an ineluctably differentiated humanity.

Notes

Introduction

1. Martin Luther King Jr., "A Time to Break the Silence" (1967), in James Melvin, ed., *Testament of Hope: The Essential Writings of Martin Luther King Jr.* (Washington, D.C.: Harper & Row, 1986), p. 232.
2. Jervis Anderson, *A. Philip Randolph* (Berkeley: University of California Press, 1986), p. 300.
3. Martin Luther King Jr., *The Trumpet of Conscience* (New York: Harper & Row, 1967), p. 31.
4. King, "A Time to Break the Silence," in *Testament of Hope*, p. 242.
5. "I knew that America would never invest the necessary funds of energies in rehabilitation of its poor so long as adventures like Vietnam continued to draw men and skills and money like some demoniacal destructive suction tube," King, *Trumpet of Conscience*, p. 31.
6. King, "A Time to Break the Silence," in *Testament of Hope*, p. 234.
7. King, "The American Dream" (1961), in *Testament of Hope*, p. 212.
8. King, "A Time to Break the Silence," in *Testament of Hope*, p. 234; Martin Luther King Jr., "Honoring Dr. Du Bois," published as the introduction to W. E. B. Du Bois, *Dusk of Dawn* (New York: Schocken Books, 1968), p. viii.
9. See King, *The Trumpet of Conscience*, p. 31. Also Taylor Branch, "Interview with David Barsamian," *The Progressive* 65 (May 1988): 34–38; Steven Lawson and Charles Payne, *Debating the Civil Rights Movement, 1945–1968* (New York: Rowman and Littlefield, 1998), p. 132. The slogan of the Southern Christian Leadership Conference (SCLC) was "saving the soul of America."
10. King, "I Have a Dream" (1963), in *Testament of Hope*, pp. 217–220.

11. King, "Black Power Defined" (1967), in *Testament of Hope,* p. 312.

12. King, "Where Do We Go from Here" (1968), in *Testament of Hope,* p. 251.

13. The phrase "freedom dreams" comes from Robin Kelley, *Freedom Dreams: The Black Radical Imagination* (Boston: Beacon Press, 2002).

14. "King's life," Taylor Branch writes in his epic study, "is the best and most important metaphor for American history in the watershed postwar years." Taylor Branch, *Parting the Waters: America in the King Years, 1954–1963* (New York: Simon and Schuster, 1988), p. xii. Most significant about King, historian David Hollinger asserts, is that he led a movement of the excluded that also "widened the circle of the we . . . affirming a national American 'we' and the solidarity of black people at the same time." David Hollinger, *Postethnic America: Beyond Multiculturalism* (New York: Basic Books, 1995), p. 171.

15. Branch, *Parting the Waters,* p. 887.

16. Etienne Balibar and Immanuel Wallerstein, *Race, Nation, Class: Ambiguous Identities* (New York: Verso, 1991), p. 86.

17. "King-centric" is Charles Payne's phrase. Charles Payne, *I've Got the Light of Freedom: The Organizing Tradition and the Mississippi Freedom Struggle* (Berkeley: University of California Press, 1995), p. 419. Payne is primarily concerned with challenging the propensity toward "top-down" histories of the movement in which King serves a "normative role" affirming the "general liberalization of post-war America" (421). The approach here shares this critique of a conventional normative framing of the civil rights era, not by rejecting a normative approach altogether, but by showing how black activist thought works to expose the self-limiting, exclusionary, and often violent underpinnings of national norms (i.e., freedom, democracy, tolerance) and to generate more inclusive alternatives.

18. King, "The American Dream," in *Testament of Hope,* p. 208.

19. National Advisory Commission on Civil Disorders (Kerner Commission), *Report* (New York: Bantam, 1968).

20. Thomas Byrne Edsall and Mary D. Edsall, *Chain Reaction: The Impact of Race, Rights, and Taxes on American Policy* (New York: Norton, 1991); Jim Sleeper, *The Closest of Strangers: Liberalism and the Politics of Race in New York* (New York: W. W. Norton, 1990); Harry Ashmore, *Civil Rights and Wrongs: A Memoir of Race and Politics, 1944–1994* (New York: Pantheon Books, 1994); Stephan and Abigail Thernstrom, *America in Black and White: One Nation, Indivisible* (New York: Simon and Schuster, 1997); Tamar Jacoby, *Someone Else's House: America's Unfinished Struggle for Integration* (New York: Free Press, 1998).

21. Thomas Sugrue, *Origins of the Urban Crisis: Race and Inequality in Postwar Detroit* (Princeton, N.J.: Princeton University Press, 1996); George Lipsitz, *The Possessive Investment in Whiteness: How White People Profit from Identity Politics* (Philadelphia: Temple University Press, 1998); Arnold Hirsh, *Making the Second Ghetto: Race and Housing in Chicago, 1940–1960* (Cambridge: Cambridge University Press, 1983).

22. Harold Isaacs, *The New World of American Negroes* (New York: Viking Press, 1963), pp. 13–18.

23. Melvin Oliver and Thomas Shapiro, *Black Wealth/White Wealth: A New Perspective on Racial Inequality* (New York: Routledge, 1995); Michael Brown, *Race, Money and the American Welfare State* (Ithaca, N.Y.: Cornell University Press, 1999).

24. Troy Duster, "The Morphing Properties of Whiteness," in Birgit Brander Rasmussen et al., eds., *The Making and Unmaking of Whiteness* (Durham, N.C.: Duke University Press, 2001), p. 119. The quote is from Lipsitz, *The Possessive Investment in Whiteness*, p. 5.

25. Douglas Massey and Nancy Denton, *American Apartheid: Segregation and the Making of the Underclass* (Cambridge, Mass.: Harvard University Press, 1993).

26. Kim Moody, *Workers in a Lean World: Unions in the International Economy* (London: Verso, 1997), p. 156.

27. Penny Von Eschen, *Race against Empire: Black Americans and Anticolonialism, 1937–1957* (Ithaca, N.Y.: Cornell University Press, 1997); Mary Dudziak, *Cold War Civil Rights: Race and the Image of American Democracy* (Princeton, N.J.: Princeton University Press, 2000).

28. King, "A Testament of Hope," in *Testament of Hope*, p. 313.

29. Kevin Phillips, *The Emerging Republican Majority* (New Rochelle, N.Y.: Arlington House, 1969).

30. Ronald Reagan is quoted in Eric Foner, *The Story of American Freedom* (New York: W. W. Norton, 1994) p. 315; Lipsitz, *The Possessive Investment in Whiteness*, p. 175.

31. The most trenchant contemporary analyst of the new "prison-industrial complex" is Angela Davis. See Angela Davis, *The Angela Davis Reader* (Malden, Mass.: Blackwell Publishing, 1998). Glen Loury, *Anatomy of Racial Inequality* (Cambridge, Mass.: Harvard University Press, 2002), pp. 80–81, 201; Loic Waquant, "From Slavery to Mass Incarceration: Rethinking the Race Question in the U.S.," *New Left Review* 13 (2001): 41–60. Mike Davis, "Who Killed L.A? Political Autopsy," *New Left Review* 197 (1993): 25; Mike Davis, *City of Quartz: Excavating the Future in Los Angeles* (London: Verso, 1990); Lawrence Bobo, "From Jim Crow Racism to Laissez-Faire Racism: The Transformation of Racial Attitudes," in Wendy F. Katkin, Ned Landsman, and Andrea Tyree, eds., *Beyond Pluralism: The Conception of Groups and Group Identities in America* (Urbana: University of Illinois Press, 1998); Adolph Reed, *Class Notes: Posing as Politics and Other Thoughts on the American Scene* (New York: New Press, 2000).

32. Scalia is quoted in Jeffrey Rosen, "The Color-Blind Court," *New Republic* (July 31, 1995): 23.

33. Lani Guinier and Gerald Torres, *The Miner's Canary: Enlisting Race, Resisting Power, Transforming Democracy* (Cambridge, Mass.: Harvard University Press, 2002). Lawrence Bobo has described this as "laissez-faire rac-

ism." See Bobo, "From Jim-Crow Racism to Laissez-Faire Racism." For further developments of this idea see Kimberle Crenshaw, "Race, Reform, and Retrenchment: Transformation and Legitimation in Anti-Discrimination Law," in Kimberle Crenshaw et al., eds., *Critical Race Theory* (New York: New Press, 1995), pp. 103–126. On the defeat of school desegregation see Peter Irons, *Jim Crow's Children: The Broken Promise of the Brown Decision* (New York: Viking, 2002).

34. I am quoting from the five-to-four majority decision penned by Justice Sandra Day O'Connor. "Justices Back Affirmative Action by 5 to 4, but Wider Vote Bans a Racial Point System," *New York Times* (June 24, 2003): A1.

35. *One America in the Twenty-First Century: Forging a New Future* (Washington, D.C.: Advisory Board to the President, 1998); Nikhil Pal Singh, "Notes on a Nominal Report," *Souls: A Critical Journal of Black Politics, Culture and Society* 1(3) (1998): 45–52.

36. William Julius Wilson, *The Bridge over the Racial Divide: Rising Inequality and Coalition Politics* (New York: Russell Sage Foundation, 1999), p. 19; "Blacks Lose Better Jobs as Middle-Class Work Drops," *New York Times* (July 12, 2003): A1.

37. The recent overturning of the 1989 convictions of five black youths in New York's infamous "Central Park Jogger" rape case is revealing on this score. This case exemplifies the human costs of the racially invidious fantasies and media orchestrated panics that in the postsegregation era have in many ways hardened antiblack beliefs and policies. Widely viewed at the time as an instance of an epidemic of "wilding" by unsupervised black youths, the case was decided in the tabloid court of public opinion even before the trial. Despite a lack of forensic evidence, police misconduct, and confessions riddled with inconsistencies, the youths were convicted. It has now come to light that a lone serial rapist committed the crime and the youths have been freed. Against a false naiveté about why the youths confessed to crimes they did not commit that once again blames the victims, it is important to reckon the extent of the damage done, not just in terms of the five young lives lost to prison for the past thirteen years, but to our social capacity to transform the distorting powers of racialized reason.

38. The term "racial formation" is useful for discussing "race" as a symbolic and structural category rather than a set of unchanging biological characteristics or essences. It suggests that racial demarcation, at least in the modern United States, is coextensive with the social formation itself. In other words, racial marking is a signifying practice whose effects are registered across central aspects of our common social life and social relations (i.e., economic class, gender, sexuality, and political participation) that might otherwise appear neutral with respect to race. Finally, the idea of a "formation" suggests that racial practice has a historical dimension, and it changes over time in relationship to economic, social, and political forces. "The effort must be made," write Michael Omi and Howard Winant, "to under-

stand race as an unstable and decentered complex of social meanings constantly being transformed by political struggle." Michael Omi and Howard Winant, *Racial Formation in the United States: From the 1960s to the 1980s* (New York: Routledge & Kegan Paul, 1986), p. 68. Also see Evelyn Brooks Higginbotham, "African American Women's History and the Metalanguage of Race," *Signs* (Winter 1992): 255.

39. Quoted in Thernstrom and Thernstrom, *America in Black and White,* p. 11.
40. Ibid., p. 158.
41. King, "A Testament of Hope," in *A Testament of Hope,* p. 314.
42. Ibid., p. 316.
43. Ibid., p. 317.

1. Rethinking Race and Nation

1. "Jacob Lawrence Retrospective," Henry Art Gallery at the University of Washington, Seattle, 1998.
2. A note on usage: by using the term "racialized" I want to suggest the active sense of racial demarcation as a signifying practice that inscribes its effects within social relations and social history.
3. This can be understood as an instance of the production of what Adrienne Rich has called singular universals. Adrienne Rich, *On Lies, Secrets, and Silence: Selected Prose, 1966–1978* (New York: Norton, 1979), p. 35.
4. The Negro History movement was pioneered by Carter G. Woodson's Association of Negro Life and History (ASNLH) founded in 1915.
5. Like the Migration series, *Struggle* was to have sixty panels, of which Lawrence only completed thirty. "Over the Line: The Art of Jacob Lawrence," Seattle Art Museum, April–May, 2003.
6. Ross Posnock, "Before and After Identity," *Raritan 15* (Summer 1995): 101–102. Also see David Hollinger, "Nationalism, Cosmopolitanism and the United States," in Noah Pickus, ed., *Immigration and Citizenship in the 21st Century* (Lanhan, Md.: Rowman and Littlefield, 1998), pp. 85–99.
7. John Higham, "Multiculturalism and Universalism: A History and Critique," *American Quarterly* 44 (Winter 1992): 197.
8. Philip Gleason, "American Identity and Americanization," in W. Petersen, M. Novak, and P. Gleason, eds., *Concepts of Ethnicity* (Cambridge, Mass.: Harvard University Press, 1980), pp. 62–63. Gleason is quoted in Rogers Smith, *Civic Ideals: Conflicting Visions of Citizenship in U.S. History* (New Haven, Conn.: Yale University Press, 1997), p. 14.
9. Bruce Ackerman, *We the People: Foundations* (Cambridge, Mass.: Harvard University Press, 1991). For a strong defense of American ideology as Christian-derived liberalism demonstrating an unprecedented capacity to mediate tensions between liberty and equality, see James Kloppenberg, *The Virtues of Liberalism* (New York: Oxford University Press, 1998).
10. Ackerman, *We the People,* p. 3.

11. Todd Gitlin, "From Universality to Difference: Notes on the Fragmentation of the Idea of the Left," *Contention*, vol. 2, no. 2 (Winter, 1993): 24. Also see Todd Gitlin, *The Twilight of Common Dreams: Why America Is Wracked by Culture Wars* (New York: Metropolitan Books, 1995), p. 88.

12. Paine is quoted in Eric Foner, *The Story of American Freedom* (New York: W. W. Norton, 1998), p. 15. Also see Arthur Schlesinger Jr., *The Disuniting of America: Reflections on a Multicultural Society* (New York: W. W. Norton, 1992), p. 138.

13. Rogers Smith, *Civic Ideals*, p. 31; Etienne Balibar, "Racism as Universalism," in *Masses, Classes, Ideas* (New York: Routledge, 1994); Warren Montag, "The Universalization of Whiteness," in Mike Hill, ed., *Whiteness: A Critical Reader* (New York: New York University Press, 1997), pp. 281–294; David Theo Goldberg, *Racist Culture: Philosophy and the Politics of Meaning* (Cambridge: Blackwell Publishers, 1993).

14. Etienne Balibar and Immanuel Wallerstein, *Race, Nation, Class: Ambiguous Identities* (New York: Verso, 1991), p. 93. Ideologies of racial and ethnic belonging gain their force in the context of, and not in contradistinction to, universalizing properties of nationalism, precisely as a way of inventing tradition, or as Balibar puts it, "creating lived ties and affects and common evidences among people in a society where . . . kinship has ceased to be a central social structure." Balibar, "Racism as Universalism," p. 201. Also see Benedict Anderson, *Imagined Communities: Reflections on the Origins and Spread of Nationalism* (New York: Verso, 1990).

15. Etienne Balibar, "Ambiguous Universalism," *Differences* (Spring 1995): 61–2.

16. David Hollinger, *Post-Ethnic America: Beyond Multiculturalism* (New York: Basic Books, 1995), p. 19.

17. Ross Posnock, *Color and Culture: Black Writers and the Making of the Modern Intellectual* (Cambridge, Mass.: Harvard University Press, 1998), p. 12.

18. "Multiracism" helps to convey the manifold, multiple, and flexible uses of racist ascription and projection within U.S. history. It is a term I borrow from Vijay Prasad, "Bruce Lee and the Anti-Imperialism of Kung-Fu: A Polycultural Adventure," *Positions* 11(1) (2003): 51–90.

19. Edmund Morgan, *American Slavery, American Freedom* (New York: W. W. Norton, 1975); Francis Jennings, *The Invasion of America: Indians, Colonialism and the Cant of Conquest* (New York: W. W. Norton, 1975); Matthew Frye Jacobson, *Whiteness of a Different Color: Immigrants and the Alchemy of Race* (Cambridge, Mass.: Harvard University Press, 1998), p. 25; Cheryl I. Harris, "Whiteness as Property," in Kimberle Crenshaw et al., eds., *Critical Race Theory* (New York: New Press, 1995), pp. 276–292.

20. "Liberty," according to the Lockean definition from which Jefferson drew, was a natural right that stemmed from man's capacity for reason. The an-

swer to the question, "What is freedom?," in other words, was preceded
by answering the question, "What is man?," which is where racialization
enters. Thomas Jefferson, *Notes on the State of Virginia* (New York: Harper
and Row, 1964), pp. 132–134.

21. Foner, *The Story of American Freedom*, p. 39. Also see Jacobson, *Whiteness
of a Different Color*, p. 22.

22. J. Hector St. John Crevecoeur, *Letters from an American Farmer*, ed. Albert
E. Stone (London: Penguin, 1986), p. 68. Also see Ned Landsman, "Plural-
ism, Protestantism and Prosperity: Crevecoueur's American Farmer and the
Foundations of American Pluralism," in Ned Landsman et al., eds., *Beyond
Pluralism: The Conception of Groups and Group Identities in America*
(Chicago: University of Illinois Press, 1998), p. 114.

23. David Hollinger, "How Wide the Circle of 'We,' American Intellectuals and
the Problem of the Ethnos since World War II," *American Historical Review* 57 (Spring 1993): 318.

24. The fullest account of this is Jacobson, *Whiteness of a Different Color.*

25. James Madison eloquently captured the different ways the multiracist imagination was shaped in relation to blacks and Indians. "Next to the case of
the black race within our bosom, that of the red on our borders is the
problem most baffling to the policy of our country." Michael Rogin has
suggested that borders and bosoms suggest the different racist regimes, tactics, and imaginings applied to blacks and Indians. If blacks represented a
type of embodiment and productivity that needed to be repressed and harnessed, then Indians represented a threat of madness or regression that
needed to be exterminated or expelled. Madison is quoted in Michael P.
Rogin, *Fathers and Children: Andrew Jackson and the Subjugation of the
American Indian* (New York: Knopf, 1975), p. 319.

26. Jefferson, *Notes on the State of Virginia*, p. 134.

27. Smith, *Civic Ideals*, p. 133.

28. Jacob Lawrence, *Harriet Tubman* series, panel #2. The position of free
blacks demonstrated even better how race defined an underlying condition
of citizenship as state after state in the North began to restrict the political
rights of black populations living within them. This was codified in the famous 1857 *Dred Scott* decision, in which Supreme Court Justice Roger
Taney asserted that blacks possessed "no rights which the white man was
bound to respect." Jacobson, *Whiteness of a Different Color*, p. 27.

29. Eric Lott, *Love and Theft: Blackface Minstrelsey and the American
Working-Class* (New York: Oxford, 1993); Alexander Saxton, *The Rise
and Fall of the White Republic* (New York: Verso, 1990).

30. Saxton, *The Rise and Fall of the White Republic*, p. 259; Barbara Fields,
"Racism in America," *New Left Review* 181 (1990): 95–118.

31. Here I am quoting David Roediger who argues that modern racism in the
United States developed prominently from working-class meditations upon
the loss of republican freedoms: the "American heritage of artisan egalitari-

anism," in a society marked by increasing class division in the North and racial slavery in the South. The conflation of whiteness and freedom, he suggests, established "herrenvolk republicanism" as the primary language of class in nineteenth-century America. David Roediger, *The Wages of Whiteness* (New York: Verso, 1991), p. 57. Leon Litwack describes white supremacy as part of "universal American convictions" in the nineteenth-century. See Leon Litwack, *North of Slavery: The Negro in the Free States, 1790–1860* (Chicago: University of Chicago Press, 1961), p. vii.

32. Chantal Mouffe, *The Democratic Paradox,* (New York: Verso, 2000), p. 12.

33. Quoted in Rayford Logan, *The Negro in American Life and Thought, 1877–1901: The Nadir* (New York: Collier, 1965), p. 7.

34. Alexander Saxton has suggested that one way to understand U.S. history is through the periodic oscillations of hard and soft forms of racism. The virtue of this account is that it acknowledges the heterogeneity and plurality of racisms, while keeping sight of the way in which a broad, flexible politics of white supremacy has been irreducible to the consolidation of state, party, and regional alliances in U.S. history. Hard racism is often what has been articulated from below, a racism predicated on the mobilization of class resentment. It has manifested itself in the terrorist violence of lynching and the pogrom, as well as in land-grabs and programs of extermination. Soft racism is the racism associated with elite strategies of social management and paternalism. It has often been part and parcel of "divide-and-rule" tactics, including attacks on working-class unity, through, for example, the importation of black strike-breakers. Soft racism can obviously stoke hard racism, although it can also proceed through the toleration of bigotry as long as the latter does not erupt in challenges to systemic prerogatives. Saxton, *The Rise and Fall of the White Republic,* p. 388.

35. John Cell, *The Highest Stage of White Supremacy: The Origins of Segregation in South Africa and the U.S. South* (New York: Oxford University Press, 1982), p. 47; Stanley Greeberge, *Race and the State in Capitalist Development* (New Haven, Conn.: Yale University Press, 1980); C. Vann Woodward, *The Origins of the New South* (Baton Roughe: Louisiana State University Press, 1951).

36. Gompers quoted in Woodward, *Origins of the New South,* p. 361; Catt quoted in Angela Davis, *Women, Race and Class* (New York: Random House, 1978), p. 122; Debs quoted in Harvard Sitkoff, *A New Deal for Blacks: The Emergence of Civil Rights as a National Issue in the Depression Decade* (New York: Oxford University Press, 1978), p. 20. Also see C. Vann Woodward, *Tom Watson: Agrarian Rebel* (New York: MacMillan, 1938); Michael Dawson, "A Black Counter-Public?: Economic Agendas, Racial Earthquakes and Black Politics," in *The Black Public Sphere* (Chicago: University of Chicago Press, 1995), pp. 199–229.

37. Rogers Smith develops this argument at greater length in *Civic Ideals,* pp. 13–40. Also see Harris, "Whiteness as Property," pp. 276–292; Michael

Sandel, *Liberalism and the Limits of Justice* (Cambridge: Cambridge University Press, 1982); and Michael Sandel, *Democracy's Discontent: America in Search of a Public Philosophy* (Cambridge: Cambridge University Press, 1996).

38. The theory of the "permanence of racism" in the United States is associated with legal scholar Derek Bell. See Derek Bell, *Faces at the Bottom of the Well: The Permanence of Racism* (New York: Basic Books, 1992). Here I am paraphrasing from Derek Bell, *Race, Racism and American Law* (Boston: Little, Brown, 1988), p. 60.

39. Evelyn Brooks Higginbotham, "African American Women's History and the Metalanguage of Race," *Signs* (Winter 1992): 251–274. Another way to think about racism is as a mode of symbolic power. Pierre Bourdieu, "Social Space and Symbolic Power," in *In Other Words* (Stanford, Calif.: Stanford University Press, 1990), p. 138.

40. Hegemony is a concept that defines episodic periods of political settlement in which ruling groups undertake social projects and in which the "cultural" community of the nation takes precedence over substantive political and economic divisions. Antonio Gramsci, *The Gramsci Reader*, ed. David Forgacs (New York: Schocken, 1990), p. 205.

41. Smith, *Civic Ideals*, pp. 6–10; Balibar and Wallerstein, *Race, Nation, Class*, p. 95.

42. Uday Singh Mehta, "Liberal Strategies of Exclusion," in Ann Laura Stoler and Frederick Cooper, eds., *Tensions of Empire* (Berkeley: University of California Press, 1997), p. 60. Also see Uday Singh Mehta, *Liberalism and Empire* (Chicago: University of Chicago Press, 1999). Marx defines the colonial system as integral to an era of "primitive accumulation": "The discovery of gold and silver in America, the extirpation, enslavement, and entombment in mines of the indigenous population of that continent, the beginnings of the conquest and plunder of India, and the conversion of Africa into a preserve for the commercial hunting of black skins, are all things which characterize the dawn of the era of capitalist production." Karl Marx, *Capital*, vol. 1 (New York: Vintage, 1977), p. 915. For a brilliant account of the racial matrix of modernity as "a race-reproduction bind" see Alys Eve Weinbaum, *Wayward Reproductions: Genealogies of Race and Nation in Trans-Atlantic Modern Thought* (Durham, N.C.: Duke University Press, 2004).

43. The phrase itself comes from Rudyard Kipling's poem celebrating U.S. victory in the Spanish-American War of 1898. In other words, it originates in a trans-Atlantic Anglo-American crucible. Also see Balibar and Wallerstein, *Race, Nation, Class*, p. 60.

44. Rayford Logan, *The Negro in American Life and Thought, 1877–1901: The Nadir* (New York: Collier, 1965); David Oshinsky, *Worse than Slavery: Parchman Farm and the Ordeal of Jim Crow Justice* (New York: Free Press, 1996).

45. Gareth Stedman Jones notes that the phrase "domestic territorial empire"

was used interchangeably with "Federal Union" by Washington, Adams, Hamilton, and Jefferson. See Gareth Stedman Jones, "The Specificity of U.S. Imperialism," *New Left Review* 60 (1972): 59–86. Also see Amy Kaplan, *The Anarchy of Empire in the Making of U.S. Culture* (Cambridge, Mass.: Harvard University Press, 2002).

46. I am indebted to Paul Gilroy for this insight.

47. Perry Anderson, "Internationalism—A Breviary," *New Left Review* 14 (March/April 2002): 5–26; Bill Mullen, "Du Bois, Dark Princess and the Afro-Asian International," *Positions* 11(1) (Spring 2003): 217–240. Also see Oswald Spengler, *Decline of the West* (New York: Knopf, 1926); Madison Grant, *The Passing of the Great Race* (New York: Scribner's, 1916); Lothrop Stoddard, *The Rising Tide of Color against White World Supremacy* (New York: Scribner's, 1920).

48. The legal benchmark of the new dispensation remained *Plessy vs. Ferguson* (1896), which established the constitutional framework for segregation in the summary doctrine "separate-but-equal." No longer strictly "other than" citizens—part person, part property—blacks were recognized as political agents, but, as such, now potentially subject to legally "enforced separation." Neil Gotanda, "A Critique of 'Our Constitution Is Color-Blind,'" in *Critical Race Theory*, p. 263.

49. Matthew Guterl, *The Color of Race in America, 1900–1940* (Cambridge, Mass.: Harvard University Press, 2001).

50. Jacobson, *Whiteness of a Different Color*, p. 12.

51. Gleason, "American Identity and Americanization," p. 62; Michael Waltzer, "What Does It Mean to Be an American," *Social Research* 57: 591; Hollinger, "How Wide the Circle," p. 335.

52. Schlesinger Jr., *The Disuniting of America*, p. 18.

53. Ibid., p. 138.

54. Crevecour, *Letters from an American Farmer*, p. 70. Crevecour concludes this passage with the following invocation of manifest destiny: "Americans are the western pilgrims who are carrying along with them that great mass of arts, sciences, vigour and industry which began long since in the East; they will finish the great circle."

55. Hollinger, *Post-Ethnic America*, p. 160.

56. Balibar and Wallerstein, *Race, Nation, Class*, p. 98.

57. Balibar, "Ambiguous Universalism," p. 70. On the retrospective ruse that sustains the causal fiction of popular sovereignty, see Jacques Derrida, "Declarations of Independence," *New Political Science* 15 (Summer 1986).

58. Balibar, "Ambiguous Universalism," p. 71.

59. Karl Marx, "On the Jewish Question," in Robert Tucker, ed., *The Marx-Engels Reader* (New York: Norton, 1972), pp. 26–52.

60. Balibar and Wallerstein, *Race, Nation, Class*, p. 96.

61. Gunnar Myrdal, *An American Dilemma: The Negro Problem and Modern Democracy*, vol. 1 (New York: Harper & Brothers, 1944), p. 3.

62. Arnold Rose, *The Negro in America [The Classic Condensation of Gunnar Myrdal's The American Dilemma]* (Boston: Beacon Press, 1948), p. 312.

63. Kenneth Stampp, *The Peculiar Institution: Slavery in the Antebellum South* (New York: Knopf, 1956); Jules Tygiel, *Baseball's Great Experiment: Jackie Robinson and His Legacy* (New York: Oxford University Press, 1983), p. 308. Glazer quoted in Michael Omi and Howard Winant, *Racial Formation in the United States from the 1960s to the 1980s* (New York: Routledge, 1986), p. 142.

64. See Ishmael Reed, "Is Ethnicity Obsolete?" in Werner Sollors, ed., *The Invention of Ethnicity* (New York: Oxford University Press, 1989). (One final irony of the metaphor of color blindness is that it literally implies seeing the world in black and white.)

65. Ralph Bunche, Fisk University Address, July 1, 1949, quoted in Charles Henry, *Ralph Bunche: Model Negro or American Other?* (New York: New York University Press, 1999), p. 161.

66. E. Franklin Frazier, *The Black Bourgeoisie* (New York: Collier, 1957), p. 193.

67. I call this a "negative dialectic" in the sense proposed by Adorno: "The truth which idealistic dialectics drives beyond every particular, as one-sided and wrong, is the truth of the whole, and if that were not preconceived, the dialectical steps would lack motivation and direction. We have to answer that the object of a mental experience is an antagonistic system in itself—antagonistic in reality, not just in its conveyance to the knowing subject that rediscovers itself therein . . . Regarding the concrete utopian possibility, dialectics is the ontology of the wrong state of things. The right state of things would be free of it: neither a system, nor a contradiction . . . To change the direction of this conceptuality, to give it a turn toward non-identity, is the hinge of negative dialectics." Theodore Adorno, *Negative Dialectics* (New York: Schocken, 1973), pp. 10–12.

68. In formulating these understandings I am indebted to Ato Sekyi Otu, *Fanon's Dialectic of Experience* (Cambridge, Mass.: Harvard University Press, 1996), p. 24.

69. Frederick Douglass, "What to the Slave Is the Fourth of July?: An Address Delivered in Rochester, New York, on 5 July 1852," in *The Frederick Douglass Papers, 1847–1854,* vol. 2, (New Haven, Conn.: Yale University Press, 1982), p. 360.

70. Douglass, "What to the Slave Is the Fourth of July," p. 387.

71. Frederick Douglass, "A Nation in the Midst of a Nation: An Address Delivered in New York, New York, on 11 May 1853," *The Frederick Douglass Papers,* p. 428.

72. Douglass, "What to the Slave Is the Fourth of July," p. 387.

73. Douglass, "Nation in the Midst of a Nation," p. 437.

74. August Meier, *Negro Thought in America, 1880–1915* (Ann Arbor: University of Michigan Press, 1968), p. 104.

75. Quoted in Woodward, *Origins of the New South,* p. 368.
76. Dawson, "A Black Counter-Public?," p. 204. Also see Hazel Carby, *Race Men* (Cambridge, Mass.: Harvard University Press, 1998); Adolph Reed, *W. E. B. Du Bois and American Political Thought* (New York: Oxford University Press, 1999).
77. W. E. B. Du Bois, *Crisis* (May 1919): 12.
78. W. E. B. Du Bois, "The Negro Mind Reaches Out," in Alain Locke, ed., *The New Negro* (1925) (New York: MacMillan, 1968), p. 385.
79. Quoted in David Levering Lewis, *W. E. B. Du Bois: The Fight for Equality and the American Century* (New York: Henry Holt, 2000), p. 14.
80. W. E. B. Du Bois, "The Souls of Whitefolk," in *Darkwater: Voices within the Veil* (New York: Dover, 1920), p. 27.
81. "If we had to put our finger upon the year which marked the beginning of modern race relations," Cox wrote, "we should select 1493–1494." Oliver Cromwell Cox, *Caste, Class and Race* (New York: Monthly Review Press, 1970), p. 486. Cox is quoted in Michael Denning, *The Cultural Front: The Laboring of American Culture* (New York: Verso, 1996), p. 452. For a brilliant, unsurpassed account of the international shape of black intellectual culture between the wars see Brent Hayes Edwards, *The Practice of Diaspora: Literature, Tranlsation and the Rise of Black Internationalism* (Cambridge, Mass.: Harvard University Press, 2003).
82. W. E. B. DuBois quoted in E. U. Essien-Udom, *Black Nationalism: The Search for Identity in America* (Chicago: University of Chicago Press, 1962), p. 25.
83. Ralph Ellison, "The Negro and the Second World War," in Eric Sundquist, ed. *Cultural Contexts for Ralph Ellison's Invisible Man* (New York: Bedford/St. Martin's, 1995), 236.
84. C. L. R. James, "The Historical Developments of the Negro in American Society" (1943), in Scott Mclemmee, ed., *C. L. R. James and the Negro Question* (Jackson: University of Mississippi Press, 1996), p. 86.
85. Du Bois, *Souls of Black Folk,* p. 124; Richard Wright, *Twelve Million Black Voices* (New York: Viking Press, 1941), p. 147.
86. Wright, *Twelve Million Black Voices,* p. 146.
87. Ralph Ellison, *Shadow and Act* (New York: Random House, 1963), p. 301.
88. Azza Salama Layton, *International Politics and Civil Rights Policies in the United States, 1941–1960* (Cambridge: Cambridge University Press, 2000); William L. Patterson, *The Man Who Cried Genocide: An Autobiography* (New York: International Publishers, 1971); Lewis, *W. E. B. Du Bois.*
89. Ellison's protagonist cautions in *Invisible Man* (1952): "(Beware of those who speak of the *spiral* of history; they are preparing a boomerang. Keep a steel helmet handy). I know; I have been boomeranged across my head so much that I now can see the darkness of lightness." Ralph Ellison, *Invisible Man* (New York: Vintage, 1995), p. 6.
90. Bernadette Callier, "If the Dead Could Only Speak: Reflections on Texts by

Niger, Hughes, and Fodeba," in V. Y. Mudimbe, *The Surreptitious Speech* (Chicago: University of Chicago Press, 1992), p. 189.

91. Ellison, *Invisible Man*, pp. 196–223.
92. Mark Tucker, ed., *The Duke Ellington Reader* (New York: Random House, 1994), p. 150.
93. Kloppenberg, *The Virtues of Liberalism*, p. 20.
94. James Baldwin, "The Discovery of What It Means to Be an American," *Nobody Knows My Name* (New York: Dell Publishing, 1961), pp. 3–12.
95. Richard Rorty, *Achieving Our Country* (Cambridge, Mass.: Harvard University Press: 1998), pp. 12–13.
96. James Baldwin, *No Name in the Street* (New York: Dell Publishing, 1972), p. 10.

2. Reconstructing Democracy

1. W. E. B. Du Bois, "Dr. Du Bois Resigns, the Board's Resolution," in Daniel Walden, ed., *The Crisis Writings* (Greenwich, Conn.: Fawcett Publications, 1972), p. 439.
2. W. E. B. Du Bois, "The Right to Work" (April 1933), in Herbert Aptheker, ed., *Selections from the Crisis, 1926–1934*, vol. 2, (Millwood, N.Y.: Kraus-Thompson Organization, 1983), p. 692.
3. Du Bois, "Segregation" (January 1934), *Selections*, p. 728.
4. Du Bois, "On Being Ashamed of Oneself; An Essay on Race Pride" (September 1933), *Selections*, pp. 716–717.
5. Du Bois, "On Being Ashamed of Oneself; An Essay on Race Pride," *Selections*, p. 717.
6. W. E. B. Du Bois, "The Negro and Social Reconstruction" (1936), in Herbert Aptheker, ed., *Against Racism: Unpublished Essays, Papers and Addresses* (Amherst: University of Massachusetts Press, 1985), p. 157.
7. Du Bois, "The Negro and Social Reconstruction," *Against Racism*, p. 155.
8. Du Bois, "Segregation in the North" (April 1934), *Selections*, p. 745.
9. Du Bois, "The Negro and Social Reconstruction," *Against Racism*, p. 150. Du Bois recognized that there was a strong and perhaps necessary link between nationalism and democracy in the formation of modern political publics. "Nationalism," as Craig Calhoun writes, "allowed the domestic public life of democracies to proceed with a tacit assumption of the boundaries of the political communities, and democratic theory and discourse had—and has—little coherent answer to why such boundaries should exist." At the same time, as Calhoun continues, "nationalist ideas fixed the most basic of collective political identities in advance of public life" in ways that were often "sharply repressive of claims to various competing identities." Du Bois's description of black people as "a nation" can be understood in this sense as an effort to imagine and represent a *black* people as political

subjects in the face of exclusion by U.S. *nationalist* publics. Craig Calhoun, *Critical Social Theory,* (Cambridge, Mass.: Blackwell, 1995), p. 273.

10. David Levering Lewis's definitive biography, *W. E. B. Du Bois: The Fight for Equality and the American Century* (New York: Henry Holt, 2001), which covers the second half of Du Bois's life and career as a black public intellectual—should begin to revise this picture.

11. Kwame Anthony Appiah, "Du Bois and the Illusion of Race: The Uncompleted Argument," in Henry Louis Gates, ed., *Race, Writing and Difference* (Chicago: University of Chicago Press, 1986).

12. Frances Broderick, *W. E. B. Du Bois: Negro Leader in a Time of Crisis* (Stanford, Calif.: Stanford University Press, 1959), pp. 190, 229.

13. John Dewey, *The Public and Its Problems* (New York: G. P. Putnam and Sons, 1927), p. 35. Dewey defines "the public" as follows: "Those indirectly and seriously affected for good or for evil form a group distinctive enough to require recognition and a name. The name selected is The Public. This public is organized and made effective by means of representatives, who as guardians of custom . . . regulate the conjoint actions of individuals and groups. Then and in so far, association adds to itself political organization, and something which may be government comes into being: the public is a political state." (35)

14. W. E. B. Du Bois, *Black Reconstruction in America: An Essay toward the History of the Part Which Black Folk Have Played in the Effort to Reconstruct Democracy in America* (1935) (New York: Atheneum, 1985), p. 700. As Du Bois wrote, "It must be remembered that the white group of laborers, while they received a low wage, were compensated by a sort of public and psychological wage." Contemporary historians have expanded greatly on this insight following the lead of David Roediger, *Wages of Whiteness: Race and the Making of the American Working-Class* (New York: Verso, 1991).

15. John Dewey, *Liberalism and Social Action* (New York: G. P. Putnam and Sons, 1935), p. 27.

16. Graham Burchell, Colin Gordon, and Peter Miller, eds., *The Foucault Effect: Studies in Governmentality* (Chicago: University of Chicago Press, 1991), p. 15.

17. Quoted in William Leuchtenberg, *Franklin Delano Roosevelt and the New Deal, 1932–1940* (New York: Harper and Row, 1963), p. 337. Also see William Leuchtenberg, "The Achievement of the New Deal," in *The F.D.R. Years* (New York: Columbia University Press, 1995), p. 239.

18. John Maynard Keynes, "The End of Laissez-Faire," in *Essays in Persuasion,* (New York: Harcourt Brace and Company, 1932), pp. 313–314, 319.

19. Antonio Negri, "Keynes and the Capitalist Theory of the State," in Michael Hardt, ed., *Labor of Dionysus* (Minneapolis: University of Minnesota Press, 1994), pp. 44–45.

20. Dewey, *The Public and Its Problems,* pp. 87–88. Dewey rejected the liberal idea that "the sole end of government was the protection of individuals in

the rights which were theirs by nature," and proposed that the public sphere of citizen discourse and organization could be a site for and the pursuit of "actual liberty" by which he meant the "effective power to do specific things." Also see Robert Westbrook, *John Dewey and American Democracy* (Ithaca, N.Y.: Cornell University Press, 1991), p. 435.

21. Thus even as eminent a historian as Daniel Rogers concludes that the liberal reformism of the New Deal era "constitutes the defining moment of twentieth-century politics," even if much of "its logic still eludes us." Daniel Rogers, *Atlantic Crossings: Social Politics in a Progressive Age* (Cambridge, Mass.: Harvard University Press, 1998), p. 405.

22. W. E. B. Du Bois, *Dusk of Dawn: An Essay Toward an Autobiography of a Race Concept* (1940) (New York: Schocken Books, 1968), p. 133.

23. W. E. B. Du Bois, "The Position of the Negro in the American Social Order: Where Do We Go from Here?," *Journal of Negro Education* vol. VII (1939): 570.

24. Du Bois, "On Being Ashamed of Oneself; An Essay on Race Pride," *Selections*, p. 716.

25. Du Bois, *Dusk of Dawn*, p. 311.

26. Ibid., p. 6.

27. Harvard Sitkoff, *A New Deal for Blacks: The Emergence of Civil Rights as a National Issue: The Depression Decade* (New York: Oxford University Press, 1978); Lewis, *W. E. B. Du Bois*; Cheryl Greenberg, *"Or Does It Explode": Black Harlem in the Great Depression* (New York: Oxford University Press, 1991); Jervis Anderson, *A. Philip Randolph: A Biographical Portrait* (New York: Harcourt Brace Jovanovich, 1973); William Scott, *Sons of Sheba's Race: African Americans and the Italo-Ethiopian War, 1935–1941* (Bloomington: Indiana University Press, 1993); Nancy Weiss, *Farewell to the Party of Lincoln: Black Politics in the Age of F.D.R.* (Princeton, N.J.: Princeton University Press, 1983); Lawrence Wittner, "The National Negro Congress: A Reassessment," *American Quarterly* 22 (Winter 1970): 883–901; Herbert Garfinkel, *When Negroes March: The March on Washington Movement in the Organizational Politics for an FEPC* (New York: Atheneum, 1969); Charles Henry, *Ralph Bunche: Model Negro or American Other?* (New York: New York University Press, 1999); Barbara Ransby, *Ella Baker and the Black Freedom Movement* (Chapel Hill: University of North Carolina Press, 2003), p. 86.

28. Jervis Anderson, *Bayard Rustin: The Troubles I've Seen* (Berkeley: University of California Press, 1998), p. 61.

29. Joanne Grant, "National Negro Congress: The Call" (1935), in *Black Protest: History, Documents and Analysis* (Greenwich, Conn.: Fawcett Publications, 1974), p. 242; W. E. B. Du Bois, "The Strategy of the Negro Vote," *Selections*; Henry Lee Moon, *The Negro Vote: The Balance of Power* (New York: Doubleday, 1948); John Hope Franklin, *From Slavery to Freedom* (New York: Knopf, 1947), p. 456. Franklin was one of the first to recognize

the Italian invasion of Ethiopia as the beginning of an uninterrupted internationalization of black politics. On this point also see Brenda Gayle
Plummer, *A Rising Wind: Black Americans and U.S. Foreign Affairs, 1935–
1960* (Chapel Hill: University of North Carolina Press, 1996).

30. Nancy Fraser, "Re-Thinking the Public Sphere: A Contribution to the Critique of Actually Existing Democracy," *Social Text* 25/26 (1990): 56–80.

31. Du Bois's ideas prefigure more recent arguments for cultural justice, such as
"multicultural citizenship" and "multiple publics." See in particular Will
Kymlica, *Multicultural Citizenship* (Oxford: Oxford University Press,
1995); Iris Marion Young, *Justice and the Politics of Difference* (Princeton,
N.J.: Princeton University Press, 1990); and Nancy Fraser, *Unruly Practices: Power, Discourse and Contemporary Social Theory* (Minneapolis:
University of Minnesota Press, 1989).

32. Du Bois, "The Negro and Social Reconstruction," *Against Racism*, p. 178.

33. Young, *Justice and the Politics of Difference*, p. 183.

34. For three substantively similar variations on this argument see Richard
Hofstadter, *The Age of Reform* (New York: Knopf, 1955); Rogers, *Atlantic
Crossings;* and Bruce Ackerman, *We the People: Transformations* (Cam-
bridge, Mass.: Harvard University Press, 1998), p. 310.

35. *The Crisis* (October 1940): 11; Also see Anderson, *A. Philip Randolph*,
p. 243.

36. This is Steven Skowronek's phrase. See his *Building a New American State:
The Expansion of National Administrative Capacity, 1877–1920* (Cambridge: Cambridge University Press, 1982).

37. Howard Odum, *Race and Rumors of Race: The American South in the
Early 1940s* (1943) (Baltimore: John's Hopkins University Press, 1997),
p. xxxiii; Roosevelt quoted in Sitkoff, *A New Deal for Blacks*, p. 62.

38. Sitkoff, *A New Deal for Blacks*, 175; Raymond Wolters; *Negroes and the
Great Depression*, (Westport, Conn.: Greenwood Publications, 1970);
Mary McLeod Bethune, *Building a Better World: Essays and Selected Doc-
uments*, ed Audrey Thomas Mcluskey and Elaine Smith, (Bloomington:
University of Indiana Press, 1999).

39. C. Vann Woodward, *The Strange Career of Jim Crow* (New York: Oxford
University Press, 1955); E. Franklin Frazier, *The Complete Report of Mayor
La Guardia's Commission on the Harlem Riot of March 19, 1935* (New
York: Arno Press, 1969); James Young, *Black Writers of the 1930s* (Baton
Rouge: Louisiana State University Press, 1973), p. 49; Douglas McAdam,
Political Process and the Development of Black Insurgency, 1930–1970
(Chicago: University of Chicago Press, 1982).

40. I have been influenced in this account by Michael Dawson's essay, "A Black
Counter-Public?: Economic Earthquakes, Racial Agendas, and Black Politics," in *The Black Public Sphere* (Chicago: University of Chicago Press,
1995), pp. 199–229. For a sharp critique of the self-serving aspects of the
idea of the black public intellectual see Adolph Reed, *Stirrings in the Jug:
Black Politics in the Post-Segregation Era* (Minneapolis: University of Min-

nesota Press, 2000) and Adolph Reed, "Black Particularity Reconsidered," *Telos* 39 (Spring 1979): 71–93.

41. Michael Warner, "The Mass Public and the Mass Subject," in Craig Calhoun, ed., *Habermas and the Public Sphere* (Cambridge, Mass.: MIT Press, 1992), p. 379; Pierre Bourdieu, "Social Space and Symbolic Power," in *In Other Words* (Stanford, Calif.: Stanford University Press, 1990); Katherine Verdery, *National Ideology under Socialism* (Berkeley: University of California Press, 1991), pp. 12, 17; Antonio Gramsci, *Selections from the Prison Notebooks* (New York: International Publishers, 1971).

42. Du Bois, "The Position of the Negro," *Journal of Negro Education;* Sitkoff, *A New Deal for Blacks,* p. 31; Patrick Washburn, *A Question of Sedition: The Federal Government's Investigation of the Black Press during World War II* (New York: Oxford University Press, 1986); Penny Von Eschen, *Race against Empire* (Ithaca, N.Y.: Cornell University Press, 1998).

43. Du Bois, "The Negro and Social Reconstruction," *Against Racism,* p. 140.

44. Aubrey Thomas and Elaine Smith, *Mary McLeod Bethune: Building a Better World: Essays and Selected Documents* (Bloomington: Indiana University Press, 1997), p. 243.

45. Young, *Black Writers of the Thirties,* p. 148.

46. Ralph Bunche, "A Critical Analysis of the Tactics and Programs of Minority Groups" (1935), in Charles Henry, ed., *Ralph J. Bunche: Selected Speeches and Writings,* (Ann Arbor: University of Michigan Press, 1995), pp. 49–63; Horace Cayton, *Long Old Road* (New York: Trident Press, 1964); Young, *Black Writers of the Thirties,* p. 36. A rich and textured account of the Howard intellectuals is given in Jonathan Holloway, *Confronting the Veil* (Chapel Hill: University of North Carolina Press, 2002).

47. As Peggy Pascoe has argued, the modernizing view was plagued from the start by circular reasoning, in which "the eradication of racism" depended "upon the deliberate non-recognition of race." See Peggy Pascoe, "Miscegenation Law, Court Cases and Ideologies of 'Race' in Twentieth-Century America," *Journal of American History* vol. 83(1): 48. As I suggest later, Du Bois was astutely critical of the emerging dominance of this view. In *Dusk of Dawn,* Du Bois sought to derive a definition of "race" that precisely did not rely upon essentialisms of biology, color, and vision. "But what is this group; how do you differentiate it; and how can you call it 'black' when you admit it is not black?" states Du Bois's imaginary interlocutor. "I recognize it quite easily and with full legal sanction," Du Bois replies, "the black man is a person who must ride 'Jim Crow' in Georgia." See Du Bois, *Dusk of Dawn,* p. 153.

48. Frazier quoted in Young, *Black Writers of the Thirties;* E. Franklin Frazier, "The Status of the Negro in the American Social Order," *Journal of Negro Education* (July 1935); E. Franklin Frazier, "The Du Bois Program in the Present Crisis," *Race* vol. 1(1) (Winter 1935–1936); Bunche quoted in Charles Henry, *Ralph Bunche: Model Negro or American Other,* p. 104.

Also see Ralph Bunche, "Conceptions and Ideologies of the Negro Problem," *Contributions in Black Studies* 9/10 (1990–1992): 104.

49. Lewis, *W. E. B. Du Bois,* p. 298; Young, *Black Writers of the Thirties,* p. 7.

50. Du Bois, *Dusk of Dawn,* pp. 299–300.

51. Du Bois, "Employment," *The Crisis Writings,* p. 412.

52. Du Bois, "The Right to Work," *Selections,* p. 692.

53. Du Bois, *Dusk of Dawn,* p. 321.

54. Du Bois, "The Negro and Social Reconstruction, *Against Racism,* p. 143.

55. Ibid., p. 146.

56. In other words, no claim is being made that Du Bois was an especially acute economic thinker. What must be recognized is that his proposal for a black consumer "commonwealth" appeared in the context of a broader discussion about transforming civil rights activism from what he called "the foray of self-assertive individuals to the massed might of an organized body." Du Bois, *Dusk of Dawn,* p. 304.

57. Ibid., p. 297.

58. Du Bois, "The Right to Work," *Selections,* p. 694.

59. Du Bois, "The Position of the Negro," *Journal of Negro Education* (Winter 1939): 564.

60. W. E. B. Du Bois, "Social Planning for the Negro, Past and Present," *Journal of Negro Education* vol. 5 (1) (January 1936): 120.

61. Du Bois, "Segregation in the North," *Selections,* p. 748.

62. G. W. F. Hegel, *Lectures on the Philosophy of World History* (New York: Cambridge University Press, 1975), pp. 165, 174, 185–186, 190. Here is the important quote in full: "We shall now attempt to define the universal spirit and form of the African character in light of the particular traits which such accounts enumerate. This character, however, is difficult to comprehend, because it is so different from our own culture, and so remote and alien in relation to our own mode of consciousness. We must forget all the categories which are fundamental to our own spiritual life." (176) Hegel believed enslavement by Europeans had "at least . . . awakened more humanity among negroes." (183) In general terms, however, Negroes embodied a "contempt for humanity," the distinguishing feature of which was a "lack of respect for life," which rendered them incapable of "political constitution." (185)

63. Quoted in Dipesh Chakrabarty, *Provincializing Europe* (Princeton, N.J.: Princeton University Press, 2000) pp. 41, 101. I am broadly indebted to Chakrabarty in the formulation of this argument.

64. Frazier made the first statement in the context of an attack on Melville Herskovits's idea of African cultural retentions among Atlantic world blacks. As James Young suggests, Frazier hoped "to achieve the race's salvation through its eventual disappearance, culturally and biologically." Young, *Black Writers of the Thirties,* p. 53. Also see E. Franklin Frazier, "Racial Self Expression," in Cary Wintz, ed., *The Politics and Aes-*

thetics of New Negro Literature, (New York: Garland Publishers, 1996), p. 113.

65. Ralph Bunche, "Organizations Devoted to Improving the Status of the Negro" (1939), *Ralph Bunche: Selected Speeches,* p. 83; Ralph Bunche, "Fisk University Address" (1949), quoted in Henry, *Ralph Bunche: Model Negro,* p. 158.

66. E. Franklin Frazier, *The Negro Family in the United States* (Chicago: University of Chicago Press, 1939); Ruth Feldstein, *Motherhood in Black and White: Race and Sex in American Liberalism, 1930–1965* (Ithaca, N.Y.: Cornell University Press, 2000).

67. 1933 O.E.D. is quoted in Steven Feierman, "African Histories and the Dissolution of World History," in Robert Bates, V. Y. Mudimbe, and Jean O'Barr, eds., *Africa and the Disciplines* (Chicago: University of Chicago Press, 1993), p. 176.

68. Du Bois, *Black Reconstruction,* p. 703.

69. Ibid., pp. 156–7. As Du Bois put it elsewhere, "Of course, we believe in the ultimate uniting of mankind and in a unified American nation with economic classes and racial barriers leveled but we believe that this ideal is to be realized only by such intensified class and race consciousness as will bring irresistible force rather than mere sentimental and moral appeal to bear on the motives and actions of men for justice and equality." Du Bois, "The Negro and Social Reconstruction," *Against Racism,* p. 148.

70. Bunche, "Organizations Devoted to Improving the Status of the Negro," *Ralph Bunche: Selected Speeches,* p. 73 (emphasis added).

71. E. Franklin Frazier, "The Du Bois Program in the Present Crisis," *Race* vol. 1(1) (Winter 1935–1936): 12.

72. Abram Harris, "Reconstruction and the Negro," *New Republic* (August 7, 1935): 367.

73. Frazier substantively dismantled Du Bois's arguments. In an uncharitable moment that he would later regret, Frazier publicly questioned Du Bois's new fondness for grassroots struggles, (without acknowledging his own position as an intellectual implicated in a process of shaping and regulating public opinion). Du Bois, Frazier wrote, "has only an occasional romantic interest in the Negro as a distinct race. Nothing would be more unendurable for him than to live within a Black Ghetto or within a black nation—unless perhaps he were king, and then probably he would attempt to unite the whites and blacks through marriage of the royal families . . . If a fascist movement should develop in America, Du Bois would play into the hands of its leaders through his program for the development of Negro racialism." Frazier, "The Du Bois Program in the Present Crisis," *Race* vol. 1(1) (Winter 1935–1936): 12.

74. George Streator, "In Search of Leadership," *Race* vol. 1(1) (Winter 1935–1936): 14–21.

75. John P. Davis, "A Survey of the Problems of the Negro under the New Deal," *Journal of Negro Education* vol. V(1) (January 1936): 11.

76. Davis, "A Survey of the Problems of the Negro," p. 12.

77. Ernest Rice McKinney, "The Worker's Party's Way Out for the Negro," *Journal of Negro Education* vol. V(1) (January 1936): 98.

78. A. Philip Randolph, "The Trade Union Movement and the Negro," *Journal of Negro Education* vol. V(1) (January 1936): 54.

79. Norman O. Thomas, "The Socialist's Way Out for the Negro," *Journal of Negro Education* vol. V(1) (January 1936): 102.

80. James Ford, "The Communist's Way Out for the Negro," *Journal of Negro Education* vol. V(1) (January 1936): 95.

81. Ralph Bunche, "A Critique of New Deal Social Planning as It Affects Negroes," *Ralph Bunche: Selected Speeches,* p. 66. (This is a longer version of Bunche's original JCNR presentation.)

82. Bunche, "A Critique of New Deal Social Planning," *Journal of Negro Education* vol. V(1) (January 1936): 65. Or, as he wrote elsewhere, "The New Deal at best can only fix the disadvantages, the differentials and the discriminations under which the Negro population has labored all along." See Bunche, "A Critique of New Deal Social Planning," *Ralph Bunche: Selected Speeches,* p. 66.

83. Thus it was, Bunche concluded that "in its unblushing role of the political coquette, it [that is, the New Deal] turns now to the left, now to the right." Bunche, "A Critique of New Deal Social Planning," *Ralph Bunche: Selected Speeches,* p. 59.

84. Bunche, "A Critique of New Deal Social Planning," *Ralph Bunche: Selected Speeches,* p. 61.

85. Quoted in Brian Urquhart, *Ralph Bunche: An American Life* (New York: W. W. Norton, 1993), p. 59.

86. Mark Solomon, *The Cry Was Unity: Communists and African Americans, 1917–1936* (Jackson: University of Mississippi Press, 1998); Michael Denning, *The Cultural Front: The Laboring of American Culture in the Twentieth Century* (New York: Verso, 1996); Bill Mullen, *Popular Fronts: Chicago and African American Cultural Politics, 1935–1946* (Urbana: University of Illinois Press, 1998).

87. Gramsci, *The Prison Notebooks.* Indeed, much like the intellectual proponents of the new liberalism, Gramsci argued that one of the most important characteristics of the modern nation-state was that its publics had achieved a substantial degree of autonomy with respect to exchange relations. At least in part this was the result of the expansion and elaboration of educative activity itself: the development of vast bureaucracies, party formations, news media, and political pundits and propagandists. (16)

88. Gramsci, *The Prison Notebooks,* p. 21.

89. Gary Gerstle, *Working-Class Americanism: The Politics of Labor in a Textile City, 1914–1960* (New York: Cambridge University Press, 1989); Lizbeth Cohen, *Making a New Deal: Industrial Workers in Chicago* (New York: Cambridge University Press, 1990).

90. Quoted in Richard Polenberg, *The Era of Franklin Delano Roosevelt and the New Deal, 1933–1945* (Boston: Bedford St. Martin's, 2000), p. 2.

91. I have adapted the idea of a "parallel proletarian civil society" from Mike Davis, "Why the U.S. Working-Class Is Different," *Prisoners of the American Dream* (London: Verso, 1986), p. 31. On the question of working-class "incorporation" see Negri, "Keynes and the Capitalist Theory of the State," *Labor of Dionysus.*

92. This is from Roosevelt's acceptance speech at the 1936 Democratic convention in Philadelphia. Quoted in Ackerman, *We the People*, p. 308. Ackerman has astutely argued "not corporatism, but nationalism" was the "watchword" of Roosevelt's New Deal (298). On the United States as a model for the development of modern welfare-state politics, see Antonio Negri, "What Can the State Still Do?" *Polygraph* 10 (1998): 15; also see William Leuchtenberg, "The Europeanization of America," *The F.D.R. Years*, pp. 283–305. Leuchtenberg offers the following interesting quotation from Leon Blum's biographer, Joel Colton: "Not socialism, but a 'French New Deal' was his objective, Roosevelt not Marx, his guide." (296).

93. The idea of "classification struggles" is from Adam Przeworski, *Capitalism and Social Democracy* (Cambridge: Cambridge University Press, 1985), pp. 70–80. Another way of putting this would be to say that the modern state does not merely emerge as an effort to monopolize the physical instruments of power (Max Weber), but develops as a set of institutions that concentrate and monopolize what Pierre Bourdieu calls "symbolic power": the power to produce the "principles of social vision and division that conform to its own structure," which is in an exemplary sense "the power to produce groups." See Pierre Bourdieu, "Re-Thinking the State: Genesis and Structure of the Bureaucratic Field," in George Steinmetz, ed., *State/Culture: State-Formation after the Cultural Turn* (Ithaca, N.Y.: Cornell University Press, 1999), p. 63; Bourdieu, "Social Space and Symbolic Power," *In Other Words*, p. 138.

94. Michael Brown, *Race, Money and the American Welfare State* (Ithaca, N.Y.: Cornell University Press, 1999); George Lipsitz, *The Possessive Investment in Whiteness* (Philadelphia: Temple University Press, 1998).

95. Walter White, *A Man Called White,* (New York: Viking, 1948), p. 169.

96. Steve Fraser and Gary Gerstle, *The Rise and Fall of the New Deal Order, 1930–1980* (Princeton, N.J.: Princeton University Press, 1989), p. xix.

97. Stuart Hall, *Policing the Crisis: Mugging, the State, and Law and Order* (New York: Holmes and Meier, 1978), p. 313.

98. Quoted in William Banks, *Black Intellectuals* (New York: W. W. Norton, 1996), p. 108.

99. Du Bois, "The Position of the Negro," *Journal of Negro Education*: 563–564.

100. Du Bois, *Dusk of Dawn*, pp. 288, 290.

101. Du Bois, "The Negro and Social Reconstruction," *Against Racism,* p. 142.
102. Benjamin Barber, "More Democracy, More Revolution," *The Nation* (October 26, 1998): 13.
103. Du Bois, "The Negro and Social Reconstruction," *Against Racism,* p. 144.
104. Du Bois's brilliant insight was not just that race needed to be considered in addition to class, but that racism had distorted U.S. class struggles to the point of rendering them meaningless. As he argued in *Black Reconstruction,* "It was easy to transfer class hatred so that it fell upon the black worker." (103) In the South, "race philosophy came as a new and terrible thing to make labor unity or labor class consciousness impossible." (680) This in turn became the general pattern throughout the country. "Thus in America," Du Bois wrote, "we have seen a wild and ruthless scramble of labor groups over each other in order to climb to wealth on the backs of black labor and foreign immigrants. The Irish climbed on the Negroes. The Germans scrambled over the Negroes and emulated the Irish. The Scandinavians fought forward next to the Germans and the Italians and "Bohunks" are crowding up, leaving Negroes still at the bottom chained to helplessness, first by slavery, then by disfranchisement, and always by the color bar." Du Bois, "Marxism and the Negro Question," *The Crisis Writings,* p. 406.
105. Du Bois, *Dusk of Dawn,* p. 205.
106. Du Bois, "The Negro Mind Reaches Out," *The New Negro* (1925) (New York: MacMillan, 1968), p. 386.
107. Du Bois, *Black Reconstruction,* p. 15.
108. Du Bois, *Dusk of Dawn,* p. 289.
109. Du Bois, "Marxism and the Negro Problem," *Selections,* p. 699. Black workers, "doubly exploited" by race and class, could imagine a more expansive kind of freedom than that conceived in liberal or Marxist orthodoxies. Here is Du Bois again: "Why do you know the two finest things in the industry of the West, finer than factory, shop or ship? One is the black laborer's Saturday off . . . The second thing is laughter . . . If you want to feel humor too exquisite and subtle for translation, sit invisibly among a gang of Negro workers. The white world has its gibes and cruel caricatures; it has its loud guffaws; but to the black world alone belongs the delicious chuckle." Du Bois, *Dusk of Dawn,* p. 148.
110. Du Bois, "The Negro and Social Reconstruction," *Against Racism,* p. 143. If this was Marxism, and Du Bois believed it was, it was a heterodox and highly inventive variety. This has led Manning Marable to suggest that the phrase "radical democrat" (rather than "socialist") might best describe Du Bois's thinking of the 1930s. Manning Marable, *W. E. B. Du Bois: Black Radical Democrat* (Boston: Twayne, 1986). More interesting is the idea that Du Bois believed "radical democracy" was an aspect of "the progress of socialistic ideas in general." See Du Bois, *Black Reconstruction,* p. 46.
111. Recall Harris described Du Bois's Marxism as undisciplined; Frazier viewed

it as a form of poetic license, and Du Bois's first biographer Broderick called it "eccentric" and "bordering on burlesque." Singling out Du Bois's passage on the "dark and vast sea of human labor" for special ridicule, Broderick pronounced the book "passable as polemic or melodrama," but "not history." Broderick, *W. E. B. Du Bois,* p. 185. Howard Beale's assessment was fairer, "in describing the Negro's role Du Bois has presented a mass of material, formerly ignored, that every future historian must reckon with." Howard K. Beale, "On Writing Reconstruction History," *American Historical Review* (July 1940): 808.

112. Sterling Spero, "The Negro's Role," *The Nation* (July 24, 1935): 108.

113. Ibid.: 139; Harris, "Reconstruction and the Negro," *New Republic:* 367.

114. Jacques Ranciere, *The Names of History: On the Poetics of Knowledge* (Minneapolis: University of Minnesota Press, 1994), p. 102.

115. Ibid., p. 97.

116. Du Bois, *Black Reconstruction,* p. 121.

117. I am indebted to Fred Moten for his thoughts on "the knowledge of freedom." See Fred Moten, *In the Break* (Minneapolis: University of Minnesota Press, 2003).

118. Aptheker, "The Historian," *W. E. B. Du Bois,* p. 269.

119. It is of passing interest to note that this idea was akin to the Trotskyist notion of "permanent revolution" or the steady (and even potentially nonviolent) passing of a bourgeois-democratic revolution into a socialist one. See Michael Lowy, *Permanent Revolution* (London: Verso, 1981).

120. As Ranciere notes, "the name *proletarian* is explicit about its Latin etymology (the multitude given to simple reproduction) much more than the 'rigorous' definitions over which historians and sociologists wear themselves out." Ranciere, *The Names of History,* p. 97.

121. Ato Sekyi-Otu, *Fanon's Dialectic of Experience* (Cambridge, Mass.: Harvard University Press, 1999), p. 15.

122. Quoted in Aldon Nielsen, *C. L. R. James: A Critical Introduction* (Jackson: University of Mississippi Press, 1997), p. 59. As James added, "Only the future can tell to what degree the historical audacities of Du Bois are viable. . . Quotation can scarcely do him justice but his awareness of the intricacies and subtleties of politics and social movement on an international scale rest firmly on a deep and passionate humanity." C. L. R. James, *The Future Is in the Present: Selected Essays* (Westport, Conn.: L. Hill, 1977), p. 211.

123. Du Bois, *Black Reconstruction,* p. 721.

124. Ibid., p. 725.

125. Hayden White, "Introduction," *The Names of History,* p. ix.

126. Lewis, *W. E. B. Du Bois,* p. 367. "Had he ventured to paraphrase Marx," Lewis writes, "Du Bois might well have observed that he had set reconstruction historiography upright after finding it standing on its head."

127. Du Bois's master work still stands outside the formal canons of the "profession." See Peter Novick, *That Noble Dream: The "Objectivity" Question*

and the American Historical Profession (Cambridge: Cambridge University Press, 1988), pp. 232–233.

128. Chakrabarty, *Provincializing Europe*, p. 43.

129. W. E. B. Du Bois, "What the Negro Has Done for Texas" (1936), in Philip Foner, ed., *W. E. B. Du Bois Speaks: Speeches and Addresses, 1920–1963* (New York: Pathfinder Press, 1970), p. 92.

130. This phrase is taken from Lisa Lowe, *Immigrant Acts* (Durham, N.C.: Duke University Press, 1996).

131. Du Bois, *Black Reconstruction*, p. 727.

132. C. L. R. James, "The Revolutionary Answer to the Negro Question," in Scott McLemee, ed., *C. L. R. James on the "Negro Question"* (Jackson: University of Mississippi Press, 1996), p. 139. Also see Robin D. G. Kelley, *Freedom Dreams: The Black Radical Imagination* (Boston: Beacon Press, 2002), p. 54.

133. W. E. B. Du Bois, *The Correspondence of W. E. B. Du Bois, Selections, 1934–1944,* ed. Herbert Aptheker (Amherst: University of Massachusetts Press, 1976), p. 137.

134. Wolters, *Negroes in the Great Depression*, p. 277.

135. Du Bois, "The Negro and Social Reconstruction," *Against Racism*, p. 149.

136. Du Bois, "The Position of the Negro," *Journal of Negro Education*, p. 568.

137. E. Franklin Frazier, "The Failure of the Negro Intellectual," in G. Franklin Edwards, ed., *On Race Relations: Selected Writings* (Chicago: University of Chicago Press, 1968), p. 269.

138. Frazier, "The Complete Report of Mayor La Guardia's Commission on the Harlem Riot of March 19, 1935." The report was typed from an account that first appeared in the July 18, 1936 edition of the *Amsterdam News*.

139. Bunche, "Triumph or Fiasco," *Race* 1(2)(Summer 1936): 93–96.

140. Wittner, "The National Negro Congress," *American Quarterly:* 900.

141. Ibid.: 901.

142. Quoted in Polenberg, *The Era of Franklin Delano Roosevelt*, p. 32. Also see Garfinkel, *When Negroes March;* on the U.A.W., see Joanne Grant, *Ella Baker: Freedom Bound* (New York: Wiley, 1998), p. 56.

143. Ralph Bunche, *The Political Status of the Negro in the Age of F.D.R.* (1940; reprint, Chicago: University of Chicago Press, 1973), p. 104. Also see Reed, *Stirrings in the Jug,* p. 33.

144. Du Bois, *Dusk of Dawn,* p. 2.

145. Ibid., p. 199.

3. Internationalizing Freedom

1. Herbert Garfinkel, *When Negroes March* (New York: Atheneum, 1969), p. 24; Walter White, *A Rising Wind* (New York: Doubleday, 1945); Walter White, *A Man Called White* (New York: Viking, 1948). Richard Dalfiume,

"The Forgotten Years of the Negro Revolution," *Journal of American History 55(1)* (June 1967), pp. 90–106.

2. Garfinkel, *When Negroes March,* p. 24.
3. C. L. R. James, "The Historical Developments of the Negro in American Society" (1943), in Scott McLemmee, ed., *C. L. R. James on the Negro Question* (Jackson: University of Mississippi Press, 1996), p. 66. The full quote reads: "The tumultuous world situation, the loud-voiced shrieking of "democracy" by Anglo-American imperialism and the increasing demands of organized labor for greater and greater extensions of its democratic rights, stimulated in the Negro people by the beginning of World War II a more than usually intensive desire to struggle for equality."
4. Garfinkel, *When Negroes March,* p. 88.
5. Arnold Rampersad, *The Life of Langston Hughes, 1941–1967,* vol. 2, (New York: Oxford University Press, 2002), p. 47; Barnett quoted in Garfinkel, *When Negroes March,* p. 114; Michael Denning, *The Cultural Front* (New York: Verso, 1996), p. 34. Note the NAACP went from just 300,000 members in 1939 to over one million by 1947.
6. Cedric Robinson, *Black Movements in America* (New York: Routledge, 1997), p. 129.
7. David Hollinger, "How Wide the Circle of 'We': American Intellectuals and the Problem of the Ethnos since World War II," *American Historical Review* 57 (Spring 1993): 318.
8. Roosevelt is quoted in Carey McWilliams, *Brothers under the Skin* (Boston: Little, Brown, 1943), p. 34. As McWilliams wrote, in what proved to be a seminal contribution to the discursive field of wartime nationalism, "For several centuries now we have been victimized by a kind of myopia and have come to think of Western Europe and America as the world. (17)
9. Willkie is quoted in Eric Foner, *The Story of American Freedom* (New York: W. W. Norton, 1998), p. 246. Speaking in the House of Commons, Churchill expressly stated that the charter was not "applicable to the Coloured Races in colonial empire." Churchill is quoted in Penny Von Eschen, *Race against Empire: Black Americans and Anti-Colonialism, 1937–1957* (Ithaca, N.Y.: Cornell University Press, 1997), p. 26. Also see Melani McCalister, *Epic Encounters* (Berkeley: University of California Press, 2002), p. 48.
10. Michael Hunt, "Conclusions: The Decolonization Puzzle in U.S. Policy: Promise versus Performance," in David Ryan, ed., *The United States and Decolonization* (New York: MacMillan, 2000), p. 225.
11. Ralph Ellison, "Introduction" (1981), *Invisible Man* (1952) (Vintage: New York, 1995), p. xii.
12. Charles Johnson, *To Stem This Tide: A Survey of Racial Tension Areas of the US* (Boston: The Pilgrim Press, 1943); Howard Odum, *Race and Rumors of Race* (1943) (Baltimore: Johns Hopkins University Press, 1997), p. 101.

13. Thomas Sugrue, *Origins of the Urban Crisis: Race and Inequality in Postwar Detroit* (Princeton, N.J.: Princeton University Press, 1996); Cheryl Greenberg, *Or Does It Explode* (New York: Oxford University Press, 1991); Rampersad, *The Life of Langston Hughes,* p. 75.

14. McWilliams, *Brothers under the Skin,* p. 39.

15. Arnold Hirsh, *The Making of the Second Ghetto: Race and Housing in Chicago, 1940–1960* (Chicago: University of Chicago Press, 1998), p. 9. Douglas Massey and Nancy Denton point out that the highest index of segregation recorded for any U.S. ethnic group in an urban area—Milwaukee's Italians following World War I—was lower than the lowest rates recorded for blacks in the urban ghettoes of the North across the twentieth century. Massey and Denton, *American Apartheid: Segregation and the Making of the Underclass* (Cambridge, Mass.: Harvard University Press, 1993).

16. George Lipsitz, *The Possessive Investment in Whiteness: How White People Profit from Identity Politics* (Philadelphia: Temple University Press, 1998).

17. McWilliams, *Brothers under the Skin,* pp. 26, 28, 42.

18. Gunnar Myrdal, *An American Dilemma: The Negro Problem and Modern Democracy* (1944) (New York: Pantheon, 1962), p. 80.

19. Chester Himes, "Zoot Suit Riots are Race Riots" (1943), in Bucklin Moon, ed., *Primer for White Folks* (New York: Doubleday, 1945), pp. 220, 224; Langston Hughes, "Fair Play in Dixie" (1945), in Christopher De Santis, ed., *Langston Hughes and the Chicago Defender* (Chicago: University of Illinois Press, 1995), p. 81. In other words, if the South was becoming Americanized, it was only one side of a dynamic in which the United States and perhaps the world was at risk of being "Southernized." James N. Gregory, "The Southern Diaspora and the Urban Dispossessed: Demonstrating the Census Public Use Microdata Samples," *Journal of American History* vol. 82(1) (June 1995): 111–134; James N. Gregory, "Southernizing the American Working Class," *Labor History* vol. 39(2) (1998).

20. Roi Ottley, *A New World-a-Coming* (Boston: Houghton Mifflin Company, 1943), p. 344. Chester Himes, "Now Is the Time! Here Is the Place," *Primer for White Folks,* p. 215.

21. This idea of a black popular front is coined by Von Eschen: "if the communist popular front of the 1930s had a second incarnation after Hitler's invasion of the Soviet Union and the formation of the US-British-Soviet wartime alliance, black civil rights and anti-colonial activists—invigorated by the crumbling of European hegemony and the domestic upheavals of war—created a black popular front." *Race against Empire,* p. 19.

22. St. Clair Drake and Horace Cayton, *Black Metropolis: A Study of Negro Life in a Northern City,* vol. 2 (New York: Harper and Row, 1945), p. 736.

23. "Negro Editors Look at Communism," *Crisis* (May 1932): 13. Perhaps the most important legacy of American Marxism was the practical, if not theoretical, elevation of antiracism as a central framework for radical politics.

By winning the first Supreme Court victories on behalf of blacks in 1935 (two decades before *Brown vs. Board of Education*) for the denial of due process by the Alabama courts in the Scottsboro verdicts, the Communist Party's International Labor Defense arguably scored the first substantive victories of the long civil rights era. In Harvard Sitkoff's accurate and succinct summary of the period: the far left may have "failed to destroy capitalism in the 1930s, but it succeeded in revolutionizing the status of civil rights issues." Harvard Sitkoff, *A New Deal for Blacks* (New York: Oxford University Press, 1978), pp. 139, 149.

24. Padmore's exit foreshadowed black declarations of independence from the left during U.S.-Soviet wartime alliance from 1942 to 1945, when the American Communist Party (CPUSA) revived the policy of the Popular Front in an effort to reconcile itself with U.S. liberal-nationalism. Indeed, one-time party head William Z. Foster had already publicly denigrated the "black belt thesis" as a "fantastic scheme designed to capture sections of the disintegrating Garvey Movement." James Hooker, *Black Revolutionary: George Padmore's Path from Communism to Pan-Africanism* (New York: Prager, 1970), p. 12.

25. Harold Cruse, "Les Noires et L'idée de la Revolte," in *Rebellion or Revolution* (New York: William and Morrow, 1968), p. 191; George Lipsitz, "'Frantic to Join . . . the Japanese Army': The Asia Pacific War and the Lives of African American Soldiers and Civilians," in Lisa Lowe and David Lloyd, eds., *The Politics of Culture in the Shadow of Capital* (Durham, N.C.: Duke University Press, 1997); Ralph Ellison, "Letter to Richard Wright, May 28, 1940," Richard Wright Papers Personal Correspondence, James Weldon Johnson Collection, MSS3, Series II, Box 97, Folder 1314, Ralph Ellison, 1937–1953.

26. Indeed, it is arguable that the Communist Party attracted the most talented black intellectuals and activists when it was most uncompromising in its own criticisms of U.S. capitalism, for example, the third period of the 1930s, the waning of the Popular Front in 1939, and the period immediately following World War II. (One thinks, for example, of George Padmore, Langston Hughes, Richard Wright, Ralph Ellison, Harold Cruse, or Jack O'Dell.) The Party invariably lost these self-same figures to some variety of independent black radicalism the moment it compromised, or the moment that black organizations appeared that could more effectively nurture and sustain black struggle. This suggests neither a relation of unhealthy antipathy, nor one of unhealthy dependency, between black activists and the far left. Rather, it shows how racial oppression in the United States shaped a shared spectrum of radical commitment to social change, and at the same time, how black activists have been remarkably flexible and nondoctrinaire in choosing the vehicles and instruments of their radicalism.

27. Richard Wright, *Black Boy/American Hunger* (1944) (New York: Harper Collins, 1993); Harold Cruse, *The Crisis of the Negro Intellectual* (New

York: William and Morrow, 1967); Robin D. G. Kelley, *Freedom Dreams: The Black Radical Imagination* (Boston: Beacon Press, 2002), p. 54; Jervis Anderson, *Bayard Rustin: Troubles I've Seen* (Berkeley: University of California Press, 1998), p. 59.

28. Gary Gerstle, *American Crucible: Race and Nation in the Twentieth Century* (Princeton, N.J.: Princeton University Press, 2001), p. 187.

29. Barbara Savage, *Broadcasting Freedom: Radio, War and the Politics of Race, 1938–1948* (Chapel Hill: University of North Carolina Press, 1999).

30. According to Werner Sollors, the American neologism "ethnicity" was first coined in 1941 by sociologist Lloyd Warner in his study, *Yankee City*. It refers to a type of intranational difference *different* from "race," the kind of difference, in other words, that supplements the national narrative of tolerance, inclusion, and global promise without destabilizing it. See Werner Sollors, *Beyond Ethnicity: Consent and Descent in American Culture* (New York: Oxford University Press, 1986). Also see Matthew Frye Jacobson, *Whiteness of a Different Color* (Cambridge, Mass.: Harvard University Press, 1998), pp. 94, 108.

31. Louis Adamic, "The Crisis Is Our Opportunity," *Common Ground* (Autumn 1940): 71.

32. Michael Denning, *The Cultural Front: The Laboring of American Culture* (New York: Verso, 1997), p. 445.

33. Myrdal, *American Dilemma*, p. 13. The process of assimilation was imagined as so successful that after the war, the dean of U.S. immigration historians, Oscar Handlin, could argue that it was no longer "appropriate at all to refer to minorities as a feature of American life," and that the "attributes of Americanism were . . . appropriate to the people of the whole world." Oscar Handlin, *Race and Nationality in American Life* (Boston: Little, Brown, 1957), pp. 173, 198.

34. Hughes, "Get Together Minorities, June 17, 1943," *Langston Hughes and the Chicago Defender*, p. 30.

35. Clayton Koppes and Gordon Black, *Hollywood Goes to War: How Politics, Profits and Propaganda Shaped World War II Movies* (New York: Free Press, 1986), p. 17.

36. Savage, *Broadcasting Freedom*, p. 62. It's unsurprising finally, that Frank Capra's officially sanctioned effort to document the black contribution to the war effort, "The Negro Soldier," contained a similar racial subtext. Its soundtrack, by Irving Berlin, opens with the old minstrel tune, "Putting on the Ritz," a piece that mocked black pretensions to higher social status. I'm indebted to Matt Jacobson for this insight.

37. Richard Wright, "Introduction: Blueprint for Negro Writing" (1937), in Addison Gayle, ed., *The Black Aesthetic* (New York: Doubleday and Company, 1971), p. 323.

38. Richard Wright, *Lawd Today* (Boston: Northeastern University Press, 1963), p. 6.

39. Ralph Ellison, "Letter to Richard Wright, May 26, 1940," JWJ MSS3, Series II, Box 97, Folder 1314.

40. Martin Dies, *A Trojan Horse in America* (New York: Dodd and Mead, 1940), pp. 118–129; Melvin Leffler, *The Specter of Communism* (New York: Hill and Wang, 1999).

41. Bunche quoted in Brian Urquhart, *Ralph Bunche: An American Life* (New York: W. W. Norton, 1993), p. 95. Also see Ben Keppel, *The Work of Democracy: Ralph Bunche, Kenneth B. Clark, Lorraine Hansberry and the Cultural Politics of Race* (Cambridge, Mass.: Harvard University Press, 1995), p. 52.

42. Ralph Ellison, "Editorial," *Negro Quarterly* vol. 1(4) (Winter 1943): 300.

43. Richard Wright, *Conversations with Richard Wright,* (Jackson: University of Mississippi Press, 1993), p. 26.

44. C. L. R. James, "The Twilight of the British Empire" (1938), quoted in Scott McLemee, ed., *C. L. R. James on the Negro Question*, p. xiii.

45. Paul Gilroy, *The Black Atlantic: Modernity and Double Consciousness* (Cambridge, Mass.: Harvard University Press, 1995), p. 4.

46. "The Result of Hate," *Chicago Defender* (March 26, 1938), quoted in Von Eschen, *Race against Empire*, p. 41; Paul Robeson, *Paul Robeson Speaks* (New York: Citadel Press, 1978), p. 147; Aimé Césaire, *Discourse on Colonialism* (New York: Monthly Review Press, 2000), p. 36.

47. Quoted in Timothy Tyson, *Radio Free Dixie: Robert Williams and the Roots of Black Power* (Chapel Hill: University of North Carolina Press, 1999), p. 29.

48. Rampersad, *Langston Hughes,* p. 24; Langston Hughes, "The Brazenness of Empire: From Here to Yonder," *Chicago Defender* (January 27, 1945), quoted in Von Eschen, *Race against Empire*, p. 34.

49. Horace R. Cayton, "An Awakening: The Negro Now Fights for Democratic Rights of All the World's Peoples," *Pittsburgh Courier* (February 27, 1943), quoted in Von Eschen, *Race against Empire*, p. 40.

50. Ralph Ellison, "Letter to Wright, November 3, 1941," JWJ, MSS3, Series II, Box 97, Folder 1314, p. 17.

51. Richard Wright, "I Tried to Be a Communist" (1944), in Richard Crossman, *The God That Failed* (New York: Harper and Row, 1949), p. 118.

52. Wright, *Black Boy/American Hunger,* p. 394.

53. Ibid., p. 341.

54. Richard Wright, *White Man Listen!* (New York: Anchor Books, 1957), p. 20; Richard Wright, "How Bigger Was Born," *Native Son* (New York: Harper and Row, 1966), pp. xx, xxiv.

55. Barbara Foley, "The Rhetoric of Anti-Communism in *Invisible Man*," *College English* vol. 59(5) (September 1997): 530–547; Bill Mullen, *Popular Fronts: Chicago and African American Cultural Politics, 1935–1946* (Urbana: University of Illinois Press, 1999).

56. Wright, "I Tried to Be a Communist," p. 167.

57. Ellison, "Letter to Wright, August 5, 1945," JWJ, MSS3, p. 28.

58. Richard Crossman, "Introduction," *The God That Failed,* p. 9.

59. Ellison, "Editorial," *Negro Quarterly* vol. 1(4) (Winter 1943): 300–301. Also see Alan Wald, *Exiles from a Future Time: The Forging of Mid-Century Literary Culture* (Chapel Hill: University of North Carolina Press, 2003), p. 284.

60. Ellison, *Invisible Man,* pp. 439–441.

61. Michel Fabre, *The Unfinished Quest of Richard Wright,* (Urbana: University of Illinois Press, 1993), p. 251.

62. Fabre, *The Unfinished Quest,* p. 258.

63. Ellison, "Editorial," *Negro Quarterly* vol. 1(4) (Winter 1943): 298; C. L. R. James, "Letter to Constance Webb" (1945), in Anna Grimshaw, ed., *The C. L. R. James Reader* (London: Blackwell, 1992), p. 146. This echoed Richard Wright's injunction that black writers must "accept the concept of (black) nationalism because, in order to transcend it, they must possess and understand it." Wright, "Blueprint for Negro Writing," *The Black Aesthetic.*

64. Wright quoted in Fabre, *The Unfinished Quest,* p. 224.

65. Himes, "Now Is the Time! Here Is the Place," *Primer for White Folks,* p. 215.

66. C. L. R. James, *American Civilization* (1950) (Cambridge, Mass.: Blackwell, 1993), p. 211.

67. James, "The Revolutionary Answer to the Negro Question," *C. L. R. James on the Negro Question,* p. 139.

68. James, "The Historical Development of Negroes," p. 74.

69. James, *American Civilization,* p. 201.

70. McWilliams, *Brothers under the Skin,* p. 24.

71. Frederick Keppel, "Foreword," *An American Dilemma,* p. xlviii.

72. Ottley, *A New World-a-Coming,* p. 5.

73. Abby Arthur Johnson and Ronald Mayberry Johnson, *Propaganda and Aesthetics: The Literary Politics of Afro-American Magazines in the Twentieth Century* (Amherst: University of Massachusetts Press, 1979), p. 125.

74. Hughes, "No Half-Freedoms, January 16, 1943," *Langston Hughes and the Chicago Defender,* p. 25.

75. Himes, "Now Is the Time! Here Is the Place," *Primer for White Folks,* p. 218.

76. L. D. Reddick, "The Test of the Atlantic Charter," *Crisis,* 50(7) (1943): 202, quoted in Von Eschen, *Race against Empire,* p. 28.

77. George Padmore, "Nigeria Questions Intent of the Atlantic Charter," *Chicago Defender* (January 12, 1942): 12, quoted in Von Eschen, *Race against Empire,* p. 26.

78. Cruse, "Revolutionary Nationalism and the Afro-American" (1962), *Rebellion or Revolution,* p. 75.

79. James, "The Historical Development of Negroes," p. 87. (italics in origi-

nal). Also see Terry Eagleton, "Nationalism, Irony and Commitment," in Seamus Deane, ed., *Nationalism, Colonialism and Literature* (Minneapolis: University of Minnesota Press, 1990), p. 37.

80. James, "The Historical Development of Negroes," p. 86.
81. C. L. R. James, *Special Delivery: Constance Webb/C. L. R. James Letters,* ed. Anna Grimshaw (London: Blackwell, 1996), p. 148.
82. James, "The Historical Development of Negroes," pp. 74, 86.
83. The "figure of America" in this view failed to represent a unified national subject, becoming instead "the locus for ideological battles over the trajectory of US history, the meaning of race, ethnicity and region in the United States, and the relation between ethnic nationalism, Americanism and internationalism." See Denning, *The Cultural Front,* p. 129.
84. Henry Wallace, "The Price of Free World Victory" (1942), in Russell Lord, ed., *Democracy Reborn* (New York: Reynalt Hitchcock, 1944), pp. 190–193.
85. Henry Luce, *The American Century* (New York: Farrar and Rhinehart, 1941), p. 23. In Luce's vision, as Norman Markowitz writes, "U.S. power and ideals (which Luce defined in simple conservative terms as law, truth, charity, and freedom) would be imposed upon the world as a kind of dispensation." Luce understood U.S. prerogatives in the world in terms of the imperialist rhetoric of a "civilizing" mission. As Luce put it, "It is the manifest duty of this country to undertake to feed all the people of the world who as a result of this worldwide collapse of civilization are hungry and destitute—all of them that is, whom we can from time to time reach consistently with a very tough attitude to all hostile governments. For every dollar we spend on armaments, we should spend at least a dime in the gigantic effort to feed the world." (37) Norman Markowitz, *The Rise and Fall of the People's Century* (New York: Free Press, 1973), p. 50.
86. Luce, *The American Century,* p. 23.
87. Wallace, "The Price of Free World Victory," *Democracy Reborn,* p. 194; Ralph Ellison, "The Negro and the Second World War," in Eric Sundquist, ed., *Cultural Contexts for Ralph Ellison's Invisible Man* (Boston: Bedford/St. Martin's Press, 1995), p. 236.
88. Indeed, if Wallace's vision was "ideal," evoking the insurrectionary demand of the disenfranchised, it might make sense to introduce the term *realism* to describe Luce's prefigurative relationship to what would eventually become the dominant U.S. discourse for mapping worldly relations during the Cold War. Exponents of realism called upon one-world visionaries to be less universalist and *more* culturally specific in identifying the potential agents and members of a world civilization. David Noble, *The End of American History: Democracy, Capitalism and the Metaphor of Two Worlds in Anglo-American Historical Writing, 1880–1980* (Minneapolis: University of Minnesota Press, 1985); John Ehrmann, *Neoconservatism: Intellectuals and Foreign Affairs, 1945–1994* (New Haven, Conn.: Yale University Press, 1995).

89. Ralph Ellison and Angelo Herndon, "Editorial Comment," *Negro Quarterly* vol. 1(4) (Winter/Spring 1943): ii–iii.

90. Ralph Ellison and Angelo Herndon, "Editorial Comment," *Negro Quarterly* vol. 3(3) (Fall 1942): 196 (emphasis added).

91. George Padmore, "The New Imperialism III: Anglo-American Condominium," *Politics* (May 1944): 113.

92. Rayford Logan, "The Negro Wants First-Class Citizenship," in Rayford Logan, ed., *What the Negro Wants* (Chapel Hill: University of North Carolina Press, 1944), pp. 7–8.

93. Hughes, "Ask for Everything, January 30, 1943," *Langston Hughes and the Chicago Defender,* p. 143.

94. Richard Wright, "Introduction," *Black Metropolis,* p. xxv.

95. C. L. R. James, "The American People in One World: An Essay in Dialectical Materialism," *New International* (July 1944): 226; "The Historical Developments of the Negroes in American Society," p. 66.

96. George Kennan, "The Necessity for Containment" (1946), in William Chafe and Harvard Sitkoff, eds., *A History of Our Times: Readings on Postwar America* (New York: Oxford University Press, 1999), p. 17.

97. Drake and Cayton, *Black Metropolis,* vol. 1, p. 762; Wright, *Twelve Million Black Voices,* p. 130.

4. Americanizing the Negro

1. Walter Jackson, *Gunnar Myrdal and America's Conscience: Social Engineering and Racial Liberalism, 1938–1987* (Chapel Hill: University of North Carolina Press, 1990), p. 25; Charles Henry, *Ralph Bunche: Model Negro or American Other?* (New York: New York University Press, 2000), p. 93.

2. Woodrow Wilson, "The Making of a Nation," *Atlantic Monthly* (July 1897): 1–14.

3. Harold Isaacs, *The New World of the American Negroes* (New York: Viking Press, 1963), p. 38.

4. Frederick Keppel, "Foreword," in Gunnar Myrdal, *An American Dilemma: The Negro Problem and Modern Democracy* (1944) (New York: Harper and Row, 1962), p. xlvi.

5. Perry Anderson, "Internationalism: A Breviary," *New Left Review* 14 (March/April 2002): 23.

6. John Dower, *War without Mercy: Race and Power in the Pacific War* (Baltimore: Johns Hopkins University Press, 1986).

7. Franz Schurmann, *The Logic of World Power* (New York: Pantheon Books, 1974), pp. 57, 4.

8. Thomas McCormick, *America's Half Century: United States Foreign Policy in the Cold War* (Baltimore: Johns Hopkins University Press, 1989), p. 37.

9. Quoted in David Levering Lewis, *W. E. B. Du Bois: The Fight for Equality*

and the American Century, 1919–1963 (New York: Henry Holt, 2000), p. 503.

10. W. E. B. Du Bois, *Color and Democracy: Colonies and Peace* (New York: Harcourt Brace, 1945), p. 9.

11. Robert Hill, ed., *The F.B.I.'s RACON: Racial Conditions in the United States during World War II* (Boston: Northeastern University Press, 1995); Patrick Washburn, *A Question of Sedition: The Federal Government's Investigation of the Black Press During World War II* (New York: Oxford University Press, 1986); Kenneth O'Reilly, *Black Americans: The FBI Files* (New York: Caroll and Graf, 1994).

12. Charles Johnson, *To Stem This Tide* (Boston: The Pilgrim Press, 1943), p. 130. Also see Carey McWilliams, *Brothers under the Skin* (Boston: Little, Brown, 1943), p. 4.

13. Brian Urquhart, *Ralph Bunche: An American Life* (New York: W. W. Norton, 1993), p. 97.

14. Ralph Bunche, "The Negro in the Political Life of the U.S." (1941), in Charles Henry, ed., *Ralph Bunche: Selected Speeches and Writings* (Ann Arbor: University of Michigan Press, 1996), p. 94.

15. Urquhart, *Ralph Bunche: An American Life*, p. 115.

16. Henry, *Ralph Bunche: Model Negro or American Other?* p. 125.

17. Ibid., p. 126.

18. The governmental state, or welfare state, can be understood, after Keynes, as the growing interpenetration of governing institutions with the exchange networks of civil society. Expanding the point, the state might be the simplified name given to a more complicated modern process: the establishment of a feedback loop between practices and institutions for coordinating and normalizing human behavior and the cultural and intellectual processes for both revising those practices and making them publicly legible and legitimate. See Graham Burchell, Colin Gordon, and Peter Miller, eds., *The Foucault Effect: Studies in Governmentality* (Chicago: University of Chicago Press, 1993).

19. Gunnar Myrdal, *An American Dilemma: The Negro Problem and Modern Democracy*, 2 vols. (1942) (New York: Harper and Row, 1963). The two-volume, two-thousand-page study took six years to complete, enlisting hundreds of academics, intellectuals, and culture workers across the nation for what at the time was the unprecedented sum of $300,000. Jackson, *Gunnar Myrdal and America's Conscience*, p. 106.

20. Myrdal, *An American Dilemma*, vol. 1, pp. 25, 464.

21. Ibid., p. 510.

22. Ben Keppel, *The Work of Democracy: Ralph Bunche, Kenneth B. Clark, Lorraine Hansberry and the Cultural Politics of Race* (Cambridge, Mass.: Harvard University Press, 1995), p. 55.

23. Myrdal, *An American Dilemma*, vol. 1, p. 74.

24. Ibid., p. 75.

25. See, for example, Wilson Record's definitive Cold War text, *The Negro and the Communist Party* (Chapel Hill: University of North Carolina, 1951): "Because the aspirations of the American Negro are essentially egalitarian, a 'bourgeois' document like the American Constitution has a liberating potential in the Black Belt of Alabama and in the ghetto of Harlem that the *Communist Manifesto* could never hope to have." (315)

26. It is worth quoting more fully: "Negroes are denied identification with the nation or with national groups to a much larger degree. To them social speculation, therefore, moves in a sphere of unreality and futility. Instead of organized popular theories or ideas, the observer finds in the Negro world, for the most part, only a *fluid and amorphous mass of all sorts of embryos of thoughts.*" Myrdal, *An American Dilemma,* p. 782 (italics in original).

27. Myrdal, *An American Dilemma,* p. 927. Thus, Myrdal wrote that the study had "excluded from consideration . . . valuations which have not behind them a considerable number of citizens with a considerable actual or potential power." Also see Jackson, *Gunnar Myrdal and America's Conscience,* p. 114.

28. Uday Mehta, *Liberalism and Empire* (Chicago: University of Chicago Press, 1999), p. 17.

29. Robert Lynd, "Prison for American Genius: The Vast and Ugly Reality of Our Greatest Failure," *Saturday Review of Literature* (April 22, 1944), p. 5.

30. Myrdal, *An American Dilemma,* p. 782.

31. Ibid., pp. 781–784. Recall that both Bunche and Frazier emphasized the pathological aspects of black culture and the provincialism of black leadership. Both once again envisioned the solution of the Negro problem as involving the dissolution of black distinctiveness, which they understood in entirely negative terms. As Bunche wrote in one of his memoranda: "The Negro is a purely sociological phenomenon in this country, the product of a series of historical accidents, with his collective identification resting primarily on the color of his skin, the texture of his hair, and most importantly, the white man's conception of him as a Negro." See Jackson, *Gunnar Myrdal and America's Conscience,* p. 130.

32. David Kazandjian, "Charles Brockden Brown's Biloquial Nation: National Culture and White Settler Colonialism in Memoirs of Carwin the Biloquist," *American Literature* 73 (September 2001): 459–496. Also see David Kazandjian, *The Colonizing Trick* (Minneapolis: University of Minnesota Press, 2003).

33. Myrdal, *An American Dilemma,* p. 1017.

34. Daniel Rogers, *Atlantic Crossings: Social Politics in a Progressive Age* (Cambridge, Mass.: Harvard University Press, 1998), p. 410.

35. Myrdal, *An American Dilemma,* p. 1021.

36. Ibid., p. lviii.

37. Brenda Gayle Plummer, *A Rising Wind: Black Americans and U.S. Foreign Affairs, 1935–1960* (Chapel Hill: University of North Carolina Press, 1996), p. 327.

38. Myrdal, *An American Dilemma,* p. lxix (italics in original).
39. Indeed, the funding sources were exhausted for the next two decades. After the war, Drake wrote, no one was interested in how to conceptualize race relations; people were interested only in outcome studies framed around the teleological supposition that racial discrimination was declining and that this could then be measured. Jackson, *Gunnar Myrdal and America's Conscience,* p. 265.
40. Quoted in Plummer, *A Rising Wind,* p. 228
41. W. E. B. Du Bois, *The Autobiography of W. E. B. Du Bois* (New York: International Publishers, 1968), p. 167.
42. Ralph Ellison, *Shadow and Act* (New York: Signet Books, 1963), pp. 290–302.
43. Ellison, *Shadow and Act,* p. 301.
44. Oliver Cox, "An American Dilemma: A Mystical Approach to the Study of Race Relations" (1945), in Herbert Hunter and Sameer Abraham, eds., *Race, Class and the World-System: The Sociology of Oliver C. Cox* (New York: Monthly Review Press, 1987), pp. 19, 32.
45. Eric Williams, *Capitalism and Slavery* (Chapel Hill: University of North Carolina Press, 1944), p. 210.
46. Ibid., p. 212. Also see Cedric Robinson, "Capitalism, Slavery and Bourgeois Historiography," *History Workshop Journal* (Winter 1990):130; Thomas Holt, *The Problem of Freedom: Race, Labor and Politics in Jamaica and Britain, 1832–1938* (Baltimore: Johns Hopkins University Press, 1992), pp. 23–25.
47. Du Bois, *Color and Democracy,* p. 91.
48. Ibid., pp. 71, 73.
49. W. E. B. Du Bois, "The Negro and Imperialism" (1944), Philip Foner, ed., *W. E. B. Du Bois Speaks,* vol.2 (New York: Pathfinder Press, 1970), p. 155. Also see Hannah Arendt, *The Origins of Totalitarianism* (New York: Harcourt, Brace and Jovanovich, 1951), p. 267.
50. W. E. B. Du Bois, *Dusk of Dawn* (New York: Schocken Books, 1968), pp. 32, 127.
51. Du Bois, *Color and Democracy,* p. 3.
52. W. E. B. Du Bois, "Human Rights for All Minorities" (1945), in *W. E. B. Du Bois Speaks,* pp. 182, 184.
53. Du Bois, "Human Rights for All Minorities," p. 182.
54. Lewis, *W. E. B. Du Bois,* pp. 503, 509–510.
55. As David Levering Lewis writes, "for Du Bois, the prospect of shattered colonial empires of Britain and France being shored up by a North American colossus whose laws abided racial segregation was almost beyond enduring." Lewis, *W. E. B. Du Bois,* pp. 502–503.
56. Quoted in Marilyn Young, *The Vietnam Wars* (New York: Oxford University Press, 1992), p. 2.
57. Marilyn Young et al., *The Vietnam War: A History in Documents* (New York: Oxford University Press, 2002), pp. 26, 32, 33.

58. As Robert Hill has eloquently put it, "If the first half of the decade of the forties represented a hopeful hour for popular initiative and autonomy, the postwar half reflected a mood of national anxiety. Suddenly the feeling of hope and confidence gave way to a sense of self-doubt and fiendish reality. It is a transformation that is still difficult from this distance to appreciate." Robert Hill, "Afterword," in C. L. R. James, *American Civilization* (Cambridge, Mass.: Blackwell, 1993), p. 329.

59. Michael Hunt, "Conclusions: The Decolonization Puzzle," in David Ryan and Victor Pungong, eds., *The United States and Decolonization: Power and Freedom* (New York: St. Martin's Press, 2000), p. 207.

60. Quoted in L. S. Stavrianos, *Global Rift: The Third World Comes of Age* (New York: William & Morrow, 1981), p. 459.

61. Chalmers Johnson, *Blowback: The Causes and Consequences of American Empire* (New York: Metropolitan Books, 2000), p. 23.

62. Patricia Sullivan, *Days of Hope: Race and Democracy in the New Deal Era* (Chapel Hill: University of North Carolina Press, 1996), p. 181.

63. The division between these two trajectories was exemplified by the different institutions they sought to advance, as the former pursued the vision of a democratic United Nations, while the latter promoted the Bretton Woods system, a highly inegalitarian system of financial institutions grafted upon the economic advantages already accrued to colonial and Western powers.

64. Kennan's statement was made in 1948 at the onset of the official Cold War. It is thus revealing not only of the material underpinnings of anticommunist doctrine, but also of the cynical underside of the "American Century." As Kennan continues, "We will have to dispense with all sentimentality and day-dreaming; and our attention will have to be concentrated everywhere on our immediate national objectives. We need not deceive ourselves that we can afford the luxury of altruism and world benefaction. We should cease to talk about vague—and for the Far East—unreal objectives such as human rights, the raising of living standards, and democratization. The day is not far off when we are going to have to deal in straight power concepts. The less we are then hampered by idealistic slogans, the better." Robert Merrill, "Simulations and Terrors of Our Time," in Robert Merrill, ed., *Violent Persuasions: The Politics and Imagery of Terrorism* (New York: Routledge, 1994), p. 27; Kennan's writings are quoted in Joel Kovel, *Red-Hunting in the Promised Land* (New York: Basic Books, 1994), p. 58.

65. Quoted in McKormick, *America's Half-Century*, p. 75. Also see George Kennan, "The Necessity for Containment," reprinted in William Chafe and Harvard Sitkoff, eds., *A History of Our Time: Readings on Postwar America* (New York: Oxford University Press, 1999), p. 14–17.

66. It also obscured forms of antidemocratic and authoritarian rule that the United States and the Soviets equally spawned within their spheres of power. As Chalmers Johnson writes, there was "far more symmetry between the postwar policies of the Soviet Union and the United States than

most Americans are willing to recognize. The USSR in Eastern Europe and the US in East Asia created their satellite systems for essentially the same reasons." Indeed, Johnson adds that the United States constructed its system for more genuinely imperialist reasons (rather than as a bulwark against Soviet expansion), since the USSR unlike the U.S. actually had a real defensive security concern at the end of World War II. Moreover, "just as the Soviets intervened in Hungary and Czechoslovakia, in the interest of preserving their empire, the US intervened in Korea and Vietnam (not to mention Iran, Guatemala, Indonesia, Chile, etc. . .), and probably to much bloodier effect." Johnson, *Blowback,* p. 24.

67. Schurmann, *The Logic of World Power,* p. 150.

68. Indeed, in the early 1950s the American Medical Association (AMA) defeated proposals for national health insurance by invoking the "monstrosity of Bolshevik bureaucracy," even offering a fake quotation attributed to Lenin in which socialized medicine was described as "the keystone of the socialist state." Steven Whitfield, *The Culture of the Cold War* (Baltimore: Johns Hopkins University Press, 1996); Foner, *Story of American Freedom,* p. 257; Elaine Tyler May, *Homeward Bound: American Families in the Cold War Era* (New York: Basic Books, 1988).

69. Melvin Leffler, *The Specter of Communism: The United States and the Origins of the Cold War, 1917–1953* (New York: Hill and Wang, 1994), p. 15; Lewis, *W. E. B. Du Bois,* p. 525.

70. Arthur Schlesinger Jr., *The Vital Center: the Politics of Freedom* (New Brunswick, N.J.: Transaction Publishers, 1998).

71. "Opposition to the Military Act of 1949," U.S. Congress, House Committee on Foreign Affairs, First Session, 28–29 July, 1949. Quoted in Sterling Johnson, *Black Globalism: The International Politics of a Non-State Nation* (London: Ashgate, 1998), p. 115.

72. Arthur Schlesinger Jr., "The Communist Party," *Life* (July 29, 1946): 90; Arthur Schlesinger Jr., "The Liberal Fifth-Column in America," *Partisan Review* (Summer 1946): 279–293; quoted in Lewis, *W. E. B. Du Bois,* p. 526.

73. This is not to say that both Du Bois and Robeson did not have popular support, particularly in black communities like Harlem. As historian David Montgomery writes of the early 1950s, "In the academic world Du Bois was not being read seriously. But I think it is safe to say that there would be no name that would be pronounced with greater respect throughout the Black working-class community in America than that of Dr. Du Bois. Henry Abelove, *Visions of History* (New York: Pantheon, 1976), p. 178.

74. Gerald Horne, *Black and Red: W. E. B. Du Bois and the African American Response to the Cold War, 1944–1963* (New York: SUNY Press, 1986); Norman Markowitz, "A Culture of Resistance," in Michael Klein, ed., *An American Half Century* (London: Pluto Press, 1994), p. 18.

75. Manning Marable, *Race, Reform and Rebellion: The Second Reconstruction in Black America, 1945–1990* (Jackson: University of Mississippi

Press, 1991), p. 22; Patricia Sullivan, *Days of Hope: Race and Democracy in the New Deal Era* (Chapel Hill: University of North Carolina Press, 1996), p. 274; Kim Moody, *Workers in a Lean World* (New York: Verso, 1997), p. 156.

76. Thomas Sugrue, "Crabgrass-Roots Politics: Race, Rights and the Reaction against Liberalism in the Urban North, 1940–1964," *Journal of American History* (September 1995): 569, 556.

77. Martin Duberman, *Paul Robeson: A Biography* (New York: Knopf, 1989), p. 314.

78. Arnold Hirsh, "Massive Resistance in the Urban North: Trumbull Park, Chicago, 1953–1960," *Journal of American History* (September 1995): 522–550.

79. St. Clair Drake, "The International Implications of Race Relations," *Journal of Negro Education* (1951): 269.

80. Plummer, *A Rising Wind,* pp. 189–204. Also see Horne, *Black and Red;* and Duberman, *Paul Robeson.*

81. Quoted in Marable, *Race, Reform and Rebellion,* p. 22.

82. Mary Dudziak, *Cold War Civil Rights: Race and the Image of American Democracy* (Princeton, N.J.: Princeton University Press, 2000); Von Eschen, *Race against Empire,* p. 113.

83. Martin Duberman, *Paul Robeson* (New York: Random House, 1989), p. 347.

84. Von Eschen, *Race against Empire,* p. 117.

85. Margaret Butcher, *The Negro in American Culture* (New York: Knopf, 1956), p. 42.

86. Quoted in Record, *The Negro and the Communist Party,* p. 315. In his 1972 autobiography, Robinson in a sense recanted his testimony against Robeson. "In those days, I had much more faith in the ultimate justice of the American white man than I have today. I would reject such an invitation if offered now." Quoted in Duberman, *Paul Robeson,* p. 362.

87. E. Franklin Frazier, *The Black Bourgeoisie: The Rise of a New Middle-Class in the United States* (1955) (New York: Collier Books, 1962), p. 193.

88. "For most Negro intellectuals, the integration of the Negro means just the opposite—the emptying of his life of meaningful content and ridding him of all Negro identification. For them integration and eventual assimilation means the annihilation of the Negro—physically, culturally and spiritually." E. Franklin Frazier, "The Failure of the Negro Intellectual," in *E. Franklin Frazier on Race Relations* (Chicago: University of Chicago Press, 1968), p. 278. Also see Anthony Platt, *E. Franklin Frazier Reconsidered* (New Brunswick, N.J.: Rutgers University Press, 1991).

89. *The Negro in American Life* explicitly celebrated the government's opposition to residential segregation, codified in the Supreme Court Decision in *Shelley vs. Kramer* (1948) outlawing racially restrictive covenants. Dudziak, *Cold War Civil Rights,* p. 47.

90. Henry, *Ralph Bunche: Model Negro or American Other,* p. 167.

91. Quoted in Mary Dudziak, "Desegregation as a Cold War Imperative," *Stanford Law Review* (Stanford, Calif.: Stanford School of Law, Stanford University, 1988), p. 65.

92. Consider, for example, the following from the *Chicago Defender* in 1950 (which shows just how far it had traveled from its wartime radicalism): Ralph Bunche, *The Defender* editorialized, gave "the lie to enemy propaganda that American democracy is limited to those who can pass a color test . . . We need the kind of leadership that Mr. Bunche could give us to turn the Asiatic our way. It will take more than dollars to win the Cold War, and Dr. Bunche has what it takes." Keppel, *The Work of Democracy,* p. 66.

93. Thus, erstwhile anti-Stalinist leftists and anti-imperialists like Dwight Mac-Donald expressly "chose the West" during this period in the name of a civilizational (and implicitly racializing discourse) that equated the Soviet Union with "the great slave societies of Egypt and the Orient." Dwight MacDonald, "I Choose the West," *Memoirs of a Revolutionist: Essays in Political Criticism* (New York: Farrar, Strauss and Giroux, 1957), p. 198.

94. Mary Anne Glendon, *A World Made New: Eleanor Roosevelt and the Universal Declaration of Human Rights* (New York: Random House, 2001), p. 205.

95. Peter Irons, *Jim Crow's Children: The Broken Promise of the Brown Decision* (New York: Viking, 2002).

96. Langston Hughes, *Good Morning Revolution: Uncollected Social Protest Writings* (New York: Lawrence Hill, 1970), p. 144.

97. Quoted in Fabre, *The Unfinished Quest,* p. 366

98. Ellison amplified his own difference from Wright in other ways. In his speech accepting the National Book Award for *Invisible Man* in 1953, Ellison took another dig at Wright, suggesting that he was attempting to oppose "the final and unrelieved despair of so much of our current fiction" with a novel that could approximate the "rich diversity" and "fluidity and freedom" of America with "all the bright magic of a fairy tale." Ralph Ellison, "Light on 'Invisible Man'," *Crisis* (March 1953): 158. Also see Fabre, *The Unfinished Quest,* p. 369.

99. James Baldwin, "The Discovery of What It Means to Be an American," in *Notes of a Native Son* (New York: Delta Books, 1961). In an interview with Harold Isaacs, Ellison described himself in the early 1960s as "vindictively American." Issacs, *New World,* p. 261.

100. Wright quoted in Fabre, *The Unfinished Quest of Richard Wright,* p. 369.

101. Wright letter to Margit Salboniere (1960), quoted in Julia Wright, "Introduction," *Haiku: This Other World* (New York: Arcade Publishers, 1998). Also see Cedric Robinson, *Black Marxism: The Making of the Black Radical Tradition* (London: Zed Press, 1988), p. 437.

102. C. L. R. James, *Mariners, Renegades and Castaways: The Story of Herman Melville and the World We Live In* (New York: C. L. R. James, 1953),

pp. 181, 199; Leroi Jones, *Blues People* (New York: Henry Holt, 1962), p. 215. The McCarran-Walter Immigration Act of 1952 further exemplified how new national security doctrines embedded racial ascription within an ostensibly universalizing discourse. The act, for the first time in U.S. history, formally abolished racial qualifications for naturalization. Yet, even as racial exclusion was theoretically abolished, it was practically upheld, as the act reaffirmed national origins quotas that severely limited immigration to the United States from every part of the world except northern and western Europe. Moreover, the law was aimed at denying all suspected subversives entry into the country, the provision under which James himself was subsequently deported, in a period that, like the present, was marked by a major spike in the number of deportations.

103. Paul Robeson, *Here I Stand* (Boston: Beacon Press, 1958), p. 79. Also see Pete Daniel, *Lost Revolution: The South in the 1950s* (Washington, D.C.: Smithsonian, 2000), p. 305.

104. Timothy Tyson, *Radio Free Dixie: Robert Williams and the Roots of Black Power* (Chapel Hill: University of North Carolina Press, 1999), p. 51; John Dittmer, *Local People: The Struggle for Civil Rights in Mississippi* (Urbana: University of Illinois Press, 1994).

105. C. L. R. James, "Black People in the Urban Areas of the U.S.," in Anna Grimshaw, ed., *The C. L. R. James Reader* (Blackwell: London, 1992), p. 378.

106. Paul Gilroy, *The Black Atlantic: Modernity and Double-Consciousness* (Cambridge, Mass.: Harvard University Press, 1993), p. 123.

5. Decolonizing America

1. Aimé Césaire, "Culture and Colonization," *Presence Africaine: Revue Culturelle du Monde Noire* (June–November 1956): 190 (author's translation).

2. John P. Davis, "Debats," *Presence Africaine* (June–November 1956): 213; James Ivy, "The NAACP as an Instrument of Social Change," *Presence Africaine* (June–November 1956): 335.

3. Davis, "Debats," p. 214.

4. Aimé Césaire, *Discourse on Colonialism* (New York: Monthly Review Press, 2000), p. 77; Mary Renda, *Taking Haiti: Military Occupation and the Culture of U.S. Imperialism, 1915–1940* (Chapel Hill: University of North Carolina Press, 2001).

5. W. E. B. Du Bois, "To the Congress of Ecrivains et Artistes Noires," *Présence Africaine* (June–November 1956): 383.

6. Richard Wright, "Tradition and Industrialization: The Plight of the Tragic Elite in Africa," *Presence Africaine* (June–November 1956): 360, 377. As Wright put it around this time, to "people oppressed so long . . . their oppression has become a tradition, in fact a kind of culture." Richard Wright,

"Introduction," to George Padmore, *Pan-Africanism or Communism* (London: Denis Dobson, 1955), p. 13.

7. Wright, "Tradition and Industrialization," p. 377.

8. Padmore, *Pan-Africanism or Communism*, p. 18. Also see Richard Wright, *The Color Curtain: A Report on the Bandung Conference* (Cleveland: World Publishing, 1956).

9. Richard Wright, *Black Power: A Record of Reactions in a Land of Pathos* (New York: Harper & Brothers, 1954), pp. 53–54. Also Kevin Gaines, "Richard Wright in Ghana: Black Radicalism and the Dialectics of Diaspora," paper in author's possession.

10. C. L. R. James, "Politics and Letters" (1957), in Anna Grimshaw, ed., *C. L. R. James Reader* (London: Blackwell, 1992), p. 275.

11. James Baldwin, "Princes and Powers," *Nobody Knows My Name* (New York: Dell Publishing, 1961), p. 18.

12. Nancy Kates and Bennett Singer, *Brother Outsider: The Life of Bayard Rustin* (South Burlington, Vt.: California Newsreel, 2002).

13. Carl Rowan, *Breaking Barriers: A Memoir* (Boston: Little, Brown, 1991), pp. 123–124. Rowan is also quoted in Vijay Prashad, *The Karma of Brown Folk* (Minneapolis: University of Minnesota Press, 2000), p. 241.

14. Powell is quoted in Charles Hamilton, *Adam Clayton Powell Jr.* (New York: Macmillan, 1991), p. 243. Also see Thomas Borstelmann, *The Cold War and the Color Line: American Race Relations in the Global Era* (Cambridge, Mass.: Harvard University Press, 2001).

15. I am indebted to Jodi Melamed for the idea of blacks as witnesses for U.S. democracy.

16. Hamilton, *Adam Clayton Powell*, p. 246.

17. Carl Rowan, "Has Paul Robeson Betrayed the American Negro," *Ebony* (September 1957): 37.

18. Rustin is quoted in Martin Duberman, *Paul Robeson: A Biography* (New York: Ballantine, 1989), p. 344.

19. Duberman, *Paul Robeson*, p. 346.

20. Robert Williams is quoted in Timothy Tyson, *Radio Free Dixie: Robert F. Williams and the Roots of Black Power* (Chapel Hill: University of North Carolina, 1999), p. 240.

21. Bayard Rustin, "From Protest to Politics: The Future of the Civil Rights Movement," *Commentary* 35 (1965).

22. E. Frankin Frazier, "The Failure of the Negro Intellectual" (1962), in G. Franklin Edwards, ed., *E. Franklin Frazier on Race Relations: Selected Papers* (Chicago: University of Chicago Press, 1968), p. 273.

23. Ibid., p. 274.

24. Ibid., p. 278.

25. Harold Cruse, "An Afro-American's Cultural Views" (1958), in *Rebellion or Revolution* (New York: William & Morrow, 1968), p. 61.

26. Cruse, "Introduction," *Rebellion or Revolution*, p. 22.

27. Cruse, "Revolutionary Nationalism and the Afro-American" (1962), *Rebellion or Revolution*, pp. 74, 76.

28. Ibid., pp. 91, 95.

29. Jerry Watts, *Amiri Baraka: The Politics and Art of a Black Intellectual* (New York: New York University Press, 2002), p. 223.

30. Tyson, *Radio Free Dixie*, p. 51.

31. Cruse, *Rebellion or Revolution*, p. 23.

32. Harold Isaacs, *The New World of American Negroes* (London: Phoenix House, 1963).

33. James Baldwin, "Fifth Avenue Uptown: A Letter from Harlem," *Nobody Knows My Name*, p. 79. In 1960, for example, *Ebony* devoted an entire issue to documenting the splendors of Ghanain independence. As Baldwin said at the time, "The image of Nkrumah getting off his plane has an effect on all the other images . . . tak[ing] a certain sting out of those pictures of the African savage." Quoted in Isaacs, *The New World of American Negroes*, p. 276.

34. James Baldwin, "An Open Letter to My Sister Angela Davis," in Angela Davis, *If They Come in the Morning* (San Francisco: The National United Committee to Free Angela Davis [NUCFAD], 1971), pp. 19–23; James Baldwin, *No Name in the Street* (New York: Dell Publishing, 1972).

35. James Boggs, *Racism and the Class Struggle: Further Pages from a Black Worker's Notebook* (New York: Monthly Review Press, 1971), p. 29.

36. Martin Luther King Jr., "My Trip to the Land of Gandhi," in *Testament of Hope: The Essential Writings of Martin Luther King Jr.* (New York: Harper and Row, 1986), p. 24.

37. Aijaz Ahmad's *In Theory: Classes, Nations and Literatures* (New York: Verso, 1992) designates the years between 1945 and 1975 the high period of decolonization, with 1965–1975 giving rise to nationalist struggles with "a distinctly socialist trajectory" (30).

38. Van Gosse, *Where the Boys Are: Cuba, Cold War America and the Making of the New Left* (New York: Verso, 1993), pp. 153–154.

39. Cruse, "Rebellion or Revolution—I," *Rebellion or Revolution*, p. 105.

40. Cruse, "Revolutionary Nationalism and the Afro-American," *Rebellion or Revolution*, pp. 75, 94.

41. Brenda Gayle Plummer, *A Rising Wind: Black Americans and U.S. Foreign Affairs, 1935–1960* (Chapel Hill: University of North Carolina Press, 1996), p. 303.

42. Plummer, *A Rising Wind*, p. 304.

43. St. Clair Drake, "The Relations of the American and the African Negro in the Context of Pan-Africanism," *American Society of African Culture, Summary Report, 4th Annual Conference* (June 21–24, 1961): 9–12.

44. Orlando Bagwell, dir., *Malcolm X: Make It Plain* (Blackside, Inc., 1994).

45. Malcolm X, *By Any Means Necessary* (New York: Pathfinder, 1970), p. 153.

46. The idea of African "survivals" was first advanced by anthropologist Melville Herskovits in the early 1940s in his book *The Myth of the Negro Past* (Boston: Beacon Press, 1990).

47. Malcolm X, *The Autobiography of Malcolm X* (New York: Ballantine, 1965).

48. This speech was republished under the title "On National Culture." See Frantz Fanon, *Wretched of the Earth* (New York: Grove Press, 1961), pp. 216, 224.

49. Ibid., p. 247.

50. Ibid., p. 232. Also see Ato Sekyi Out, *Fanon's Dialectic of Experience* (Cambridge, Mass.: Harvard University Press, 1996), pp. 44, 41.

51. Ibid., p. 80.

52. Ibid., p. 101.

53. Ibid., p. 75.

54. See Tyson, *Radio Free Dixie* for the full account. Also see Gosse, *Where the Boys Are,* pp. 153–154.

55. Robert F. Williams, *Negroes with Guns* (New York: Marzani and Munsell, 1962), p. 103.

56. Ibid., p. 109.

57. James Forman, *The Making of Black Revolutionaries* (Seattle: Open Hand Publishing, 1985), p. 174.

58. For the importance of "routes" (as opposed to "roots") as the governing metaphor for black radical thinking see Paul Gilroy, "It Ain't Where You're From, It's Where You're At. . . The Dialectics of Diasporic Identification," reprinted in *Small Acts: Thoughts on the Politics of Black Cultures* (London: Serpent's Tale, 1993), p. 120.

59. Etienne Balibar and Immanuel Wallerstein, *Race, Nation, Class: Ambiguous Identities* (London: Verso, 1991), p. 18.

60. This is Max Weber's famous axiom defining the modern state.

61. Quoted in Emmanuel Hansen, *Frantz Fanon: Social and Political Thought* (Columbus: Ohio State University Press, 1977), p. 6.

62. Eldridge Cleaver, *Soul on Ice* (New York: Dell Publishing, 1968), p. 27.

63. David Hilliard and Lewis Cole, *This Side of Glory: The Autobiography of David Hilliard and the Story of the Black Panther Party* (Boston: Little, Brown, 1993), p. 115.

64. Boggs, *Racism and the Class Struggle,* p. 39.

65. Harry Haywood, *Black Bolshevik: Autobiography of an Afro-American Communist* (Chicago: Liberator Press, 1978).

66. Quoted in Boggs, *Racism and the Class Struggle,* p. 41.

67. Huey P. Newton, *To Die for the People,* ed. Toni Morrison (New York: Writers & Publishers, 1995), p. 36.

68. If the founding ethos of the post–World War II civil rights movement was said to be America's fulfillment of "the main trend in its history" or "the gradual realization of the American Creed," the self-assertion of the ghetto

destructured the imaginary space of the nation-state as a place of historicist becoming for black people and as an integral territorial and ideological unit to which they belonged. Gunnar Myrdal, *An American Dilemma* (New York: Harper and Row, 1962), p. 3. For the general reconceptualization of "space" in social theory and politics see Edward Soja, *Postmodern Geographies: The Reassertion of Space in Critical Social Theory* (London: Verso, 1989); Neil Smith, *Uneven Development: Nature, Capital and the Production of Space* (London: Basil Blackwell, 1984).

69. Fanon, *Wretched of the Earth,* pp. 129–130; Hilliard and Cole, *This Side of Glory,* p. 180.

70. William Gardner Smith, *Return to Black America* (Englewood Cliffs, N.J.: Prentice-Hall Publishers, 1970), p. 173.

71. Stuart Hall et al., *Policing the Crisis: Mugging, the State and Law and Order* (New York: Holmes and Meier, 1978), p. 387.

72. Bobby Seale, *Seize the Time: The Story of the Black Panther Party and Huey P. Newton* (1970) (Baltimore: Black Classic Press, 1991), pp. 80–83.

73. Hilliard and Cole, *This Side of Glory,* p. 232.

74. Eldridge Cleaver, *Post-Prison Writings and Speeches* (New York: Vintage Books, 1970); Forman, *The Making of Black Revolutionaries,* p. 541; Angela Davis, *With My Mind on Freedom: An Autobiography* (New York: Bantam Books, 1974); George Jackson, *Soledad Brother* (London: Penguin Books, 1970); Carlos Munoz Jr., *Youth, Identity and Power: The Chicano Movement* (New York: Verso, 1989), p. 86; Dan Georgakas and Marvin Surkin, *Detroit: I Do Mind Dying: A Study in Urban Revolution* (New York: St. Martin's Press, 1975), p. 61; Ward Churhill and Jim Vander Wall, *Agents of Repression: The F.B.I.'s Secret Wars against the Black Panther Party and the American Indian Movement* (Boston: South End Press, 1988); Cornel West, "The Paradoxes of the Afro-American Rebellion," in Sonya Sahres et al., eds., *The Sixties without Apology* (Minneapolis: University of Minnesota Press, 1984), p. 53; Hilliard and Cole, *This Side of Glory,* pp. 247, 278; Hall et al., *Policing the Crisis,* pp. 386–388.

75. Arnold Hirsch, *The Making of the Second Ghetto: Race and Housing in Chicago, 1940–1960* (New York: Cambridge University Press, 1983); Mike Davis, *City of Quartz: Excavating the Future in Los Angeles* (New York: Vintage Books, 1992); Douglas Massey and Nancy Denton, *American Apartheid: Segregation and the Making of the Underclass* (Cambridge, Mass.: Harvard University Press, 1993).

76. Robert Self, "To Plan Our Liberation: Black Power and the Politics of Place in Oakland, California, 1965–1977," *Journal of Urban History* (September 2000): 767. Oakland's black population rose from 47,000 in 1950 to 125,000 in 1970.

77. Fanon, *Wretched of the Earth,* p. 208.

78. Ibid., p. 38.

79. Newton, *To Die for the People,* p. 92; Hilliard and Cole, *This Side of Glory,* p. 121.

80. Here I am paraphrasing Stuart Hall, who writes that the Panthers forged "a form of black revolutionary politics alternative to the worlds of low wage work, hustling, the middle-class politics of civil rights and the separatism of cultural nationalism." Hall et al., *Policing the Crisis*, p. 387.

81. Huey P. Newton, "We Are Nationalists and Internationalists," in John Gerassi, *The Coming of the New International* (New York: The World Publishing Co., 1971), p. 575.

82. Quoted in Hilliard and Cole, *This Side of Glory*, p. 122.

83. Erik Erikson and Huey P. Newton, *In Search of Common Ground* (New York: W. W. Norton & Co., 1973), p. 133.

84. Hilliard and Cole, *This Side of Glory*, p. 319.

85. Richard J. Barnet and Ronald Muller, *Global Reach: The Power of Multinational Corporations* (New York: Simon and Schuster, 1974), p. 334.

86. Ernesto Laclau emphasizes the populist dimension of counter-hegemonic, anticapitalist struggles that effectively articulate heterogeneous identities and antagonisms into a single antithetical structure: "the people" versus "the power bloc," in *Politics and Ideology in Marxist Theory* (London: Verso, 1977), p. 135. Panther rhetoric was indeed populist in the sense that Laclau suggests, in particular in its effort to weld contemporary, anticolonial, and anticapitalist ideologies together with the revolutionary, democratic demands of the Declaration of Independence and the Constitution. See the last paragraph of the Panthers' famous ten-point program, which begins, "We hold these truths to be self-evident. . ." Newton, *To Die for the People*, p. 5.

87. In this vein, Rubin Hurricane Carter, the unjustly imprisoned black middleweight, described the nation-state for black people as a little more than a "penitentiary with a flag." Quoted in Bruce Franklin, *Prison Literature in America* (New York: Oxford University Press, 1978), p. 242.

88. Davis, *City of Quartz*, p. 297; Hilliard and Cole, *This Side of Glory*, p. 238; John Valadez, dir., *Passing It On: A Story of a Black Panther's Search for Justice*, videotape (Dhoruba Bin Wahad) (New York: First Run Features, 1993).

89. Franklin, *Prison Literature in America*, p. 273.

90. Stanley Crouch, "The Nationalism of Fools," in *Notes of a Hanging Judge: Essays and Reviews, 1979–1989* (New York: Oxford University Press, 1990), p. 166; Hilliard and Cole, *This Side of Glory*, p. 258. David Hilliard is most stark on the Panthers' slide into undisciplined violence and criminal activities by the early 1970s: "Before we've used Cuba, Algeria, and China as examples of revolutionary struggle. Now, Mario Puzo's *Godfather* provides the organization map, a patriarchal family divided into military and political wings" (339).

91. Erikson and Newton, *In Search of Common Ground*, p. 44.

92. Quoted in Ward Churchill and Jim Vander Wall *Agents of Repression* (Boston: South End Press, 1988), pp. 77, 68 (my emphasis).

93. Tom Wolfe, *Radical Chic and Mau-Mauing the Flak Catchers* (New York:

Farrar, Strauss and Giroux, 1970); David Horowitz and Peter Collier, *Destructive Generation: Second Thoughts about the Sixties* (New York: Simon and Schuster, 1990); Hugh Pearson, *The Shadow of the Panther: Huey P. Newton and the Price of Black Power in America* (New York: Addison Wesley, 1994); Elaine Brown, *A Taste of Power: A Black Woman's Story* (New York: Anchor Books, 1992).

94. For a fuller elaboration of many of these points see Nikhil Pal Singh, "The Black Panthers and the Undeveloped Country of the Left," in Charles E. Jones, ed., *The Black Panther Party Reconsidered* (Baltimore: Black Classic Press, 1998), pp. 57–109.

95. Seale, *Seize the Time,* p. 4.

96. The idea of domestication is deliberately polyvalent, if insufficiently elaborated. The Panthers resisted domestication not only to a narrative of nation, but also to conservative, racialist narratives of family and kinship advanced in the seemingly opposed, but ultimately symbiotic, discourses of black cultural nationalism and the Moynihan report. Also see Paul Gilroy, "It's a Family Affair," *Small Acts,* p. 205.

97. Ronald Fraser, *1968: A Student Generation in Revolt* (New York: Pantheon, 1988), p. 238.

98. Jean Genet, *Prisoner of Love* (Middletown, Conn.: Wesleyan University Press, 1992), p. 85.

99. Ibid., 84.

100. *Eyes on the Prize II: A Nation of Law, 1968–1971* (Boston: Blackside, 1991).

101. Pierre Bourdieu, "Social Space and Symbolic Power," in *In Other Words* (Stanford, Calif.: Stanford University Press, 1990), p. 138. In this sense we must also understand that the state is always performative. As Philip Abrams puts it, in slightly different terms, "[the state is] a public reification that acquires an overt symbolic identity progressively divorced from practice as an illusory account of practice." Quoted in Michael Taussig, "Malfecium: State Fetishism," in Emily Apter and William Peitz, eds., *Fetishism as Cultural Discourse* (Ithaca, N.Y.: Cornell University Press, 1993), p. 220.

102. Newton, *Revolutionary Suicide,* p. 322.

103. Eldridge Cleaver, "The Land Question and Black Liberation," in *Post-Prison Writings and Speeches* (New York: Random House, 1967), p. 67.

104. Davis, *City of Quartz,* p. 297.

105. Balibar and Wallerstein, *Race, Nation, Class,* p. 95.

106. Isaacs, *The New World of American Negroes,* p. 11.

107. Quoted in Isaacs, *The New World of American Negroes,* p. 13.

108. George Jackson, *Blood in My Eye* (New York: Random House, 1972), p. 47; James Baldwin, *The Fire Next Time* (New York: Dell Publishing, 1963).

109. Here, Panther imagery and language was itself translated immediately into popular, idiomatic expressions and figurations. Newton suggested that coining the term "pig" was meant to dispel the "fear-image" attached to the

police in the minds of black people. Those who think this sort of thing doesn't count in struggles should take note of the fact that the FBI, in its attempts to combat the Panthers' inventive and effective labeling of the police, circulated an anonymous cartoon lamely deriding "the panther" as "an animal with a small head." See Churchill, *Agents of Repression*, p. 44.

110. Steven Lawson, "View from the Nation," in Steven Lawson and Charles Payne, *Debating the Civil Rights Movement, 1945–1968* (New York: Rowman & Littlefield, 1998), p. 31. The phrase "simulacrum of inclusion" is owed to Lisa Lowe, *Immigrant Acts* (Durham, N.C.: Duke University Press, 1998).

111. Quoted in Charles Payne, "A View from the Trenches," *Debating the Civil Rights Movement*, p. 125.

112. Ella Baker, "Excerpt from Bigger Than a Hamburger" (1966), in *Debating the Civil Rights Movement*, p. 140; Charles Payne, *I've Got the Light of Freedom: The Organizing Tradition and the Mississippi Freedom Struggle* (Berkeley: University of California Press, 1995).

113. Jackson is quoted in R. Radhakrishnan, "Toward an Effective Intellectual: Foucault or Gramsci," in Bruce Robbins, ed., *Intellectuals, Aesthetics, Politics and Culture* (Minneapolis: University of Minnesota Press, 1990), p. 59.

114. Here I am paraphrasing Kobena Mercer's illuminating essay, "1968: Periodizing Politics and Identity," in Lawrence Grossberg, ed., *Cultural Studies* (London: Routledge, 1992), p. 434. Newton himself undertook a self-critical appraisal of black masculinism, sexism, and homophobia, producing a pamphlet entitled "The Women's Liberation and Gay Liberation Movements," in which he observed that "homosexuals" might actually be the most oppressed, and the most revolutionary, participants in a coalition of oppressed peoples. Newton, *To Die for the People*, pp. 152–155. On women's and gay liberation see Alice Echols, *Daring to Be Bad: Radical Feminism, 1967–1973* (Minneapolis: University of Minnesota Press, 1993), pp. 222–223; Karla Jay and Allen Young, *Out of the Closets: Voices of Gay Liberation* (1972) (New York: New York University Press, 1992); Andrew Kopkind, "The Real SDS Stands Up" (1969), in *The Thirty Years Wars: Dispatches and Diversions of a Radical Journalist, 1965–1994* (New York: Verso, 1995), p. 166.

115. Joanne Grant, *Ella Baker: Freedom Bound* (New York: John Wiley & Sons, 1998); Beth Tomkins Bates, *Pullman Porters and the Rise of Protest Politics in Black America, 1925–1945* (Chapel Hill: University of North Carolina Press, 2001).

116. King, "The American Dream" (1961), "Black Power Defined" (1967), *Testament of Hope*, pp. 212, 303, 318.

117. Malcolm X, "The Ballot or the Bullet," speech at Cory Methodist Church, Cleveland, Ohio, April 3, 1964. (Pamphlet printed by Pathfinder Press, New York, 1965, in author's possession.)

118. Ralph Bunche, "The Black Revolution" (1968), in Charles Henry, ed.,

Ralph J. Bunche: Selected Speeches and Writings (Ann Arbor: University of Michigan Press, 1995), pp. 297–305.

119. In the early 1970s, political scientist Samuel P. Huntington famously voiced the concern that the 1960s had produced such an "excess" of democratic demands that the country was becoming ungovernable. See Holly Sklar, *Trilateralism: The Trilateral Commission and Elite Planning for World Management* (Boston: South End Press, 1980), p. 27. The quotation is from Daniel Patrick Moynihan: see Sheila Collins, *The Rainbow Challenge* (Boston: South End Press, 1986), p. 57.

Conclusion

1. This phrase was later used by Du Bois to open his chapter entitled "The Dawn of Freedom" in *Souls of Black Folk* (New York: Vintage, 1990), p. 16. The initial context for this prophetic utterance, however—an international congress addressing questions of imperialism and racism—is often forgotten. See George Sheperson, "Notes on Negro American Influences on the Emergence of African Nationalism," *Journal of African History* 1(2) (1960): 307.

2. Du Bois, *Souls of Black Folk*, p. 4.

3. W. E. B. Du Bois, *W. E. B. Du Bois Speaks: Speeches and Addresses, 1890–1919,* ed. Phillip Foner (New York: Pathfinder Press, 1970), p. 84.

4. Wilson Moses, *The Golden Age of Black Nationalism* (New York: Oxford University Press, 1987); Albert Murray, *The Omni Americans: Black Experience and American Culture* (New York: Da Capo Press, 1970), p. 22.

5. Du Bois, *Souls of Black Folk,* p. 4.

6. W. E. B. Du Bois, "The Negro Mind Reaches Out" (1925), in *The New Negro* (New York: Da Capo, 1968), p. 386.

7. Du Bois, *Black Reconstruction in America* (New York: Atheneum, 1985), p. 14.

8. Anthony Appiah, "Du Bois and the Illusion of Race: The Uncompleted Argument," in Henry Louis Gates, ed., *Race, Writing and Difference* (Chicago: University of Chicago Press, 1988).

9. Lani Guinier and Gerald Torres, *The Miner's Canary* (Cambridge, Mass.: Harvard University Press, 2002), p. 98.

10. Antonio Gramsci, *The Gramsci Reader,* ed. David Forgacs (New York: New York University Press, 2002).

11. The American exceptionalist formula of Cold War civil rights generally applied to King has been transferred to the even more amenable figure of Powell. It is Powell today who appears as the embodiment of America's self-transcendence of the racist past. Indeed, he has self-consciously embraced this mantle. In his U.S. Senate confirmation hearing, Powell described himself as the heir to both Thomas Jefferson and King, who "answered Jefferson's prayers for freedom for black Americans." Talk about papering over a

contradiction! Despite his limited role in formulating foreign policy in the Bush administration, Powell arguably plays a more important role vindicating America's universalism for global publics. As he put it in a revealing comment to an audience at Howard University: "It's just terrific to be able to walk into a room somewhere in Africa, Russia, Asia, and Europe, and you know they're looking at you. You know how they be. They're looking at you and they recognize your position and who you are, and they also recognize that you're black. And it's always a source of inspiration and joy to see people look at me and through me see my country and see what promise my country offers to all people to come to these shores for a better life." "Embattled, Scrutinzed Powell Soldiers On," *New York Times* (July 25, 2002): A5.

12. Thomas Byrne Edsall and Mary D. Edsall, *Chain Reaction* (New York: Norton, 1991). See also David Roediger's useful critique of these positions in "The Racial Crisis of American Liberalism," in *Towards the Abolition of Whiteness* (New York: Verso Books, 1994), p. 122.

13. Charles Murray, *Losing Ground: American Social Policy, 1950–1980* (New York: Basic Books, 1984).

14. Harold Cruse, *Crisis of the Negro Intellectual* (New York: William & Morrow, 1968), p. 13.

15. Clayborne Carson, *In Struggle: SNCC and the Black Awakening of the 1960s* (Cambridge, Mass.: Harvard University Press, 1981).

16. The notion of black people as "anti-citizens . . . enemies rather than members of the social compact" is from David Roediger. See David Roediger, *The Wages of Whiteness* (New York: Verso, 1991), p. 57.

17. Guinier and Torres, *The Miner's Canary*, p. 45; Andrew Hacker, *Two Nations: Black and White, Separate and Unequal* (New York: Macmillan, 1992), p. 102; Loïc Waquant, "From Slavery to Mass Incarceration," *New Left Review* (January/February 2002): 58; Glen Loury, *Anatomy of Inequality* (Cambridge, Mass.: Harvard University Press, 2002), p. 104; Bob Herbert, "What Is It Good For" *New York Times* (April 21, 2003): A23.

18. William Julius Wilson, *The Declining Significance of Race: Black Politics and Changing American Institutions* (Chicago: University of Chicago Press, 1980).

19. "Since 1979, the median wage for Americans overall, after adjustments are made for inflation, has dipped 10 percent, and the hardest hit have been workers without a college degree—a category that represents three-quarters of the workforce." William Julius Wilson, *Bridge over the Racial Divide* (Berkeley: University of California Press, 1999), p. 25.

20. Ibid., p. 121.

21. Michael Brown, *Race, Money and the Welfare-State* (Ithaca, N.Y.: Cornell University Press, 1999), p. 3.

22. Paul Nichols, "Jesse Jackson Jr.: A Different Vision," *The Nation* (September 18, 2000): 18.

23. C. L. R. James, *American Civilization* (London: Basil Blackwell, 1994).

24. Gunnar Myrdal, *An American Dilemma: The Negro Problem and Modern Democracy,* vol. 1 (Pantheon Books: New York, 1944), p. 3.

25. Ralph Ellison, *Shadow and Act* (New York: Signet Books, 1963), p. 301.

26. Richard Wright, *White Man Listen!* (New York: Anchor Books, 1957), p. 101.

27. Ibid., p. 72 (my emphasis).

28. Ralph Ellison, *Invisible Man* (New York: Random House, 1952), p. 440.

29. Kobena Mercer, "1968: Periodizing Politics and Identity," in Lawrence Grossberg and Cary Nelson, eds., *Cultural Studies* (New York: Routledge, 1992), pp. 424–449.

30. See Cedric Robinson, *Black Marxism* (London: Zed Press, 1983) for the notion of "racial capitalism." Also see Manning Marable, *How Capitalism Underdeveloped Black America: Problems in Race, Political Economy and Society* (Boston: South End Press, 1983).

31. Douglas Massey and Nancy Denton, *American Apartheid* (Cambridge, Mass.: Harvard University Press, 1993), p. 30.

32. Quoted in Randy Holland, dir., *The Fire This Time* (Rhino Films, 1985).

33. Bayard Rustin, "From Protest to Politics: The Future of the Civil Rights Movement," *Commentary* 39(2) (February 1965): 25–31.

34. Michel Foucault, *Society Must Be Defended* (New York: Picador, 2003), pp. 253–254. I am indebted to Foucault for the idea of racism as the creation of "caesuras" in human populations by state powers, though he is silent on the specific historical forms these caesuras have taken.

Acknowledgments

This project was completed over many years of shifting jobs and cities, old and new colleagues and friendships. Many people have helped me along the way. I regret that I cannot thank every one of them.

While in graduate school in American Studies at Yale, I was lucky to be part of a group of intellectuals and activists who believed that it was not desirable to separate struggles for institutional transformation and intellectual creation. I thank Stephanie Smallwood, Mark Harding, Adam Green, Gordon Lafer, Ivanna Kracinovic, David Waldsteicher, Sandhya Shukla, Michelle Stephens, and Faulkner Fox for learning and practicing this idea with me. I also thank Michael Denning, a wonderful teacher to many of us, and the best I've ever had. For her support and attention to detail, I will always be grateful to Nancy Cott.

The Program in American Studies at New York University, where I briefly worked, is an inspiring example of what it means to train for intellectual activism. I thank Andrew Ross, Lisa Duggan, Robin D. G. Kelley, Phil Harper, and Walter Johnson for the good fights we fought together. For helping me to always remember the personal stakes of this work, I am indebted to a number of current and former graduate students, including Alondra Nelson, Davarian Baldwin, Kitty Krupat, Sujani Reddy, Nathalie Bimel, Amy Bass, Andrew Schroeder, Danny Widener, and Todd Tietchen.

Some extraordinary people in Seattle and at the University of Washington enrich my work and my life each day. I cherish my conversations with Chandan Reddy, whose brilliance and generosity never cease to amaze me. Gillian Harkins, Moon Ho Jung, Jodi Melamed, and Jonathan Warren are comrades in the truest sense of the word. Priscilla Wald, Joe Donahue, Ranji Khanna, Srinivas Aramavudan, and Andrew Jones have been greatly missed since their various departures to points south. I was lucky to know, though too briefly, the late Tyree Scott, mentor, visionary, and fighter for social justice.

A number of colleagues across the country invited me to present, or commented upon, parts of this book over the past few years. I thank Gary Gerstle, Matt Jacobson, Paul Gilroy, Manning Marable, Kevin Gaines, Herman Bennett, Vijay Prashad, Lewis Gordon, Gay Seidman, David Kazanjian, and Howie Winant for engaging with my ideas. Amy Kaplan, Stephanie Camp, Moon Ho-Jung, Chandan Reddy, Jodi Melamed, Bruce Burgett, Bill Rorabaugh, and especially Brent Edwards generously read parts of the manuscript at different stages, offering valuable suggestions. Portions of Chapters 3, 5, and the conclusion were published in earlier forms in *American Quarterly, The Black Panther Party Reconsidered,* and *Race and Reason.* I thank Lucy Maddox, George Lipsitz, Charles E. Jones, and Manning Marable for these opportunities.

I will always be indebted to Joyce Seltzer, my editor at Harvard University Press, for her unwavering belief in this project, despite its at times glacial progress. Jan Bultmann revealed to me the joys of writing. Her kindness and insight into the creative process led me on paths of discovery that I'm still traveling. Peggy Crastnopol helped me to know what I did not always know that I knew, or could do. Christina Miller provided timely research and editorial assistance. Douglas Jensen saved the day at the copy-editing stage, when illness and tight deadlines loomed. Kaesmene Harrison expertly shepherded the manuscript into production.

A small web of people scattered across the globe help me to hold on to my sense of the meaning and significance of writing for a different kind of world. Brad Stam and Patrick Powdermaker have been loyal fellow-travelers for almost twenty years. Henry Abelove has been a true mentor; the pleasure of his conversation has been sustaining through many life turns. My brother, Karam Singh, never fails to uplift me with his sense of humor and passion for justice. Sandy and Shelly Weinbaum welcomed me into their family and overwhelm me with their wisdom and generosity. Anita, Nick, Andrew, and Michael Sudano have given me immense joy with their company. Finally, I thank my amazing parents, Maureen and Kultar Singh, for their worldliness, love, and unfailing support.

A few individuals have closely inhabited the tempo of my thoughts while I have been working on this book. Early on, Penny Von Eschen and I realized we were grappling with many of the same questions; we've been sharing joys of discovery ever since. Matt Jacobson has been a wonderful interlocutor from innocent days when we rode the Northern State Parkway rapt in the adventure of ideas. Adam Green and I have been engaged in a generative dialogue for over a decade—from New Haven to Los Angeles to New York, Seattle, Chicago, and back again—that is now foundational to my thinking. Brent Edwards and Nora Nicolini are co-conspirators. Their rare passion and subtle genius have been a gift and inspiration. Finally, Alys Weinbaum has lived this project with me and shaped its course. Her brilliance and beauty light up my world.

Index